FORENSIC
DNA
TECHNOLOGY

EDITED BY

MARK A. FARLEY
JAMES J. HARRINGTON

 LEWIS PUBLISHERS, INC.

Library of Congress Cataloging-in-Publication Data

Forensic DNA technology / editors, Mark A. Farley, James J. Harrington.
     p. cm.
     Includes bibliographical references and index.
     ISBN 0-87371-265-X
     1. Forensic genetics — Technique. 2. DNA fingerprints. I. Farley,
Mark A. II. Harrington, James J.
RA1057.5.F67   1991
614′.1—dc20   90-13449
                                            CIP

LEWIS PUBLISHERS, INC.
121 South Main Street, Chelsea, MI 48118

PRINTED IN THE UNITED STATES OF AMERICA
   4 5 6 7 8 9 0

Printed on acid-free paper

Preface

The decade of the 1990s promises to be the age of biotechnology. Recent discoveries in this field have resulted, for example, in major advances in understanding disease, in the treatment of environmental pollutants, and in the development of new pharmaceutical products. One of the most exciting applications of this field of science has been the implementation of DNA print technology in the analysis of physiological evidence uncovered during the course of criminal investigations and its related use in the investigation of issues relating to paternity.

DNA, or deoxyribonucleic acid, is the genetic material that provides the code that determines each person's individual characteristics. A number of analytical techniques, previously utilized for a variety of applications by molecular biologists, have recently been utilized to determine the unique characteristics of DNA and thus to permit its use in identifying the source of biological stains such as blood or semen deposited at a crime scene. Since many of these recent discoveries lie at the frontier of biotechnology, however, potential problems in their application to forensic investigation and issues relating to their weight and admissibility in court are only now coming into focus.

Forensic DNA Technology examines both the legal and scientific issues relating to the implementation of DNA print technology in both the crime laboratory and the courtroom. The book has been written for use by nonscientists as well as by those having a degree of technical expertise in the areas covered. Chapters written by a number of the country's leading experts trace the underlying theory and historical development of this technology, as well as the methodology utilized in the restriction fragment length polymorphism (RFLP) and polymerase chain reaction (PCR) techniques. The effect of environmental contaminants on the evidence and the statistical analysis of population genetics data as it relates to the potential of this technology for individualizing the donor of the questioned sample are also addressed. Another chapter deals with proposed guidelines for the use of this technology in the crime laboratory, while still others set forth, from the perspective of the prosecution and the defense, the legal standards for determining the admissibility and weight of such evidence at trial. Finally, the issues of the validation and proposed standards for interpretation of autoradiograms are brought into focus in a detailed study of actual case work.

In view of the rapidly increasing importance of DNA typing technology, the need for a reliable, up-to-date reference dealing in a single volume with both the legal and the technical issues inherent in this area has prompted the publication of *Forensic DNA Technology*.

About the Editors

Mark A. Farley, Esq. is an attorney with the law firm of Pennie & Edmonds. The firm, with offices in New York City and Washington, D.C., specializes in the protection of intellectual property assets, including patents, trademarks, copyrights, and trade secrets, with a particular emphasis in the field of biotechnology. Mr. Farley was formerly employed from 1977–1984 with the Suffolk County, New York, Division of Medical-Legal Services and Forensic Sciences as Supervisor of the Chemistry Section of the Suffolk County Criminalistics Laboratory. His duties at the laboratory included the chemical and instrumental analysis of pharmaceutical products as well as crime scene investigation and analysis. He has testified as an expert witness in pharmaceutical analysis in over 30 criminal trials.

Mr. Farley is registered to practice before the U.S. Patent and Trademark Office. He holds a Juris Doctor degree (1985) from the Jacob D. Fuchsberg Law Center of the Touro School of Law, where he was a Senior Editor of the Touro Law Review. In addition, he holds a Master of Science degree in Forensic Chemistry (1977) from John Jay College of Criminal Justice of the City University of New York and a Bachelor of Science degree (1974) in Biology from Saint John's University, Jamaica, New York.

He is an active member of the American Chemical Society's Division of Chemistry and the Law, serving on its Executive Committee as Chairman of the Forensic Chemistry Committee. He is a member of the American Bar Association, the New York State Bar Association, the New York Patent, Trademark and Copyright Law Association, and the Northeastern Association of Forensic Scientists.

Mr. Farley has organized and moderated a number of symposia at ACS National Meetings dealing with issues such as the analysis and abuse of steroids, the clandestine manufacture of illicit pharmaceutical products, and the role of the scientist as an expert witness. He served as Cochairman for the Forensic DNA Symposium held during the American Chemical Society's national meeting in Los Angeles in September, 1988.

His professional interests include the protection and licensing of technology and the education of the public concerning the role of the forensic scientist in the analysis of physiological evidence.

James J. Harrington is a Senior Scientist with New Jersey's North

Regional Forensic Science Laboratory, where he has been employed in the Department of Biochemistry for the past 5 years. He holds a Bachelor of Science degree in Biochemistry from the University of Scranton; a Master of Science degree in Forensic Science (Biochemistry) from The City University of New York, John Jay College of Criminal Justice; and is currently completing the requirements for a Juris Doctor degree at Pace University School of Law.

Mr. Harrington is an experienced forensic biochemist and has testified as an expert witness on over 40 occasions. He has written and lectured extensively on the applications and admissibility of conventional biochemical marker analysis and DNA print technology. Mr. Harrington was the cochairperson for the forensic DNA symposium held during the American Chemical Society's 1988 national meeting in Los Angeles, California and is currently actively involved in the development of New Jersey's DNA analysis unit.

Chapter Authors
Forensic DNA Technology

DWIGHT E. ADAMS, Ph.D.
Forensic Science Research and Training Center, FBI Academy, Quantico, Virginia

FRANK S. BAECHTEL, Ph.D.
Forensic Science Research and Training Center, FBI Academy, Quantico, Virginia

MICHAEL L. BAIRD, Ph.D.
Lifecodes Corporation, Valhalla, New York

JAN BASHINSKI, M.S.
California Department of Justice, Oakland, California

BRUCE BUDOWLE, Ph.D.
Forensic Science Research and Training Center, FBI Academy, Quantico, Virginia

SIMON FORD, Ph.D.
Molecular Biologist, Public Policy Research Organization, University of California, Irvine, California

ROCKNE P. HARMON, ESQUIRE
Senior Deputy District Attorney, Alameda County District Attorney's Office, Oakland, California

ALLAN D. HYMER, ESQUIRE
Trial Attorney, Alameda County Public Defender's Office, Oakland, California

ROGER KAHN, Ph.D.
Biology/Serology Section, Crime Laboratory Bureau, Metro-Dade Police Department, Miami, Florida

LAURENCE MUELLER, Ph.D.
University of California, Department of Ecology and Evolutionary Biology, Irvine, California

GEORGE SENSABAUGH, D. CRIM.

Forensic Science Group, Department of Biomedical and Environmental Health Sciences, School of Public Health, University of California, Berkeley, California

WILLIAM C. THOMPSON, Ph.D.

Associate Professor, Program in Social Ecology, University of California, Irvine, California

CECILIA VON BEROLDINGEN, Ph.D.

Forensic DNA Specialist, Oregon State Police Crime Detection Laboratory, Portland, Oregon

JAN A. WITKOWSKI, Ph.D.

The Banbury Center, Cold Spring Harbor Laboratory, Cold Spring Harbor, New York

About The Authors

Jan A. Witkowski is the director of the Banbury Center, Cold Spring Harbor (Long Island) Laboratory. He was formerly director of the Kleberg DNA Diagnostic Laboratory, Institute for Molecular Genetics, Baylor College of Medicine. Dr. Witkowski's degrees include a B.Sc. from the University of Southampton and a Ph.D. in biochemistry from the University of London, United Kingdom. His special interest is human molecular genetics, especially in the uses made by society of the ever-increasing technical advances in this field. He organized one of the first meetings on DNA fingerprinting that dealt with social concerns, and he was a member of the New York State Panel on DNA fingerprinting. Dr. Witkowski is also an historian of 20th century experimental biology and has published articles in this area as well as numerous papers based on his laboratory research.

Roger Kahn is the director of the DNA Identification Unit of the Metro-Dade Police Crime Laboratory in Miami, Florida. He has occupied this position since the inception of the DNA Unit in October, 1988. He holds a Ph.D in human genetics from Yale University and a B.A. in biology from the University of California at Santa Barbara. Dr. Kahn is a member of the Technical Working Group on DNA Analysis Methods (TWGDAM) and is an adjunct Associate Professor of Molecular Genetics at Florida International University. He is involved in the shaping of policies and protocols for the application of DNA techniques in the forensic sciences.

Michael L. Baird is Director of Business Development at Lifecodes Corporation. He has been with Lifecodes since its inception in 1982 and has served as Senior Research Scientist and Director of Forensics and Paternity. He pioneered the introduction of DNA RFLP analysis for the investigation of biological material and has testified about DNA in over 60 court cases. He holds a Ph.D. degree from The University of Chicago in genetics, an M.S. from the State University of New York, and a B.S. from Drew University. Before joining Lifecodes, he was a postdoctoral Fellow at the University of Michigan in the Department of Human Genetics for one year and a research associate at Columbia University in the Department of Human Genetics and Medicine for three years where he studied the organization of beta globin genes. He has over 75 publications in the field of genetics.

Laurence D. Mueller is an Associate Professor of Ecology and Evolutionary Biology at the University of California, Irvine. He received a Ph.D. in Ecology in 1979 from the University of California, Davis and was a postdoctoral Fellow in the Department of Biological Sciences at Stanford University from 1979 to 1983. His research interests include the theory of kin selection and density-dependent natural selection, the maintenance of genetic variation in natural populations, and the evolution of life histories.

George F. Sensabaugh is a professor of forensic science and biomedical sciences in the Department of Biomedical and Environmental Health Sciences, School of Public Health, University of California, Berkeley. He received his doctorate in Criminology from the University of California (Berkeley) and did post-doctoral research in the Chemistry Department at the University of California at San Diego and at the National Institute for Medical Research, Mill Hill, London, England. He has been a visiting professor at the University of Strathclyde, Glasgow, Scotland. He belongs to a number of professional societies and serves on the editorial boards of several journals. His research interests blend biochemical genetics and forensic science; he publishes in both areas.

Cecilia H. Von Beroldingen is a forensic DNA specialist with the Oregon State Police Crime Detection Laboratory in Portland, Oregon. She received her Ph.D. in biology from the University of Oregon and did post-doctoral research at Oregon State University and at the Research Institute of the Scripps Clinic in La Jolla, California. From 1986 to 1989, she was a research associate in the Forensic Science Group of the School of Public Health at the University of California, Berkeley.

Bruce Budowle is director of the Forensic Science Research and Training Center, Laboratory Division, at the FBI Academy in Quantico, Virginia. He received his Bachelor of Arts degree in Biology from King College, Bristol, Tennessee in 1975 and his Ph.D. in Genetics from Virginia Polytecnic Institute and State University. He is a member of numerous scientific organizations, including The Electrophoresis Society, The Mid-Atlantic Association of Forensic Scientists, and the American Association for the Advancement of Science, and has authored or co-authored a number of professional publications.

Frank S. Baechtel is a research chemist at the Forensic Science Research and Training Section, Laboratory Division, at the FBI Academy in Quantico, Virginia. He received his Bachelor of Science degree in Biology-Chemistry from Lynchburg College, Lynchburg, Virginia in 1964 and his Master of Science and Ph.D. degrees in Biochemistry from Virginia Polytechnic Institute and State University.

Dwight E. Adams is a Supervisory Special Agent of the DNA Unit in the Forensic Science Research and Training Section, Laboratory Division, at the FBI Academy in Quantico Virginia. He received his Ph.D. degree from the University of Oklahoma in 1982 and joined the FBI in 1983.

William C. Thompson, an attorney and psychologist, is an associate professor in the Program in Social Ecology at the University of California, Irvine. He has published a number of articles on human judgment and decision making and is particularly interested in the ability to draw appropriate conclusions from scientific and statistical data. His interest in forensic DNA analysis arose out of his National Science Foundation funded research on the use of mathematical evidence in criminal trials. In collaboration with molecular biologist Simon Ford, he has published four articles (in addition to the chapter in this volume) on the scientific and legal aspects of genetic identification tests. He served as lead defense counsel during the Frye hearing in *State of New Mexico v. Anderson*, one of the first cases in which the defense raised a serious challenge to the admissibility of the FBI's DNA test. He holds a J.D. from the University of California at Berkeley and a Ph.D. in Psychology from Stanford. Before retiring to the academic world in 1983, he was a civil litigator.

Simon Ford is a molecular biologist affiliated with the Public Policy Research Organization at the University of California, Irvine. Born in England, Dr. Ford holds a B.Sc. (with honors) in genetics from Leeds University and a Ph.D. in biochemistry from Bristol University. He has been working with DNA since 1977 and held research positions at Sloan Kettering Cancer Center and the University of Southern California before coming to the University of California, Irvine. He is particularly interested in the analysis of DNA extracted from samples which have been exposed to the environment, including microorganisms exposed to pollutants, and human samples from crime scenes. He was one of the first independent consultants on forensic DNA analysis.

Rockne P. Harmon is a Senior Deputy District Attorney in the Alameda County (California) District Attorney's Office, where he has been employed for 16 years. He is also co-chairman of the California District Attorneys Association Forensic Science Committee. He has written and spoken extensively on the admissibility of DNA evidence in criminal prosecutions. He was the prosecutor in *People v. Reilly*, the case which established the legal precedent for the admissibility of conventional electrophoretic bloodstain analysis in California. Mr. Harmon received his B.S. from the United States Naval Academy in 1967 and his J.D. from the University of San Francisco in 1974.

Allan D. Hymer is a trial attorney with the Alameda County Public Defender in Oakland, California, where he is currently Administrative Attorney for Superior Court Calender and Juvenile Operations and is also a Senior Attorney on the Homicide Defense team. Mr. Hymer is also an Adjunct Professor of Law at Hastings Law School in San Francisco, where he teaches evidence workshop courses. He received his A.B. degree in 1961 and his L.L.B. in 1965 from Stanford University. Mr. Hymer has defended criminal cases since 1968 and has tried several death penalty cases. In 1989 he was the defense attorney in *People v. Barney*, which was one of the initial cases in California in which the prosecution sought to introduce the results of DNA testing and which involved an extensive Frye hearing.

Jan S. Bashinski is the manager of the DNA program of the California Department of Justice, having assumed that post in the fall of 1989 after 25 years as a criminalist and laboratory director with the Oakland Police Department Crime Laboratory. She holds a B.S. degree in chemistry and an M.Crim. in criminalistics, both from the University of California at Berkeley. Throughout her career, her research interests have centered on forensic serology, and she has been project director of two National Institute of Justice sponsored research studies on the genetic typing of sexual assault evidence. Her past professional activities have included service as President of the California Association of Criminalists, Chairman of the Criminalistics Section of the American Academy of Forensic Sciences, and Executive Secretary of the American Society of Crime Laboratory Directors Laboratory Accreditation Board. In her current position with the California Department of Justice, Ms. Bashinski is responsible for establishing a centralized DNA typing laboratory which will analyze DNA evidence as well as creating a DNA offender identification file for the State of California.

Acknowledgments

A book of a scope as wide as that of *Forensic DNA Technology* would obviously be impossible to compile without the advice of numerous legal and scientific experts. Since we relied on so many people, it would be impossible to thank all of them individually. To all of you, we would like to extend our sincere appreciation for your efforts. The editors would, however, like to individually thank a number of people who were especially instrumental in motivating us to finish this work when all appeared hopeless.

We would first like to thank the members of the Executive Committee of the American Chemical Society's Division of Chemistry and the Law, especially Chairman Michael E. Burns, for their unflagging enthusiasm and support for this project.

We would also like to thank each of our chapter authors for so unselfishly giving of their time and effort. Several of these authors, namely Drs. Budowle, Baird, and Sensabaugh, Jan Bashinski, and attorneys Rock Harmon and Al Hymer, were speakers at the ACS Forensic DNA Symposium held in Los Angeles, California in September, 1988. In addition, we are also grateful for the initial interest of Ed Lewis, of Lewis Publishers, in our project, as well as for the editorial contributions of Brian Lewis and Janice Morey.

Individually, *Mark Farley* would like to thank the partners of Pennie & Edmonds for their support and assistance in completing this project. In fact, had it not been for the Pennie & Edmonds' word processing staff, this book could never have been completed. In this regard, those most deserving of our gratitude include Philip Dorman, Albertha Eaves, Richard Bradshaw, and Bernadette Lawrence. Further thanks are due my parents, Helen and John Farley, for always encouraging my curiosity and fostering an appreciation of the role of books in answering my many questions. Finally, I would like to express my gratitude and appreciation to my wife Helen and my daughter Kathleen for sharing me with this project, which, once begun, took on a life of its own. Although neither wrote a word of the text, their support and understanding during the time required to complete "THE BOOK", as it became known, have meant more than mere words can say.

James Harrington: I would like to thank the members of the New Jersey

State Police North Regional laboratory, including Ken Salvato, Herbert Heaney, Joselito Versoza, Ajit Tungare, and Cindi McSweeney, for their understanding, encouragement, and practical help. I would also like to thank Laura Mieszerski for instilling in me the importance of reaching my full potential. Finally, I must acknowledge with deep appreciation my parents John and Dorothy Harrington, who always gave a kind word of encouragement when it was most needed.

The reader is advised that all of the opinions expressed herein are those of the authors and are not necessarily those of the editors, The American Chemical Society, the Division of Chemistry and the Law, Inc., Pennie & Edmonds, or the New Jersey State Police.

Contents

1. Milestones in the Development of DNA Technology

J.A. WITKOWSKI, Ph.D.

INTRODUCTION

DNA technology is having an increasing impact on our daily lives. The availability of DNA diagnosis for an ever-increasing number of human inherited disorders has brought significant benefits to families afflicted by these diseases.[1] DNA technology is leading the fight against AIDS[2] and recombinant DNA techniques may result in "tailor-made" drugs and other therapeutic agents.[3,4] However, one of the most spectacular, and certainly one of the most publicized, applications of DNA technology involves so-called DNA fingerprinting.[5,6] The mystique of DNA, together with the apparently infallible identifications that result, is proving to be a potent combination when the evidence analysis is presented in court. It is difficult under these circumstances to realize that DNA typing is the result of a "basic" research project that in itself was based on experiments and theories stretching back over the past 50 years. In this brief introduction DNA typing will be set in its scientific context and some of the milestones in the development of molecular biology will be described.[7]

THE DAWN OF MOLECULAR BIOLOGY

A good year to begin is 1938, the year in which the phrase *molecular biology* was first used, or at least first appeared in print. Warren Weaver, director of the Rockefeller Foundation, used it in his annual report to describe a new field of research, one that was " . . . beginning to uncover many of the secrets concerning the ultimate units of the living cell . . .".[8] It was in large part the Rockefeller Foundation, through the advocacy of Weaver, that nurtured the new field by providing support for the x-ray crystallography of biological molecules.[9] This was a particularly British science and owed its existence to the strong British tradition of x-ray crystal-lography developed by W. H. Bragg and his son W. L. Bragg, who won the Nobel Prize for Physics jointly in 1915 (W. L. Bragg was only 25, the youngest person ever to win the Nobel Prize).

1938 was also the year in which Bill Astbury and Florence Bell, at the University of Leeds in England, published the first important x-ray crystal-lographic study of DNA.[10] Astbury (see Figure 1), a student of W. L. Bragg, had worked on keratins, the major constituents of wool, because Leeds had a large weaving industry. He showed that the α-form of keratin was changed into an elongated β-form when wool was stretched, an impressive demonstration of the power of x-ray crystallography in analyzing the behavior of biological molecules. Astbury was interested in the functional significance of the structures of biological molecules, and he began to analyze all sorts of natural fibers.[11] He and Bell examined a dried film of DNA and concluded that the nucleotides were arranged one above the other at right angles to the fiber axis,[10] (Figure 2). Astbury and Bell were delighted to find that the distance between successive nucleotides in their structure was 3.4 Å, almost identical with the spacing of 3.3 Å between successive amino acids in a polypeptide chain. The experimental results seemed to be clear evidence that there was an interaction between proteins and nucleic acids, the latter acting as a framework for the former. In fact, this correspondence between nucleotide and amino acid spacing was a numerological coincidence and the "pile of pennies" model was wrong.[9,12]

DNA AS THE MOLECULE OF LIFE

Astbury seems to have been interested in DNA simply because it was another natural fiber he could analyze. The first convincing demonstration that DNA did something interesting biologically came in 1944 when Avery, Macleod, and McCarty showed that DNA could act as a carrier of hereditary information.[13,14] Up to that time DNA had been dismissed from such a role because biochemical analyses purported to show that the four nucleotides were present in equimolar amounts, and it was assumed that DNA was a polymer of a simple four-nucleotide repeated unit.[9,15] It was clear that proteins with their 23 amino acids were much more complicated and *a priori* more likely to be the hereditary material. Avery et al. showed otherwise, using the bacterium *Pneumococcus*. *Pneumococcus* type II normally forms smooth colonies when grown on agar, but Avery et al. isolated a variant that formed rough colonies. They were able to transform this rough variant into the smooth form of *Pneumococcus* III using DNA purified from the smooth form of *Pneumococcus* III. DNA alone was able to transfer a genetic character and, in addition, the transformed bacteria remained stable through successive generations. There has since been an interesting debate

Figure 1. W. T. Astbury, the British "bulldog" of x-ray crystallography, who with Florence Bell, made the first detailed analysis of DNA. Reproduced by permission of the Department of Textile Physics, University of Leeds, U.K.

as to whether Avery et al.'s paper was neglected by the scientific community.[14-17] In retrospect Avery's data is convincing evidence that DNA and not protein is the genetic material, but at the time this conclusion was not widely accepted. However, it is clear that this study of Avery et al. is one of the classics of modern biology and one that should have won the Nobel Prize.

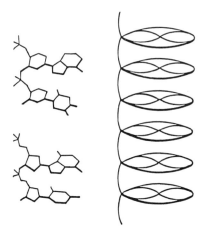

Figure 2. Bell and Astbury's "pile-of-pennies" model for DNA. "Alternative formulae for a pair of (purine and pyrimidine) nucleotides" are shown in the left part of the figure and "the idea is that of a very tall column of discs with a linking rod down one side" (right part of figure). The nucleotides project out at right angles to the axis of the single helix, one above another. Reproduced by permission from *Cold Spring Harbor Symp. Quant. Biol.* 6:109–118, 1938.

DNA AS THE DOUBLE HELIX

This part of the story hardly needs telling, having been the subject of a number of books and a television play.[9,17-19] What does need emphasizing is that it was not a question of luck, although like almost all scientific discoveries, elements of luck were involved. Rather, Watson and Crick, by using a combination of a great deal of shrewd and inspired thinking, together with x-ray crystallographic data from Rosalind Franklin[21] and Maurice Wilkins, derived a structure for DNA that, once seen, had to be right (Figure 3). The crux of the solution was the realization that nucleotides could pair with each other such that an adenine (A) paired with a thymidine (T), and a guanidine (G) paired with a cytidine (C) (Figure 4).[22] Base pairing is the essential characteristic of the DNA molecule that permits all the manipulations of recombinant DNA and DNA typing.

Base pairing was first exploited experimentally in 1960 when it was shown that the two strands of the DNA double helix could be separated and that these separated strands would then hybridize to RNA molecules.[23-25] The importance of this discovery was the demonstration that the base pairing was sufficiently precise that the single DNA strand hybridized specifically with its complementary RNA molecule. Hybridization in solution was used extensively to analyze DNA molecules, but by the mid-1970s a set of procedures, including analysis of DNA fragments by electrophoresis in agarose gels and ethidium bromide staining,[26] Southern blotting,[27] and "nick-translation" to produce radioactive probes,[28] had been developed for hybridization studies. Hybridization in solution is still a major tool in determining the degree of similarity between DNA molecules in studies of gene evolution.[29]

THE ENZYMES

At the same time that studies of RNA, protein synthesis, and the genetic code were going on apace, Arthur Kornberg's laboratory at Washington University, and later at Stanford University, was analyzing the replication of DNA. In 1958, Kornberg reported that he had found a DNA polymerase that required DNA as substrate—a small fragment of DNA to act as a primer—and all four nucleotides.[30] It was now possible to synthesize strands of DNA complementary to another strand.

In 1970, another enzyme essential for recombinant DNA techniques was discovered. Crick had postulated that the only source of genetic information was DNA, and that this information flowed from DNA via RNA to proteins, or from DNA to DNA during cell division.[31] This became known as the Central Dogma, and so the demonstration by Howard Temin and David Baltimore of a retroviral enzyme that reversed this flow of informa-

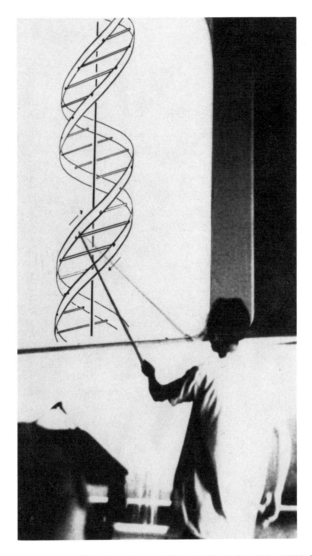

Figure 3. J.D. Watson extolling the virtues of the double helix at the 1953 Cold Spring Harbor Symposium on Quantitative Biology on Viruses. Reproduced by permission of Cold Spring Harbor Laboratory Archive.

tion was unexpected.[32,33] The retroviruses are a group of viruses that have RNA instead of DNA as their genetic information. Temin had suggested that retroviruses had first to make a DNA copy of their RNA genomes, because these viruses multiply within a cell using the cell's DNA-synthesizing enzymes. The enzyme reverse transcriptase does just that, synthesizing

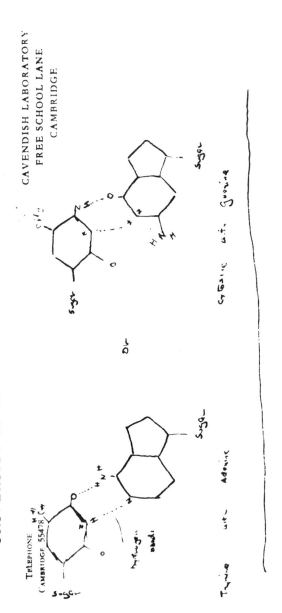

Figure 4. Part of a letter from Watson to Max Delbruck, dated March 12, 1953. The figures are Watson's sketches of the thymidine-adenine (left) and guanidine-cytosine (right) base pairs. Reproduced by permission of Cold Spring Harbor Laboratory Archive.

DNA from an RNA template. The discovery of reverse transcriptase meant that it was possible to take a cell synthesizing a large amount of a specific RNA, for example, globin RNA in a red blood cell, and to make a complementary or cDNA.

In the same year, i.e., 1970, Smith and Wilcox reported their detailed characterization of the restriction endonuclease *Hin*dIII.[34] First described some years before by Werner Arber, restriction enzymes had the curious property of rapidly degrading DNA, unless the DNA came from the same species of bacteria from which the enzyme had been isolated; *Hin*dIII prepared from the bacterium *Hemophilus influenzae* failed to degrade DNA from *Hemophilus influenzae*. Smith and Wilcox showed that *Hin*dIII cut the DNA helix specifically at the sequence:

...A A G C T T...   to give   ...A   A G C T T...

...T T C G A A...   ...T T C G A   A...

Restriction endonucleases were put to a practical use by Danna and Nathans, who used them to derive a physical map of the genome of the DNA tumor virus SV40.[35] Restriction enzymes are one of the most important tools in the molecular biology workshop. They cut DNA molecules into sizes that can be manipulated, they generate DNA fragments that can be cloned easily, and they are essential for techniques like DNA fingerprinting.

The last of the enzymes that we need to consider is T4 ligase. This enzyme, isolated from the T4 bacteriophage, is able to join together the cohesive ends of DNA molecules that have been cut with a restriction endonuclease.[36] This is exactly the opposite of the actions of restriction enzymes, and the sequential use of restriction enzymes and DNA ligase are critical steps in producing recombinant DNA molecules.

BIRTH OF RECOMBINANT DNA TECHNOLOGY[37]

In the same issue of the journal that contained the paper by Mertz and Davis, there was a paper originating from Paul Berg's laboratory at Stanford University that described the first experimental manipulations of the DNA molecule.[38] Berg's group had used a technique developed by Lobban and Kaiser[39] that added short stretches of nucleotides to the 3' ends of DNA molecules. Jackson, Symons, and Berg were able to join DNA from simian virus 40 to DNA from the bacteriophage lambda.[38] However, this inactivated the lambda DNA, so that it could not replicate in bacterial cells. (Berg did not pursue these experiments because of concern about the safety of such experiments; see below.)

The research that led to useful ways of introducing DNA into cells went on in Stanley Cohen's laboratory at Stanford. Plasmids are small circles of self-replicating DNA that occur naturally in bacteria and are responsible for transmitting antibiotic resistance between bacteria. Cohen found a way to introduce plasmids carrying antibiotic resistance genes into *E. coli* cells and to use the antibiotic to select for those bacteria that had taken up the plasmid.[40] Each resistant bacterium gave rise to an antibiotic-resistant clone, with all the bacteria of the clone containing a plasmid derived from the single plasmid in the single bacterial cell that initiated the clone.

One evening, over dinner at a delicatessen at Waikiki Beach, Cohen and Herb Boyer realized how to bring together these various elements—plasmids, restriction enzymes, and other DNA enzymes—for cloning DNA.[37,41] Cohen developed a plasmid called pSC101 that was resistant to the antibiotic tetracycline and contained a single *Eco*RI restriction enzyme site. When pSC101 is cut with *Eco*RI, it is converted into a linear molecule with "sticky" *Eco*RI sequences at each end. They cut the DNA of another plasmid that contained a kanamycin-resistant gene with *Eco*RI, mixed these fragments with the cut plasmid, and joined the fragments with DNA ligase. The DNA was introduced into bacteria, and bacteria that could grow on agar containing both kanamycin and tetracycline were isolated. These bacteria contained replicating recombinant plasmids, formed by the insertion of the kanamycin gene into the pSC101 plasmid. In the jargon of the molecular biologist, the plasmid acted as a vector carrying the cloned DNA into the cell.

The experiments of Cohen and Boyer were not recombinant in the sense that the DNA molecules they created did not combine DNA from different species. This was achieved in 1976 when the first eukaryotic gene, the rabbit β-globin gene, was cloned.[42,43] The next major advance came in 1978, when the enzyme dihydrofolate reductase[44] and proinsulin[45] were expressed in bacterial cells.

The power of cloning comes from three factors. Firstly, it gives us the ability to isolate a single gene or part of a gene from the total human genome of 3×10^9 base pairs. Secondly, once a gene is cloned, very large amounts of the gene can be produced. Each bacterial cell may contain as many as 50 copies of the plasmid with the cloned gene, and all of these are replicated each time the bacterial host cell divides. Thirdly, a gene cloned in a vector can be manipulated in ways that are simply not possible when the gene is part of the long DNA molecule that makes up the chromosome. These manipulations include mutagenesis of specific bases,[46] sequencing,[47,48] and bringing together DNA sequences in novel configurations, for example, in analyzing DNA-binding regulatory proteins.[49]

Figure 5. A cartoon by Avoine commenting on the fears of genetic engineering. Reproduced from *The DNA Story*, W.H. Freeman and Company, 1981.

SOCIAL AND POLITICAL RESPONSES[50]

The birth of recombinant DNA technology was not painless (Figure 5). It was realized that there were potential hazards in cloning certain genes into *E. coli*, a bacterial cell that lives in the human intestine. There was also considerable concern that human cancer genes would be cloned when preparing "libraries" of cloned human DNA and that the bacteria carrying these clones would be dangerous. It was not clear how to determine the degrees of hazard involved in such experiments, and a National Academy of Science Committee on Recombinant DNA Molecules was convened to examine these problems. The committee included such luminaries as Paul Berg, David Baltimore, Stanley Cohen, Herbert Boyer, Daniel Nathans, and James Watson. The result of their deliberations was a recommendation that there should be a self-imposed moratorium on certain types of experiments.[51] The first group of experiments involved the construction of plasmids containing genes for antibiotic resistance or bacterial toxins and that might be transferred to bacteria that did not contain those genes. The second group of experiments included those in which DNA fragments from cancer-causing or other animal viruses would be inserted into plasmids. Here the concern was that such DNA fragments that might cause cancer might be transferred through bacteria to human beings and other animals.

This proposal was discussed at a historic meeting of molecular biologists at Asilomar (Figure 6) in 1975,[52] held under the auspices of the National Academy of Sciences, and funded by both the National Institutes of Health and the National Science Foundation. Then, in 1976, the Department of Health, Education and Welfare introduced very restrictive guidelines governing recombinant DNA experiments.[53] These guidelines caused great consternation in the cloning world, especially amongst scientists working on viruses causing cancer. For example, adenovirus and simian virus 40 can transform normal cells in tissue culture into malignant cells. In 1978, the strict laboratory containment facilities required for using these viruses in recombinant DNA experiments were not yet available in the United States. Workers at Cold Spring Harbor Laboratory went to England to carry out recombinant DNA experiments using the less stringent containment facilities that were required there.[50]

In the meantime, the hazards involved in these experiments have been found to be minimal, except when expressing substances that are known to be dangerous, and the guidelines have thus been progressively relaxed. In fact, research on dangerous pathogens such as the human immunodeficiency virus, the cause of AIDS, has been rendered considerably safer by using recombinant DNA techniques.[2] It is possible, for example, to clone all the various parts of the virus genome and to study these separately from each other so that infectious virus particles are never handled.

Nevertheless, this controversy demonstrated that the uses of recombinant DNA technology were going to be subject to public scrutiny and that scientists could not assume that they would be permitted to do anything that they wanted. This has provided a salutary lesson for forensic applications of DNA techniques and highlights issues of public accountability that need to be addressed.

THE POWER OF RECOMBINANT DNA TECHNOLOGY

In the mid- and late-1960s, scientists like Sydney Brenner and Francis Crick had felt that most of the problems of "classical" molecular biology had been solved. Brenner, in fact, wrote of the need to move on to other problems in biology that were "new, mysterious and exciting."[54] Francis Crick turned first to developmental biology and then to neurobiology,[20] while Sydney Brenner chose to exploit the small nematode worm *C. elegans* as a model system. (This remarkable creature, with a genome of only 8×10^7 base pairs and with the developmental pathways of all its 1000 cells known, is likely to become the multicellular organism of choice for analyzing the molecular control of development.)

The seeming doldrums in molecular biology research were transformed by the ability to manipulate DNA molecules. Recombinant DNA techniques led to a radical revision of the sorts of questions that molecular biologists could ask and hope to answer. This process has continued unabated, with advances in technique leading to advances in knowledge. The methods

Figure 6.   Molecular biologists gathered at Asilomar, February 1975. Amongst the crowd are David Botstein, Rich Roberts, Stanley Cohen, Bob Williamson, and Dan Koshland. Photograph by Andrew Stern, reproduced by permission of the National Academy of Sciences.

developed in 1977 for rapid sequencing of DNA[47,48] were an extraordinary achievement, deservedly winning the Nobel Prize for Medicine for Sanger and Gilbert. Many developments have been more mundane, but nevertheless essential for the modern enterprises of molecular biology and genetics. An enormous variety of vectors have been developed for cloning DNA. The latest of these vectors are the so-called yeast artificial chromosomes that are able to accept DNA fragments as big as 600,000 base pairs[55] (this compares with 50,000 base pairs that can be cloned in some virus vectors). Southern blotting, developed by Ed Southern for the transfer of DNA from an agarose gel to a more stable support matrix, is the most familiar of the recombinant DNA techniques.[27]

The latest development to find its way into the forensic laboratory is the polymerase chain reaction.[56] It is now possible to begin with the DNA molecule in a single cell and to produce microgram quantities of a specific region of that DNA strand. Not the least of these tools is the book, *Molecular Cloning: A Laboratory Manual*, by Maniatis, Sambrook, and Fritsch.[57] Known simply as "Maniatis", it introduced the techniques of recombinant DNA to laboratories throughout the world. The manual has tripled in size between the first and second[57a] editions. Methods that were once the prerogative of a relatively small number of laboratories spread to all fields of biology.

The cumulative impact of these techniques has led to a revolution as great as that brought about by cloning. Wholly unexpected phenomena, such as RNA splicing,[58] RNA molecules as enzymes,[59] and the existence of oncogenes in normal cells[60] have been discovered. It became possible to study human genetics with almost the same ease as microbial or *Drosophila* genetics.[61] DNA applications in forensic science have grown directly out of the theoretical background and practical applications of DNA technology in medical genetics, and so these need to be discussed before turning to forensic science.

HUMAN GENETICS

There is no doubt that the last quarter of the 20th century will come to be regarded as the golden age of human genetics. It is extraordinary to recall that while the true number of human chromosomes was determined only in 1956,[62] and that the first assignment of a gene to an autosome was made in 1967,[63] the present number of cloned human genes and DNA fragments is now 3105.[64]

The first human genes to be cloned and studied in any detail were the genes for the globins, which, together with the iron-containing moiety heme, are responsible for the transport of oxygen in the blood. The globin genes were amongst the first mammalian genes to be cloned because highly purified globin mRNA was available for synthesis of globin cDNA.[42,43] There are a total of six genes in the α- and β-globin gene clusters, and mutations in these genes are responsible for an enormous amount of human disease.[65] In the United States, for example, the most familiar of these disorders is sickle cell anemia; some 1500 children with sickle cell anemia are born in the United States each year. One hundred times that number are born in Africa. The thalassemias are diseases caused by reduced amounts or the total absence of one of the globin polypeptides.[65] Conservative estimates put the number of carriers of the various thalassemias at 242 million world-wide. Other human disease genes that have been cloned as cDNAs include those for Tay-Sachs disease,[66] phenylketonuria,[67] cystic fibrosis,[67a-c] and Duchenne muscular dystrophy,[68] the latter being a huge gene having 2.3 × 10[6] base pairs.

The first application of recombinant DNA techniques in medical genetics came in 1976. The severe α-thalassemia is caused when both α-globin genes (one on each chromosome) have mutated. Kan, Golbus, and Dozy[69] ana-lyzed DNA from an α-thalassemia patient by hybridizing the patient's DNA with an α-globin cDNA in solution. They found that DNA from the patient had reduced hybridization, thus demonstrating for the first time that muta-tions could be detected directly at the DNA level. Subsequently, it was shown that the sickle cell mutation — the change of a single base pair, A-T, to G-C at codon 6 in the β-globin gene — altered a restriction endonuclease cleavage site. Normally, the enzyme MstII cuts the β-globin gene into a piece 1100 base pairs long that can be detected by hybridization with a radioactively labeled DNA fragment that is complementary to the 1100 base pair fragment. DNA from a patient with sickle cell anemia lacks this site in the β-globin gene, and a fragment of 1300 base pairs results.[70,71] This differ-ence in fragment size can be detected easily by agarose gel electrophoresis. However, only rarely does a mutation causing a disease also change a restriction enzyme site, so most diseases have to be analyzed indirectly, using linkage and restriction fragment length polymorphisms.

RESTRICTION FRAGMENT LENGTH POLYMORPHISMS (RFLPs)

There are many mutations in each individual's genome that modify DNA sequences so that restriction endonucleases fail to cut the DNA strand at sites that are susceptible to cutting in other individuals. The overwhelming majority of these mutations produce no disease, because the changes are in regions of DNA (introns) that do not code for proteins. These nucleotide changes are inherited just like a gene, and in the early 1980s it was realized[72] that these nucleotide polymorphisms were equivalent to protein polymor-phisms and that they could be used in linkage studies, just like HLA or glucose-6-phosphate dehydrogenase protein polymorphisms.[73]

RFLPs have some special advantages over protein polymorphisms. Firstly, they are very common. Secondly, they are found throughout the genome, and thus it should be possible to find an RFLP linked to any given disease. Thirdly, they are easy to analyze using techniques that are standard in molecular biology laboratories throughout the world.[57] Hard work and an element of luck are required to find RFLPs that are sufficiently close to the disease gene of interest for the polymorphism to be used in linkage diagnosis. Nevertheless RFLPs have proved invaluable in diagnoses of diseases such as Duchenne muscular dystrophy,[74] cystic fibrosis,[75] and Huntington's disease.[76]

HYPERVARIABLE PROBES

The RFLPs described above are usually two allele systems. That is, there is a polymorphic restriction site that is absent or present, producing respectively one or two fragments. In the course of studying the human myoglobin gene, Alec Jeffreys discovered a rather different polymorphism that was extremely variable.[5] These polymorphisms are so variable that there is only a very remote possibility that two individuals (other than identical twins) would by chance have the same pattern of fragments. Jeffreys recognized how these hypervariable polymorphisms could be used to identify individuals, and he chose the term *"DNA fingerprinting"* to emphasize this. The first practical application of these hypervariable polymorphisms was in establishing family relationships in immigration cases in the United Kingdom.[77] DNA "fingerprinting" was first used in criminal cases in the United Kingdom[78] and received great publicity in the Knarborough murder case.[79] The continuing development of single locus variable number tandem repeat probes is providing large numbers of loci for genetic linkage analysis and for forensic purposes.[80]

ETHICAL CONSIDERATIONS

It was noted earlier that forensic science applications had developed out of and had many parallels with similar studies in the field of medical genetics. Medical geneticists are well aware of the ethical implications of using DNA to study and characterize patients,[81,82,82a] and the American Society for Human Genetics has formed a committee that is developing guidelines that must be followed in dealing with DNA.[83] The following are some of the questions that are being considered: Do considerations of confidentiality preclude releasing information to members of the family other than the subject? What can be done when family members refuse to supply blood samples essential for a study? Should DNA diagnostic laboratories be certified?

Similar issues apply to DNA typing in the forensic setting, and there are other issues that may raise serious matters of civil liberties.[84–86] For example, should DNA samples be stored? At present we can learn little about an individual from a sample of DNA by itself, but in the future it may be possible to determine whether an individual has a predisposition to disorders such as schizophrenia and alcoholism. However, these are complex polygenic disorders with strong environmental components. An individual may be stigmatized as "schizophrenic" when there is only a probability of developing that condition. Even if it is decided to store DNA samples with strict limitations on access to them, political and economic pressures to institute screening of certain populations may become irresistible.[87] Who will then determine whether a DNA sample, taken originally for the purposes of identification, can be used for any other test?

CONCLUSIONS

There is little doubt that DNA typing is going to be a revolutionary forensic technique, although it is not clear how frequently technical problems may limit its usefulness. These problems may include insufficient quantities of DNA, DNA too degraded for analysis, or the lack of a national database for efficient searching for matches between samples. However, there are compelling reasons for introducing DNA typing into forensic practice, but this should be done with care and in a thoughtful manner. To accomplish this in New York state, the Panel on DNA Fingerprinting has made recommendations on the introduction of the technique in the state.[87a]

The continuing controversy in the courts over protein electrophoresis shows that the courts do not accept new scientific procedures uncritically.[88] In the case of DNA typing, the general acceptance by the scientific community of the basic principles underlying the procedure is beyond question.[57] The implementation of these techniques in the forensic setting is another matter. The reliability of the data for each polymorphism will have to be established before it can be used in forensic analysis. It will require a considerable amount of work to establish allele frequencies in the population, taking particular care to study ethnic groups separately. The laboratory techniques are not difficult but require particularly careful controls and critical appraisal. In this regard, the forensic laboratories should look carefully at the procedures followed in DNA diagnostics laboratories. There is no doubt that there should be an accreditation scheme for forensic laboratories performing DNA typing,[89] and that this should be a national scheme. There may be good reasons for considering licensure for forensic laboratories, and for admitting only data from licensed laboratories as evidence.

These problems have come to the fore in a recent Frye hearing in the case

"RUN FOR THE HILLS — THE RECOMBINANT DNA HAS ESCAPED !"

Figure 7. A cartoon by Sidney Harris, first published in 1980 in *Chicago Magazine*. Copyright Sidney Harris.

of *People v. Castro*.[89a-c] The basic principles of DNA typing were not challenged by the defense, but the defense witnesses pointed out serious defects in the technical quality of the analysis. These defects might have been avoided by more careful attention to controls and a more critical assessment of the quality of the data. Everyone involved in DNA typing must realize that not all analyses will yield data that can be interpreted and that inconclusive results must not be used. The *People v. Castro* case highlights the inadequacies of the Frye hearing as a forum for assessing complex scientific issues in the legal environment. The expert witnesses for prosecution and defense took the unusual step of holding a meeting to discuss the technical aspects of the case without lawyers being present. A joint statement was issued for the court's guidance. Whether such deliberations will become a regular feature of Frye hearings cannot yet be determined. The National Academy of Sciences has convened a committee to make recommendations.

The question of standardization is particularly difficult. Standardization may be desirable or even essential for a database, but it is probable that this would be premature, given the continuing rapid advances in molecular biology. The polymerase chain reaction is a recent example of a technique that was totally unexpected, yet is conceptually simple and is having an extraordinary impact in all areas of molecular biology.[90] It is impossible to plan for the unexpected, but the systems that are implemented should be flexible to meet changing circumstances.

As noted above, the Asilomar experience demonstrates that applications of recombinant DNA techniques cannot be free of political and societal scrutiny. The public's attitude toward biotechnology is ambivalent,[91] (Figure 7) as shown by the continuing debate over the release of genetically engineered bacteria,[92] the patenting of life forms,[93] and gene therapy.[94,95] The publicity already given to DNA typing has raised high expectations about its performance, and any shortcomings may have serious consequences for its further implementation. It behooves the forensic community to consider the technical and ethical issues now before they become problems.

REFERENCES

1. Caskey, C. T. "Disease Diagnosis by Recombinant DNA Methods," *Science* 236(4806):1223–1229 (1987).
2. Gallo, R. C. and L. Montagnier "AIDS in 1988," *Sci. Am.* 259(4):41–48 (1988).
3. Riechmann, L., M. Clark, H. Waldmann, and G. Winter "Reshaping Human Antibodies for Therapy," *Nature* 332 (6162):323-327 1988.
4. Lester, H. A. "Heterologous Expression of Excitability Proteins: Route to More Specific Drugs?" *Science* 241 (4869):1057-1063 (1988).
5. Jeffreys, A. J., V. Wilson, and S. L. Thein "Hypervariable 'Minisatel-lite' Regions in Human DNA," *Nature* 314 (6006):67–73 (1985).
6. Ballantyne, J., G. Sensabaugh, and J. Witkowski (eds). *DNA Technology and Forensic Science*. Banbury Report #32, Cold Spring Harbor, NY, Cold Spring Harbor Laboratory Press, 1989.
7. Witkowski, J. A. "Fifty Years On: Molecular Biology's Hall of Fame," *Trends Biotechnol*. 6(10):234–243 (1988).
8. Weaver, W. "Report of the Rockefeller Foundation," (1938), 203–225.
9. Olby, R. *The Path to the Double Helix*, (London: Macmillan Press, 1974).

10. Astbury, W. T. and F. O. Bell "X-ray Study of Thymonucleic Acid," *Nature* 141(3573):747–748 (1938).
11. Astbury, W. T. "Adventures in Molecular Biology," *The Harvey Lectures* 46:4–44 (1951).
12. Witkowski, J. A. "The Magic of Numbers," *Trends Biochem. Sci.* 10(4):139–141 (1985).
13. Avery, O. T., C. Macleod, and M. McCarty "Studies on the Chemical Nature of the Substance Inducing Transformation of Pneumococcal Types. I. Induction of Transformation by a Desoxyribonucleic Acid Fraction Isolated from Pneumococcus Type III." *J. Exper. Med.* 79(2):137–158 (1944).
14. McCarty, M. *The Transforming Principle* (New York: W. W. Norton, 1985).
15. Levene, P. A. and L. W. Bass *Nucleic Acids* (New York: American Chemical Society Monograph Series, Chemical Catalog Company, 1931).
16. Stent, G. "Prematurity and Uniqueness in Scientific Discovery," *Sci. Am.* 227(6):84–93 (1972).
17. Wyatt, H. V. "Knowledge and Prematurity: The Journey From Transformation to DNA," *Perspect. Biol. Med.* 18(1):149–156 (1975).
18. Watson, J. D. *The Double Helix* (London: Weidenfeld and Nicolson, 1968).
19. Judson, H. F. *The Eighth Day of Creation*, (London: Jonathan Cape, 1979).
20. Crick, F. *What Mad Pursuit*, (New York: Basic Books, Inc., 1988).
21. Sayre, A. *Rosalind Franklin & DNA* (New York: W.W. Norton, 1975).
22. Watson, J. D. and F. H. C. Crick "Molecular Structure of Nucleic Acids — A Structure for Deoxyribonucleic Acid," *Nature* 171(4356):737–738 (1953).
23. Marmur, J. and D. Lane "Strand Separation and Specific Recombination in Deoxyribonucleic Acids: Biological Studies," *Proc. Natl. Acad. Sci. USA* 46(4):453–461 (1960).
24. Doty, P., J. Marmur, J. Eigner, and C. Schildkraut "Strand Separation and Specific Recombination in Deoxyribonucleic Acids: Physical Chemical Studies," *Proc. Natl. Acad. Sci. USA* 46(4):461–476 (1960).
25. Rich, A. "A Hybrid Helix Containing Both Deoxyribose and Ribose Polynucleotides and its Relation to the Transfer of Information Between the Nucleic Acids," *Proc. Natl. Acad. Sci. USA* 46(80):1044–1053 (1960).
26. Sharp, P. A., B. Sugden, and J. Sambrook "Detection of Two Restriction Endonuclease Activities in Hemophilus Parainfluenzae Using Analytical Agarose-Ethidium Bromide Electrophoresis," *Biochemistry* 12(16):3055–3062 (1973).
27. Southern, E. M. "Detection of Specific Sequences Among DNA Fragments Separated by Gel Electrophoresis," *J. Mol. Biol.* 98(3):503–517 (1975).
28. Rigby, P. W. J., M. Dieckmann, C. Rhodes, and P. Berg "Labelling Deoxyribonucleic Acid to High Specific Activity In Vitro by Nick

Translation With DNA Polymerase I," *J. Mol. Biol.* 113(1):237-251 (1977).

29. "Special Issue — Molecular Evolutionary Clocks," *J. Mol. Evol.* 26:1-376 (1987).

30. Lehman, I. R., M. J. Besman, E. S. Simms, and A. Kornberg "Enzymatic Synthesis of Deoxyribonucleic Acid. I Preparation of Substrates and Partial Purification of an Enzyme From Escherichia coli," *J. Biol. Chem.* 233 (1):163-170 (1958).

31. Crick, F. H. C. "Central Dogma of Molecular Biology," *Nature* 227(5258):561-563 (1970).

32. Baltimore, D. "Viral RNA-Dependent DNA Polymerase," *Nature* 226(5252):1209-1211 (1970).

33. Temin, H. M. and S. Mizutani "RNA-Dependent DNA Polymerase in Virions of Rous Sarcoma Virus," *Nature* 226(5252):1211-1213 (1970).

34. Smith, H. O. and K. W. Wilcox "A Restriction Enzyme From Hemophilus Influenzae. I. Purification and General Properties," *J. Mol. Biol.* 51(2):379-391 (1970).

35. Danna, K. and D. Nathans "Specific Cleavage of Simian Virus 40 DNA by Restriction Endonuclease of Hemophilus Influenzae," *Proc. Natl. Acad. Sci. USA* 68(12):2913-2917 (1971).

36. Mertz, J. and R. W. Davis "Cleavage of DNA by RI Restriction Endonuclease Generates Cohesive Ends," *Proc. Natl. Acad. Sci. USA* 69(11):3370-3374 (1972).

37. Cohen, S. N. "DNA Cloning: A Personal Perspective," *Focus* 10(1):1-4 (1988).

38. Jackson, D. A., R. H. Symons, and P. Berg "Biochemical Method for Inserting New Genetic Information Into DNA of Simian Virus 40: Circular SV40 DNA Molecules Containing Lambda Phage Genes and the Galactose Operon of E. coli". *Proc. Natl. Acad. Sci. USA* 69(10):2904-2909 (1972).

39. Lobban, P. E. and A. D. Kaiser "Enzymatic End-to-End Joining of DNA Molecules," *J. Mol. Biol.* 78(3):453-471 (1973).

40. Cohen, S. N., A. C. Y. Chang, and L. Hsu "Nonchromosomal Antibiotic Resistance in Bacteria: Genetic Transformation of *Escherichia coli* by R-Factor DNA," *Proc. Natl. Acad. Sci. USA* 69(8):2110-2114 (1972).

41. Cohen, S. N., A. C. Y. Chang, H. W. Boyer, and R. B. Helling "Construction of Biologically Functional Bacterial Plasmids In Vitro," *Proc. Natl. Acad. Sci. USA* 70(11):3240-3244 (1973).

42. Maniatis, T., S. G. Kee, A. Efstratiadis, and F. C. Kafatos "Amplification and Characterization of a β-globin Gene Synthesized In Vitro," *Cell* 8(2):163-182 (1976).

43. Rabbits, T. "Bacterial Cloning of Plasmids Carrying Copies of Rabbit Globin Messenger RNA," *Nature* 260(5548):221-225 (1976).

44. Chang, A. C. Y., J. H. Nunberg, R. F. Kaufman, H. A. Erlich, R. T. Schimke, and S. N. Cohen "Phenotypic Expression in *E. coli* of a DNA Sequence Coding for Mouse Dihydrofolate Reductase," *Nature* 275(5681):617-624 (1978).

45. Villa-Kormaroff, L., A. Efstratiadis, S. Broome, P. Lomedico, R. Tizard, S. P. Naber, W. L. Chick, and W. Gilbert "A Bacterial Clone Synthesizing Proinsulin," *Proc. Natl. Acad. Sci. USA* 75(8):3727–3731 (1978).

46. Zoller, M. and M. Smith "Oligonucleotide-Directed Mutagenesis Using M13-derived Vectors: An Efficient and General Procedure for the Production of Point Mutations in Any Fragment of DNA," *Nucleic Acids Res.* 10(20): 6487–6500 (1982).

47. Maxam, A. M. and W. Gilbert "A New Method for Sequencing DNA," *Proc. Natl. Acad. Sci. USA* 74(2):560–564 (1977).

48. Sanger, F., S. Nicklen, and A. R. Coulson "DNA Sequencing with Chain-Terminating Inhibitors," *Proc. Natl. Acad. Sci. USA* 74(12):5463–5467 (1977).

49. Triezenberg, S. J., R. C. Kingsbury, and S. L. McKnight "Functional Dissections of VP16, the Transactivator of Herpes Simplex Immediate Early Gene Expression," *Genes & Devel.* 2(6):730–742 (1988).

50. Watson, J. D. and J. Tooze *The DNA Story: A Documentary History of Gene Cloning*, (San Francisco: W.H. Freeman and Company, 1981).

51. Berg, P., D. Baltimore, S. N. Cohen, R. W. Davis, D. S. Hogness, D. Nathans, R. Roblin, J. D. Watson, S. Weissman, and N. D. Zinder "Potential Biohazards of Recombinant DNA Molecules," *Science* 185(4148):303 (1974).

52. Rogers, M., *Biohazard* (New York: Alfred A. Knopf, 1977).

53. Department of Health, Education, and Welfare. "National Institutes of Health Recombinant DNA Guidelines." *Fed. Reg.* 41(131), Wednesday, July 7, 1976.

54. Brenner, S., "Foreword," in *The Nematode Caenorhabditis Elegans*, W. B. Wood, Ed., Cold Spring Harbor, NY: Cold Spring Harbor Laboratory, 1988, ix-xiii.

55. Little, R. D., G. Porta, G. F. Carle, D. Schlessinger, and M. D'Urso "Yeast Artificial Chromosomes With 200- to 800-kilobase Inserts of Human DNA Containing HLA, V_k, 5S, and Xq24-Xq28 Sequences," *Proc. Natl. Acad. Sci. USA* 86(3):1598–1602 (1989).

56. Mullis, K. B. and F. A. Faloona "Specific Synthesis of DNA in Vitro Via a Polymerase Catalyzed Chain Reaction," *Methods in Enzymology* 155:335–350 (1987).

57. Maniatis, T., E. F. Fritsch, and J. Sambrook *Molecular Cloning* (Cold Spring Harbor, NY: Cold Spring Harbor Laboratory, 1982).

57a. Sambrook, J., E. F. Fritsch, and T. Maniatis, *Molecular Cloning* 2nd ed. (Cold Spring Harbor, NY: Cold Spring Harbor Laboratory, 1988).

58. Witkowski, J. A. "The Discovery of 'Split Genes'; a Scientific Revolution," *Trends Bioch. Sci.* 13(3):110–113 (1988).

59. Cech, T. R., A. J. Zaug, and P. J. Grabowski "In Vitro Splicing of the Ribosomal RNA Precursor of Tetrahymena: Involvement of a Guanosine Nucleotide in the Excision of the Intervening Sequence," *Cell* 27(3):487–496 (1981).

60. Stehelin, D., H. E. Varmus, J. M. Bishop, and P. K. Vogt "DNA

Related to the Transforming Gene(s) of Avian Sarcoma Viruses is Present in Normal Avian DNA," *Nature* 260:170-173 (1976).

61. White, R. and C. T. Caskey "The Human as an Experimental System in Molecular Genetics," *Science* 240(4858):1483–1488 (1988).

62. Tjio, H. J. and A. Levan "The Chromosome Numbers of Man," *Hereditas* 42(1): 1-6 (1956).

63. Weiss, M. C. and H. Green "Human-Mouse Hybrid Cell Lines Containing Partial Complements of Human Chromosomes and Functioning Human Genes," *Proc. Natl. Acad. Sci. USA*, 58(3):1104–1111 (1967).

64. Kidd, K. K., A. M. Bowcock, P. L. Pearson, J. Schmidtke, H. F. Willard, R. K. Track, and F. Ricciuti "Report of the Committee on Human Gene Mapping by Recombinant DNA Techniques," *Human Gene Mapping* 9.5 (1988): Update to the Ninth International Workshop on Human Gene Mapping. Cytogenetics and Cell Genetics 49(1–3):132–218 (1988).

65. Weatherall, D. *The New Genetics and Clinical Practice* (Oxford: Oxford University Press, 1985).

66. Myerowitz, R. and R. L. Proia "cDNA clone for the α-Chain of Human β-hexosaminidase: Deficiency of α-Chain mRNA in Ashkenazi Tay-Sachs Fibroblasts," *Proc. Natl. Acad. Sci. USA* 81(17):5394–5398 (1984).

67. Woo, S. L. C., A. S. Lidsky, F. Guttler, T. Chandra, and K. J. H. Robson "Cloned Human Phenylalanine Hydroxylase Gene Allows Prenatal Diagnosis and Carrier Detection of Classical Phenylketonuria," *Nature* 306(5939):151–155 (1983).

67a. Rommens, J. M., M. C. Ianuzzi, B. S. Kerem, M. L. Drumm, et al. "Identification of the Cystic Fibrosis Gene: Chromosome Walking and Jumping," *Science* 245 (4922): 1059–1065 (1989).

67b. Riordan, J. R., J. M. Rommens, B. S. Kerem, N. Alon, et al. "Identification of the Cystic Fibrosis Gene: Cloning and Characterization of Complementary DNA," *Science* 245(4922): 1066–1073 (1989).

67c. Kerem, B. S., J. R. Rommens, J. A. Buchanan, D. Markiewicz, et al. "Identification of the Cystic Fibrosis Gene: Genetic Analysis," *Science* 245(4922): 1073–1080 (1989).

68. Koenig, M., E. P. Hoffman, C. J. Bertelson, A. P. Monaco, C. Feener, and L. M. Kunkel "Complete Cloning of the Duchenne Muscular Dystrophy (DMD) cDNA and Preliminary Genomic Organization of the DMD Gene in Normal and Affected Individuals," *Cell* 50(3):509–517 (1987).

69. Kan, W. Y., M. S. Golbus, and A. M. Dozy "Prenatal Diagnosis of Alpha-Thalassemia. Clinical Application of Molecular Hybridization," *N. Engl. J. Med.* 295(18):1165-1167 (1976).

70. Chang, J. C. and Y. W. Kan "A Sensitive New Prenatal Test For Sickle-Cell Anemia," *N. Engl. J. Med.* 307(1):30–32 (1982).

71. Orkin, S. H., P. F. R. Little, H. H. Kazazian, and C. D. Boehm "Improved Detection of the Sickle Mutation by DNA Analysis," *N. Engl. J. Med.* 307(1):32–36 (1982).

72. Botstein, D., R. L. White, M. Skolnick, and R. W. Davis "Construction of a Genetic Linkage Map in Man Using Restriction Fragment Length Polymorphisms," *Am. J Human Genet.* 32(3):314–331 (1980).
73. Cudworth, A. G. and H. Festenstein "HLA Genetic Heterogeneity in Diabetes Mellitus," *Br. Med. Bull.* 34(3):285–289 (1978).
74. Witkowski, J. A. and C. T. Caskey "Duchenne Muscular Dystrophy: DNA Diagnosis in Practice," *Curr. Neurol.* 8:1-36 (1988).
75. Harris, A., C. Quinlan, and M. Bobrow "Cystic Fibrosis Typing With DNA Probes: Experience of a Screening Laboratory," *Human Genet.* 79(1)79:76–79 (1988).
76. Meissen, G. J., R. H. Myers, C. A. Mastromauro, W. J. Koroshetz, K. W. Klinger, L. A. Farrer, P. A. Watkins, J. F. Gusella, E. D. Bird, and J. B. Martin "Predictive Testing For Huntington's Disease With Use of a Linked DNA Marker," *N. Engl. J. Med.* 318(9)535–542 (1988).
77. Jeffreys, A. J., J. F. Y. Brookfield, and R. Semeonoff "Positive Identification of an Immigration Test-Case Using DNA Fingerprints," *Nature* 317(6040):818–819 (1985).
78. Gill, P., A. J. Jeffreys, and D. J. Werrett, "Forensic Application of DNA 'Fingerprints'," *Nature* 318(6046):577–579 (1985).
79. Wambaugh, J. *The Blooding*, (New York: William Morrow Company, 1989).
80. Nakamura, Y., M. Leppert, P. O'Connell, R. Wolff, T. Holm, M. Culver, C. Martin, E. Fujimoto, M. Hoff, E. Kumlin, and R. White "Variable Number of Tandem Repeat (VNTR) Markers for Human Gene Mapping," *Science* 235(4796):1616–1622 (1987).
81. Nolan, K. and S. Swenson "New Tools, New Dilemmas: Genetic Frontiers," *Hastings Ctr. Rep.* 18(5):40–46 (1988).
82. Holtzman, N. A. "Recombinant DNA Technology, Genetic Tests, and Public Policy," *Am. J. Human Genet.* 43(4):624–632 (1988).
82a. Holtzman, N. A. *Proceed with Caution: Predicting Genetic Risks in the Recombinant DNA Era* (Baltimore, MD: Johns Hopkins University Press, 1989).
83. Ad Hoc Committee on DNA Technology, American Society of Human Genetics "DNA Banking and DNA Analysis: Points to Consider," *Am. J. Human Genet.* 43(5):781-783 (1988).
84. Motulsky, A. G. "Societal Problems of Forensic Use of DNA Technology", in J. Ballantyne, G. Sensabaugh, and J. Witkowski, Eds. *DNA Technology and Forensic Science.* Banbury Report #32 (Cold Spring Harbor, NY: Cold Spring Harbor Laboratory Press, 1989, 3–12).
85. Nelkin, D. "The Social Meaning of Biological Tests," in J. Ballantyne, G. Sensabaugh, and J. Witkowski, Eds. *DNA Technology and Forensic Science.* Banbury Report #32 (Cold Spring Harbor, NY: Cold Spring Harbor Laboratory Press, 1989, 13–23).
86. Reilly, P. "Reflections on the Use of DNA Forensic Science and Privacy Issues," in J. Ballantyne, G. Sensabaugh, and J. Witkowski, Eds. *DNA Technology and Forensic Science.* Banbury Report #32 (Cold Spring Harbor, NY: Cold Spring Harbor Laboratory Press, 1989, 43–54).

87. Kolata, G. "Genetic Screening Raises Questions For Employers and Insurers," *Science* 232(4748):317–319 (1986).

87a. Report of New York State Forensic DNA Analysis Panel. New York State Division of Criminal Justice (1989).

88. *People v. Seda*, 529 N.Y.S. 2d: 931–941 (Sup 1988).

89. Bashinski, J. S. "Laboratory Standards: Accreditation, Training, and Certification of Staff in the Forensic Context," in J. Ballantyne, G. Sensabaugh, and J. Witkowski, Eds. *DNA Technology and Forensic Science* Banbury Report #32 (Cold Spring Harbor, NY: Cold Spring Harbor Laboratory Press, 1989, 159–173).

89a. Schmeck, H. "DNA Findings are Disputed by Scientists," *New York Times*, B1, May 25, 1989.

89b. Lewin, R. "DNA Typing on the Witness Stand," *Science* 244 (4908): 1033–1035 (1989).

89c. Lander, E. "DNA Fingerprinting on Trial," *Nature* (6225) 339:501–505 (1989).

90. Erlich, H., R. Gibbs, and H. Kazazian *The Polymerase Chain Reaction*, (Cold Spring Harbor, NY: Cold Spring Harbor Laboratory Press, 1989).

91. U. S. Congress, Office of Technology Assessment, "New Developments in Biotechnology — Background Paper: Public Perceptions of Biotechnology," (Washington, D.C.: U. S. Government Printing Office, 1987).

92. U. S. Congress, Office of Technology Assessment, New Developments in Biotechnology — Field-Testing Engineered Organisms: Genetic and Ecological Issues, (Washington, D.C.: U.S. Government Printing Office, 1988).

93. U. S. Congress, Office of Technology Assessment, New Developments in Biotechnology — Patenting Life, (Washington, D.C.: U.S. Government Printing Office, 1989).

94. "Ethics in Embryo," *Harper's*, September 1988, 37–47

95. Ledley, F. D. "Somatic Gene Therapy For Human Disease: A Problem Of Eugenics?," *Trends Genetics* 3(4):112–115 (1987).

2. An Introduction to DNA Structure and Genome Organization

ROGER KAHN, Ph.D.

INTRODUCTION

All biological techniques used to identify individuals take advantage of genetic polymorphism. A method based on a genetic system that is highly polymorphic, i.e., one for which there are many possible and common alleles, is the most desirable, since it best discriminates between individuals. On the other hand, one that reveals very few allelic variants is of little use. With the ultimate individualizing test, no two individuals would share the same result. DNA identity testing often produces results that come close to providing unequivocal identification.

To best utilize the powerful technique of DNA identity testing, it is essential to have a good understanding of the molecular structure of DNA, its characteristics both inside and outside of the cell, and its organization in the genome. An understanding of the DNA structure is also important in exploring issues of reliability and admissibility of DNA test results. Fortunately, the structure of DNA and its arrangement in the cell are not difficult to describe or to understand. In fact, the molecule is remarkably beautiful and elegant in its simplicity.

THE MACROMOLECULES

Deoxyribonucleic acid, or *DNA*, together with the nearly identical molecule called *RNA* or ribonucleic acid, is one of three classes of macromolecules found in all cells. In a manner similar to polysaccharides and proteins, the nucleic acids consist of a polymer formed of repeating subunits. In the case of the polysaccharides, various sugars form the basic units. For proteins, at least 20 different amino acids compose the primary units. In DNA, four types of nucleotides serve as the fundamental subunits.

Although macromolecules all consist of a large number, but limited variety, of specific subunits, they possess very different functions. In animal cells, polysaccharides primarily provide a source of stored energy. Proteins perform a variety of functions, such as the catalysis of chemical reactions. In addition, they regulate the flow of information and serve as structural elements. However, the function of the nucleic acids is the most important, for these molecules store genetic information in a coded form, thereby making all other structure and function possible.

The term *macromolecule* is aptly used to describe these classes of molecules whose molecular weights can all exceed 10,000 daltons. Of the three classes of macromolecules, DNA is by far the largest single molecule in a human cell. The molecular weight of the average human DNA polymer is on the order of 60 billion daltons. These giant, linear DNA chains are known as chromosomes. Each human somatic cell houses 46 chromosomes in 23 pairs. There are about 100–300 million polymerized nucleotide subunits per chromosome for a total of 12 billion nucleotides per diploid human cell.

Overall, the DNA from the chromosome set of a single cell is about 1.5 m in length, a number that is remarkable since each nucleotide contributes just 3.4 Å to the length. Even more striking, the total length of the DNA in all of the 100 trillion cells of the human body is about 93 billion miles, roughly 1000 times the distance of the earth to the sun. While the chromosome is the largest unit of organization of the genetic material, the nucleotide is the smallest. It is the fundamental unit of DNA, and any discussion of the human genome should start there.

DNA STRUCTURE

DNA nucleotides are composed of three entities: a sugar (deoxyribose), a phosphate group, and a base (Figure 1). There are four bases commonly found in DNA nucleotides: adenine (A), guanine (G), thymine (T), and cytosine (C). These bases fall into two groups, purines and pyrimidines. Purine bases consist of two rings while pyrimidines have one. All of the bases are heterocyclic ring structures, composed of rings containing both carbon and nitrogen atoms. In all cases, the bases are attached to the 1' position of the sugar.

Nucleotides, when linked together, form a polymer composed of a sugar-phosphate backbone, which is always the same, and the attached bases, which vary (Figure 2). The phosphate groups link the polymeric units together via a phosphodiester linkage (two C-0 bonds) between the 5' carbon of one sugar molecule and the 3' carbon of the next. Thus, the polymer has a polarity, i.e., a polynucleotide chain always has both a 5' and a 3' end.

(a) Purine nucleotides

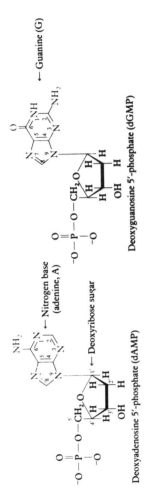

(b) Pyrimidine nucleotides

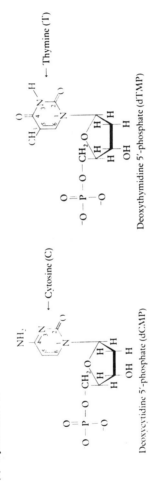

Figure 1.   The four nucleotides of DNA. Each nucleotide consists of a nitrogen-containing base, the 5-carbon sugar deoxyribose, and a phosphate group. Sugar carbon atoms are numbered with prime designators (i.e., 5′) to distinguish them from carbon and nitrogen atoms in the bases. Purine bases, e.g., adenine and guanine, contain two rings, while the pyrimidines, cytosine, and thymine, have one. Reprinted by permission from *An Introduction to Genetic Analysis*, D. T. Suzuki et al. Copyright 1986, W. H. Freeman and Company

SUGAR-PHOSPHATE BACKBONE OF DNA

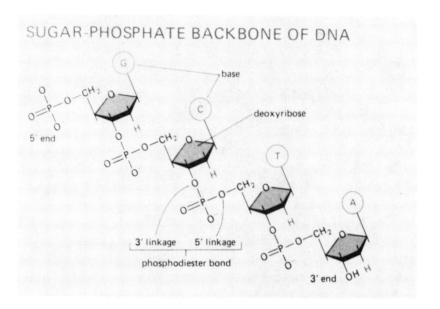

Figure 2. Chain of four polymerized nucleotides. Single-stranded DNA polymer demonstrating strand polarity, phosphodiester linkages, and the negatively charged phosphate groups of the backbone. After B. Alberts et al., *Molecular Biology of the Cell.* Copyright 1986, Garland Publishing, Inc.

The bases bind not only to the sugar moiety, but they also bind specifically, although noncovenantly, to each other; that is, adenine pairs with thymine and guanine pairs with cytosine. This binding occurs across separate strands of the sugar-phosphate backbone, with the result that DNA is generally found in a double-stranded state, with one strand wrapped around the other to form a double helix (Figures 3 and 4). The two strands, arranged with the backbone on the outside and the bases on the inside, are held together both by weak hydrogen bonds between the specifically paired bases on opposite strands and by nonspecific stacking interactions between adjacent bases on the same strand. These stabilizing forces cause the bases to align in a parallel arrangement. Since the base-pairing rule (A with T, G with C) always juxtaposes a two-ring purine with a single-ring pyrimidine, the double helix has a constant diameter (Figure 3). The combination of the double-helical form, parallel base stacking, and constant double-strand diameter bestows a marvelous regularity upon the structure of DNA (Figure 5).

In the double helix, the two DNA chains run antiparallel to one another; that is, a chain running left to right as 5′ to 3′ is always paired with a chain containing a complementary base sequence running in the opposite direction, 3′ to 5′ in this case (Figure 4). By convention, DNA sequences are read in the 5′ to 3′ direction. Although the structure of DNA is remarkably

FOUR BASES AS BASE PAIRS OF DNA

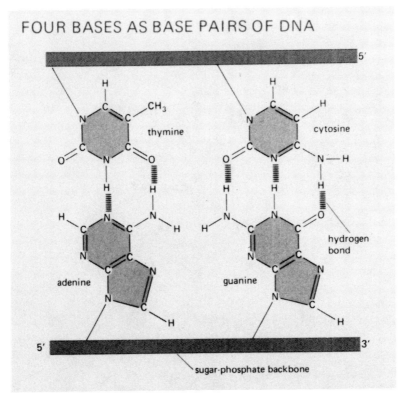

Figure 3. Specific pairing of base pairs. Structure of the four bases of DNA as hydrogen-bonded pairs. Note that cytosine-guanine base pairs are stabilized by three hydrogen bonds, while thymine-adenine have only two such bonds. After B. Alberts et al., *Molecular Biology of the Cell.* Copyright 1986, Garland Publishing, Inc.

simple, its elucidation proved to be a formidable task. The story behind this remarkable feat is set forth in Chapter 1 entitled "Milestones in the Development of DNA Technology" by Dr. Witkowski.

DNA PROPERTIES AND HANDLING CHARACTERISTICS

The weak interactions that maintain DNA in the double-stranded state are rather easily disrupted, and the two strands may thus be unwound and separated. This process, termed *denaturation* or *melting*, is an essential part of the most common DNA typing tests in use at this time. High temperature or high pH can be used to promote denaturation, although alkaline conditions are less likely to cause breakage of DNA than is elevated temperature. Low pH will also promote denaturation, but this condition must be avoided due to the tendancy of DNA to release purine bases

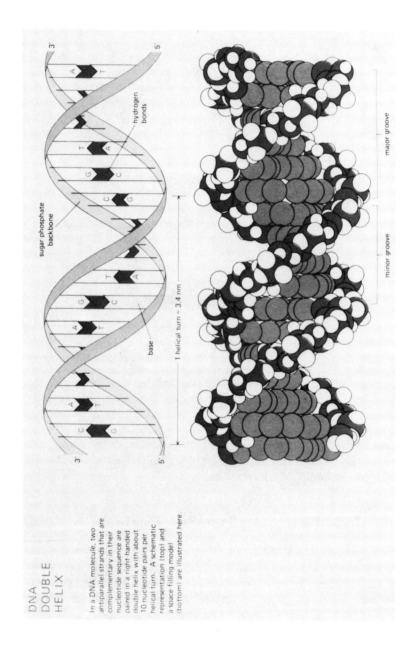

Figure 4. The double helix. The sugar-phosphate backbone forms the exterior surface, while the base pairs face the interior. After B. Alberts et al., *Molecular Biology of the Cell.* Copyright 1986, Garland Publishing, Inc.

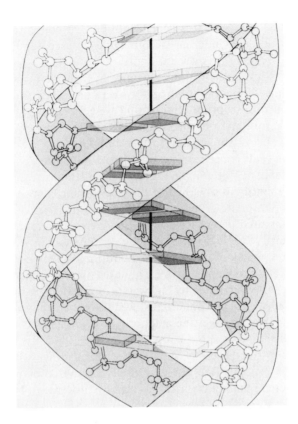

Figure 5. Another view of double-stranded DNA. The sugar-phosphate backbone is shown as ball-and-stick model; the bases are shown as a helical stairway. Reprinted by permission from *An Introduction to Genetic Analysis,* D. T. Suzuki et al. Copyright 1986, W. H. Freeman and Company.

at pH 4 or less and to hydrolyze phosphodiester bonds at pH 1 or less. Whereas DNA is stable in alkali to pH 13, exposure to acid can render it useless for analysis. For an evluation of how environmental variations may affect the analysis of DNA, the reader should see Chapter 6 entitled "Validation with Regard to Environmental Insults of the RFLP Procedure for Forensic Purposes."

DNA denaturation is reversible. The formation of duplex DNA from complementary chains of single-stranded DNA is known as renaturation, annealing (or reannealing), or hybridization. Strictly speaking, the term *hybridization* indicates that the reassociated strands were not original partners. The three terms are commonly used interchangeably, however. Unlike denaturation, which can be accomplished in minutes or even seconds, renaturation is a slow process that is dependent upon the concentrations of the hybridizing sequences. Under conditions typically used for DNA identity testing, this process requires several hours.

In addition to extended lengths of time, hybridization requires rather precise conditions of ionic strength and temperature. The temperature must be high enough to disrupt any intrastrand base pairs, but low enough to allow the stable formation of interstrand base pairs. The optimal temperature is 20–25°C below the melting temperature (T_m).

Increasing the salt concentration stabilizes base pairing and, therefore, increases the tendancy of complementary single strands to renature. This effect is due primarily to shielding of the electrostatic charges of the negatively charged phosphate groups by sodium ions and by a decrease in the solubility of unpaired bases at elevated salt levels. Typical salt concentrations in hybridization reactions range from 0.15 M to 1.0 M.

Hybridization reactions are usually performed under conditions that favor the formation of duplex DNA. Duplexes that are imperfectly paired can be subsequently eliminated by high-temperature and low-salt concentration, i.e., so-called stringent conditions. Reducing the stringency of hybridization conditions encourages the maintenance of duplexes containing mismatched or otherwise unpaired bases.

Purified DNA can be easily stored in a manner that will prevent its degradation. In general, DNA in stain materials can be more stable than enzymes or proteins commonly assayed from forensic stains. Purified DNA can be stored for many months, perhaps even years, in a sterile aqueous solution buffered at pH 7–9 at +4°C. It may be stored indefinitely if it is lyophilized or frozen in solution. DNA in blood or sperm cells that has been allowed to dry into a stain has been shown to last for months if kept in a cool, dry environment at room temperature (R. Kahn, unpublished results; D. Adams, personal communication).

The longevity of DNA in various forensic samples is the subject of ongoing investigations in several laboratories. Some of these results will be found in this volume. In general, however, degradation of DNA in stain materials will be promoted by exposure to UV light or other forms of radiation, to extremes of pH, or to wet and humid conditions. The effect of humidity on the degradation of DNA in stains can be at least partly explained by the susceptibility of DNA to attack by a variety of enzymes, known as nucleases, that are found in all cells. Nucleases are released by microorganisms into their surroundings as a part of their food accumulation effort and by lysing eukaryotic cells. Storage conditions that support the growth of microorganisms will tend to reduce the time that intact, highly polymerized DNA can be recovered from stains. Microorganisms will also contribute DNA to preparations of stain DNA, increasing the difficulty of recovering pure samples.

GENOME ORGANIZATION AND INFORMATION FLOW

The Central Dogma of biology states that information flow in a cell follows the path:

$$\text{DNA} \xrightarrow{\text{transcription}} \text{RNA} \xrightarrow{\text{translation}} \text{PROTEIN}$$

and, except for certain interesting but unusual exceptions, this scheme is ubiquitous (Figure 6). The diagram does not show the third path of information flow, that of DNA to DNA, which occurs during DNA replication.

To initiate the flow of information, DNA is copied or transcribed into the related, single-stranded nucleic acid, RNA, which is then processed in the nucleus. Processing includes a) the addition of a single, uniquely modified guanine nucleotide cap to the 5' end of the transcript; b) the addition of approximately 200 adenine nucleotides to the 3' end; and c) the removal of noncoding stretches of RNA that interrupt the coding segments.

In eukaryotes, the first process is mandatory, and the second occurs with the vast majority of transcripts. The third process occurs whenever noncoding information is encoded within the gene, as in most genes of higher eukaryotes. The RNA is then transported across the nuclear membrane into the cytoplasm where, on structures known as ribosomes, the nucleotide code is translated into the corresponding amino acid sequence (Figure 6).

There are, in fact, four classes of RNA sequences involved in the sequential phases of information flow. One of these classes, messenger RNA or mRNA, contains the code that will be translated precisely into the amino acid sequence of a protein. The three other classes, namely, ribosomal RNA (rRNA), transfer RNA (tRNA), and small nuclear and cytoplasmic RNA (snRNA and scRNA), serve specific functions as RNA molecules and are not translated into protein.

rRNAs, of which there are several species, are integral parts of the ribosome, serving a structural as well as a mRNA stabilizing function during the initiation of translation. tRNA molecules are adapters that convert nucleic acid sequences into amino acid sequences according to the triplet codon rules of the genetic code. They accomplish this by pairing in a specific, complementary fashion to the mRNA in the ribosome while carrying a specific amino acid to add to the protein under construction. There are usually several tRNA molecules for each of the 20 amino acids due to the redundancy of the genetic code. snRNA and scRNA compose a class of molecules whose functions are only partly elucidated. Some play a role in the excision of noncoding sequences of mRNA and in mRNA transport into the cytoplasm. They may have additional roles in stabilizing mRNA and other as yet undeciphered functions.

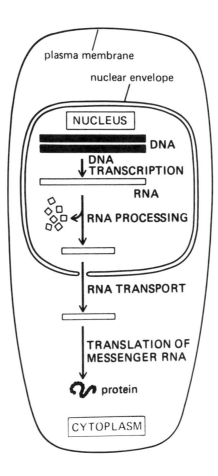

Figure 6. Information transfer in the eukaryotic cell. Information is transferred from DNA to RNA to protein in a set of discrete, compartmentalized steps. After B. Alberts et al., *Molecular Biology of the Cell*. Copyright 1986, Garland Publishing, Inc.

As previously mentioned, most of the genes of higher eukaryotes, including humans, contain internal sequences that are spliced out of primary transcripts before they are transported out of the nucleus. The excised segments are termed *introns* or *intervening sequences* and the coding sequences, which are spliced together to form the functional mRNA, are called *exons*. Introns are found in rRNA and some tRNAs, as well as in mRNA.

Introns in mRNA, however, frequently comprise the majority of the length of the original transcript, and in some cases comprise nearly all of the primary transcript. An extreme example of this is found in the gene for human Factor VIII, which is involved in blood clotting. This gene is approximately 186,000 base pairs in length, but after the removal of 25 introns, the mature transcript consists of only about 9000 nucleotides.[1] The exons vary in size from 69 to 3106 base pairs; however, all but 2 are less than 320 base pairs. This motif of relatively small exons bounded by remarkably large introns is not unusual. However, the number of introns and the number of nucleotides per intron vary widely. Some genes, such as histones, contain no introns. Although the actual proportion of intron to exon DNA in the eukaryotic genome is not known, the emerging view is one of large blocks of unique-sequence DNA that do not code for protein. These blocks are found not only as introns, but also as spacer regions of unique-sequence DNA lying between genes.

Like intron DNA, spacer DNA can markedly increase the amount of DNA in the eukaryotic genome beyond the minimally required sequences. One of the clearest examples of this phenomenon is the betalike globin gene family on human chromosome 11. This gene cluster of similar but nonidentical genes spans a region of over 50,000 base pairs. It consists of a tandem array of five functional globin genes and one dysfunctional globin gene remnant called a pseudogene. Of the 50 kilobase (kb) pairs, less than 20% is comprised of active transcription units. Of this 20%, only about 30% consists of sequences ultimately translated into protein. Overall, less than 5% of the DNA in the cluster is translated. A similar motif is found for the alphalike globin family on chromosome 16, where a 28-kb pair region contains three active genes and three pseudogenes.

Gene families are not unique to the globin system. Clustering of related genes is especially common for structural proteins, such as the tubulins and actins, and where marked diversity is desirable, such as the variable-chain immunoglobulin genes (V genes) and the transplantation or histocompatibility genes (HLA genes). In addition, the genome also contains tandemly repeated genes. Unlike a family, these are a set of identical genes and spacer elements arrayed in a head-to-tail fashion. The genes for tRNAs, rRNAs, and the histones are all tandemly repeated, hundreds of times in some organisms.

UNIQUE SEQUENCE VS. REPETITIVE SEQUENCE DNA

Hidden in the approximately 3 billion base pairs of DNA of the haploid human genome is an estimated 25,000–100,000 genes with an approximate average length of 5–10 kb pairs, including introns. In addition, DNA contains signal sequences for a variety of processes, such as gene expression regulation, DNA replication, chromosome packing, and chromosome segregation. Including spacer DNA, signal sequences, and protein coding DNA, unique sequences account for approximately 70–80% of the total

Table 1. Repetitive DNA in the Human Genome

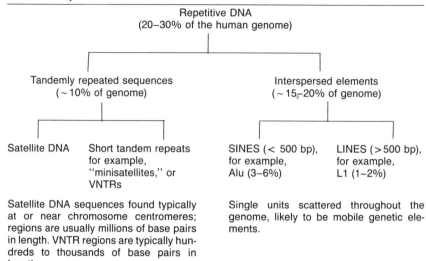

Repetitive DNA
(20–30% of the human genome)

Tandemly repeated sequences
(~ 10% of genome)

Interspersed elements
(~ 15–20% of genome)

Satellite DNA   Short tandem repeats
for example,
"minisatellites," or
VNTRs

SINES (< 500 bp),   LINES (>500 bp),
for example,   for example,
Alu (3–6%)   L1 (1–2%)

Satellite DNA sequences found typically at or near chromosome centromeres; regions are usually millions of base pairs in length. VNTR regions are typically hundreds to thousands of base pairs in length.	Single units scattered throughout the genome, likely to be mobile genetic elements.

Adapted from J. C. S. Fowler et al., "Repetitive Deoxyribonucleic Acid (DNA) and Human Genome Variation—A Concise Review to Forensic Biology," *J. Forensic Sci.*, Vol. 33, 1988. Copyright ASTM.

human genome. The remaining 20–30% of the genome consists of repetitive, primarily noncoding sequences of uncertain function.

Repetitive DNA can be divided into two classes: tandemly repetitive sequences and interspersed repeats (Table 1). For a recent review and bibliography, see Fowler et al.[2] Tandem repetitive DNA accounts for roughly one third of the repetitive DNA in the human genome, about 10% of the entire length. Like tandemly repeated genes, these regions consist of head-to-tail repeats of a particular sequence, but they are comprised of much shorter units, ranging from 5 to 250 base pairs, repeated typically hundreds of thousands of times. Regions of this type are referred to as *satellite DNA* because of the tendency of some of these sequences to form "satellite" bands in equilibrium density gradients, thus simplifying their separation from other chromosomal DNA. In humans, as in a variety of higher eukaryotes, there are several classes or families of satellite DNAs. At least some of these classes are associated with the centrome regions of the chromosomes.

A minor fraction of tandemly repeated DNA, consisting of regions much shorter than satellite DNA, exhibits an extraordinary variability in overall length (Table 1).[3] These regions, termed *minisatellites*[4] or variable number tandem repeats (VNTRs),[5] are comprised of short, i.e., 9–64 base pair, "core" sequences in tandem arrays at unique chromosomal loci.[5,6] The length of the region depends upon the number of times the core sequence is repeated.

It is possible to determine the lengths of the DNA comprising the two alleles carried by an individual by using standard molecular biological techniques. Testing of this type has revealed remarkable heterozygosities, greater than 70% at many loci and some as high as 99%.[5,6] These loci have received a great deal of attention from forensic scientists recently, as they form the basis of the most common form of DNA identity testing currently in use. For a review of this restriction fragment length polymorphism (RFLP) technique, see the following chapter by Dr. Michael Baird.

The largest class of repetitive DNA consists not of tandem arrays, but of individual units of specific sequences distributed widely throughout the eukaryotic genome. In humans, these interspersed elements account for as much as 20% of the total DNA (Table 1). The most common element of this type is termed the *Alu family* (named for the restriction enzyme *Alu*I, since these sequences generally contain a site for cleavage by this enzyme). These sequences, which are about 300 base pairs in length, account for roughly 5% of the human genome. In other words, a member of this family will be encountered, on the average, every 5–10-kb pairs. Alu DNA and other interspersed repeats that are less than 500 base pairs are categorized as short interspersed elements or SINES. Long interspersed elements, or LINES, are greater than 500 base pairs and are exemplified by the Ll or Kpn family (for the restriction enzyme *Kpn*I), which comprise 1–2% of the genome. Ll elements are found as 7-kb pair elements or truncations of the parent sequence family. Interspersed elements, as a class, appear to propogate themselves throughout the genome as mobile genetic elements or transposons.

SUMMARY

The advent of DNA identity testing has resulted in a surge of interest in the forensic community in the properties of DNA and its organization in the human genome. This chapter is intended to provide a framework from which the forensic scientist can pursue these topics in more detail. For those who desire an expanded presentation, a variety of recent texts are available, including Alberts et al.,[7] Darnell et al.,[8] Freifelder,[9] Lewin,[10] Singer,[11] Suzuki et al.,[12] and Watson et al.[13]

ACKNOWLEDGMENTS

I wish to thank Lisa Yee, M.D. and Michael Hass, Ph.D. for helpful criticism in the preparation of the manuscript. For their encouragement and support during the initial development of our DNA identity testing program, I would like to acknowledge Fred Taylor, Director; Eduardo Gonzalez, Deputy Director; Thomas J. Spurlock, Chief of Technical Services; Dr. William J. Hartner, Commander; and W.C. "Bud" Stuver, Supervisor, Biology/Serology Section, Crime Laboratory Bureau, Metro-Dade Police Department.

REFERENCES

1. Gitschier, J., W. I. Wood, T. M. Goralka, K. L. Wion, E. Y. Chen, D. H. Eaton, G. A. Vehar, D. J. Caron, and R. M. Lawn "Characterization of the Human Factor VIII Gene," *Nature* 312:326–330 (1984).
2. Fowler, J. C. S., L. A. Burgoyne, A. C. Scott, and H. W. J. Harding "Repetitive Deoxyribonucleic Acid (DNA) and Human Genome Variation — A Concise Review Relevant to Forensic Biology, *J. Forensic Sci.* 33:1111–1126 (1988).
3. Wyman, A. R., and R. White "A Highly Polymorphic Locus in Human DNA," *Proc. Natl. Acad. Sci. USA* 77:6754–6758 (1980).
4. Jeffreys, A. J., V. Wilson, and S. L Thein "Hypervariable 'Minisatellite' Regions in Human DNA," *Nature* 314:67–73 (1985).
5. Nakamura, Y., M. Leppert, P. O'Connell, R. Wolff, T. Holm, M. Culver, C. Martin, E. Fujimoto, M. Hoff, E. Kumlin, and R. White "Variable Number Tandem Repeat (VNTR) Markers for Human Gene Mapping," *Science* 235:1616–1622 (1987).
6. Wong, Z., V. Wilson, I. Patel, S. Povey, and A. J. Jeffreys "Characterization of a Panel of Highly Variable Minisatellites Cloned from Human DNA," *Ann. Hum. Genet.* 51:269–288 (1987).
7. Alberts, B., D. Bray, J. Lewis, M. Raff, K. Roberts, and J. D. Watson *Molecular Biology of the Cell* (New York: Garland Publishing, Inc., 1983).
8. Darnell, J., H. Lodish, and D. Baltimore *Molecular Cell Biology* (New York: Scientific American Books, Inc., 1986).
9. Freifelder, D. *Molecular Biology* (Boston: Jones and Bartlett Publishers, Inc., 1987).
10. Lewin, B. *Genes* (New York: John Wiley and Sons, 1987).
11. Singer, S. *Human Genetics* (New York: W.H. Freeman and Company, 1985).
12. Suzuki, D. T., A. J. F. Griffiths, J. H. Miller, and R. C. Lewontin *An Introduction to Genetic Analysis* (New York: W. H. Freeman and Company, 1986).
13. Watson, J. D., N. H. Hopkins, J. W. Roberts, J. A. Steitz, and A. M. Weiner *Molecular Biology of the Gene* (Menlo Park, CA: Benjamin/ Cummings Publishing Company, Inc., 1987).

3. Analysis of Forensic DNA Samples by Single Locus VNTR Probes

MICHAEL L. BAIRD, Ph.D.

The analysis of DNA isolated from forensic biological evidence provides powerful information relating to the identification of the source of the sample. Restriction fragment length polymorphism (RFLP) testing, using a combination of single locus probes that vary highly among individuals, produces a DNA print or profile. The frequency of occurrence of the DNA print can be calculated from the allele frequency of the components of the pattern. This chapter will outline the types of testing performed at Lifecodes Corporation with the controls and standards used to ensure accurate testing (Figure 1).

EXTRACTION

DNA is isolated from nucleated cells with the use of standard procedures, including proteinase K, SDS, EDTA, phenol, and chloroform. A small portion of the evidence is not processed and is saved for polymerase chain reaction (PCR) analysis. Different identification plasmids may be added in order to track samples being processed and may be used later to evaluate interlane mobility after electrophoresis.

Semen stains are first treated with solutions that lyse contaminating female epithelial cells.[1] This female DNA is processed separately along with the DNA from the sperm heads and can be used to generate the victim's DNA pattern. Dried blood stains and liquid blood are processed using standard procedures.[2] All DNA preparations are dialyzed against excess 1 × TE buffer. The quality and quantity of isolated DNA is evaluated by electrophoresis of a portion of undigested DNA (about 1%) on a 15-cm yield gel, which includes a set of DNAs of known concentration plus size markers (Figure 2). The intensity of the ethidium-bromide-stained DNA is used to estimate the amount of DNA available for analysis (as little as 5 ng can be seen in a band). A photograph of this gel is maintained.

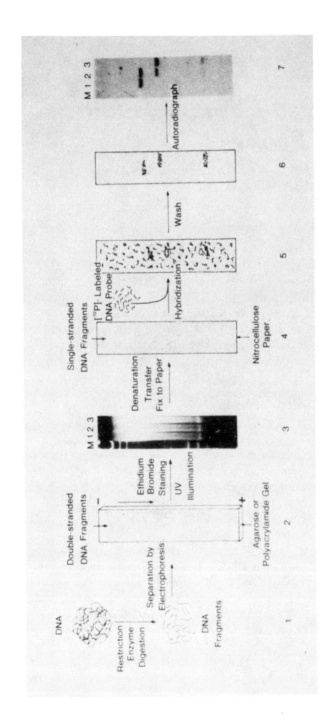

Figure 1. Diagram of the RFLP analysis used for testing of DNA isolated from forensic biological material.

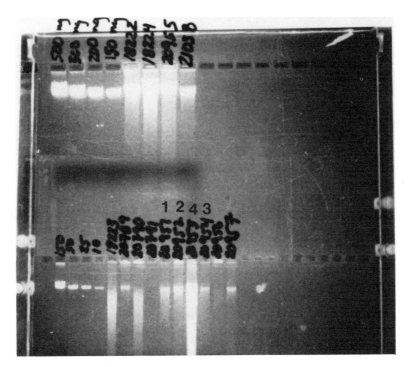

Figure 2.   Yield gel. Undigested DNA was applied to a 15-cm agarose gel, size separated by electrophoresis, and stained with ethidium bromide. Concentration controls from 500 to 10 ng in left lanes. Note sample 20953, semen stain, shows partial degradation by smear of florescence in lane 4.

The mobility of the undigested DNA indicates the quality of the isolated DNA. Uncut DNA, which is about 20 kilobase (kb) pairs in size, is considered high molecular weight. Degradation is indicated by a smear of DNA fragments. If the uncut DNA is degraded to the point where no material is apparent above 2 kb, this sample is not likely to produce results by RFLP analysis and should be saved for PCR testing. A small portion of uncut DNA is routinely saved for additional analysis by PCR. The DNA on the yield gel may be transferred to a nylon membrane and hybridized to the human Alu repeat[3] to determine the amount of human DNA present. This test is at least 10-fold more sensitive than ethidium-bromide staining.

DIGESTION

DNA is digested with the restriction endonuclease *Pst*I, which recognizes the six-nucleotide sequence CTGCAG. The first digestion is done with a 20-fold excess for 1 hr in a volume dictated by the DNA concentration.

1 2 4 3

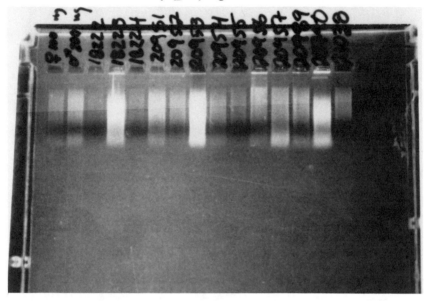

Figure 3. Test gel. An aliquot of each *Pst*I digest was applied to a 15-cm agarose gel, size separated by electrophoresis, and stained with ethidium bromide. Male and female control DNAs are on the left. 1 = rape victim 20951; 2 = vaginal swab 20952; 3 = suspect 20954; 4 = semen stain on panties 20953.

Although 50 ng of DNA can yield a result, more evidentiary DNA (about 1 μg) is usually required, because this DNA is often partially degraded. This reduces the amount of correctly cut DNA available to react with the probe.

After ethanol precipitation, the DNA is resuspended in a small volume and redigested with *Pst*I. A portion of this digestion (about 10%) is evaluated on a 15-cm test gel to determine if the sample is digested (Figure 3). A male and female control DNA plus size markers are included on each gel. After electrophoresis and staining by ethidium bromide, the gel is photographed. Digestion is indicated by a smear of DNA from the top of the gel to below 2 kb, similar to the control DNAs. Undigested DNA remains near the top of the gel. The amount of DNA loaded is estimated from the staining intensity relative to the controls.

These DNAs are then transferred to a nylon membrane and hybridized with a combination of probes that recognize the DXZ1[4] and DYZ1[5] loci. DNA that reacts with the DYZ1 locus is most likely to be from a male. A control cell-line DNA, K562, is isolated and digested along with the unknown samples to control for enzyme activity. Also, all solutions and reagents are tested before use. The *Pst*I is tested by cutting both known bacterial viral and human DNAs.

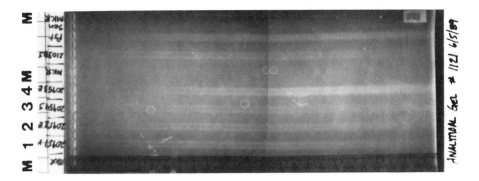

Figure 4. Analytical gel. The remainder of each *Pst*I digest was applied to a 30-cm agarose gel (gel number 1121), size separated for 3 days, and stained with ethidium bromide. These DNAs were transferred to a nylon membrane and hybridized with a series of p³²-labeled DNA probes.

ELECTROPHORESIS AND TRANSFER

Once the DNAs are digested, they are separated by size for comparative purposes by electrophoresis on a 30-cm analytical gel (Figure 4). This gel is run at room temperature for 3 days at a low voltage in TAN buffer with circulation. Size markers composed of bacterial viral DNAs cut with a variety of restriction enzymes flank the samples. These size markers generate a sizing ladder from large to small size on the final autoradiograph that is used to determine DNA fragment sizes from the samples. A control DNA is included on each gel.

Samples are loaded into the wells of the gel such that the entire sample digest is loaded, avoiding the possibility of loading the same sample twice. Lanes are skipped between samples whenever possible to avoid the possibility of sample spilling in from adjacent lanes. The gel is loaded with victim evidence, the suspect's DNA, and whenever possible, a single lane containing DNA from the evidence and the suspect for easy comparison. For a paternity analysis, samples of mother, child, alleged father, and child plus alleged father are loaded in adjacent lanes, which are flanked by size markers. A piece of numbered nylon mesh is embedded in the gel for identification. This gel is stained, photographed, and transferred to a nylon membrane by capillary action.[6]

HYBRIDIZATION AND AUTORADIOGRAPHY

DNA probes, labeled with ³²P, are applied sequentially to the membrane to generate the DNA print. The following polymorphic loci are routinely examined: D2S44,[7] D14S13,[7] D17S79,[8] DXYS14,[9] and D18S27.[10] In addition, probes that recognize constant regions within the DNA, DXZ1,[4] and

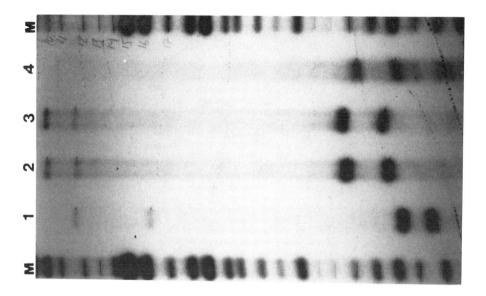

Figure 5. Results of hybridization of nylon membrane from gel 1121 to DNA probes that detects the highly polymorphic loci D2S44 (top) and D17S79 (bottom). M = size markers; 1 = victim; 2 = vaginal swab; 3 = suspect; 4 = semen stain.

DNF24[11] are used to document any interlane mobility differences[12] that may be present. They also indicate the extent of degradation. Hybridizations are performed using standard conditions at 68°C aqueous using oligonucleotide probes. The membranes are washed to $0.1 \times SSC$ at 68°C, dried briefly, wrapped in plastic, and placed against x-ray film in a cassette for 1 to 5 days to generate autoradiographs with bands within a linear range. The x-ray film is developed to produce the autoradiograph or autorad (Figure 5). The membranes are stripped of signal prior to rehybridization with 50% formamide at 68°C (Figures 6–8).

ANALYSIS

The initial analysis is performed by visual inspection of all the autoradiographs generated in the case. A match between two lanes is indicated if the patterns from all probe systems are the same. If the sample is partially degraded, the larger fragments may not be present, for example, at the D2S44 locus. It has been shown that the pattern does not change in degraded samples due to environmental conditions[13] or substrate.[14] Mobility differences may occur, especially in degraded samples, but are easily documented by the use of constant, nonvariant probes[12] (Figure 9).

Additional analysis is performed using a computerized sizing system employing either a video camera or a bit pad. These systems use the size

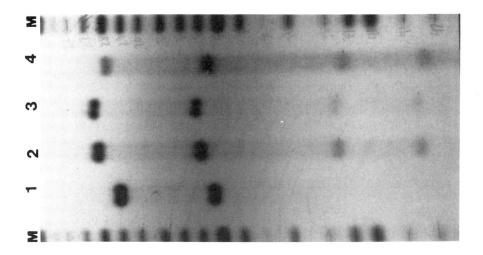

Figure 6. Results of hybridization of nylon membrane from gel 1121 to DNA probe that detects the highly polymorphic locus DXYS14.

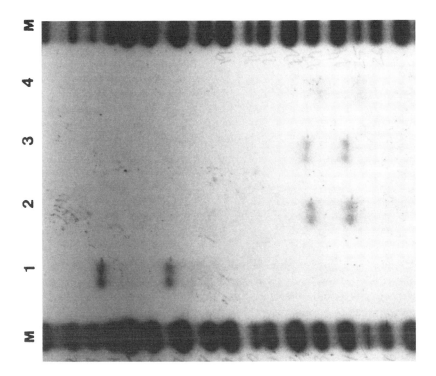

Figure 7. Results of hybridization of nylon membrane from gel 1121 to DNA probe that detects the highly polymorphic locus D14S13.

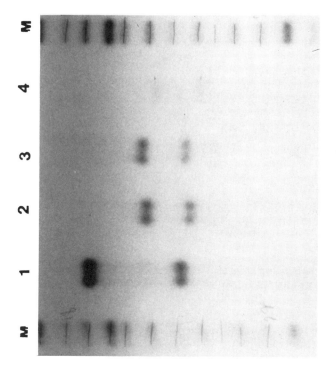

Figure 8.   Results of hybridization of nylon membrane from gel 1121 to DNA probe that detects the highly polymorphic locus D18S27.

markers to determine the fragment sizes of the samples. Computerized bit pad sizing is performed twice, and an average of the fragment sizes is determined. Video sizing is done once.

POPULATION GENETICS

The frequency of occurrence of the pattern at each locus, except for DXYS14, is calculated by multiplying the allele frequencies of the DNA fragments according to the Hardy–Weinberg equation. All frequencies within 1.8% (three average deviations) of the size of the fragment are added together to determine the final allele frequency. For the DXYS14 locus, because there are haplotypes that produce overall patterns with 1–8 bands per person, the database is merely queried to determine how frequently a particular pattern has been observed. Each of the loci appear to meet the assumptions of Hardy–Weinberg and are located on separate chromosomes, which is good evidence that there is no linkage disequilibrium.[15,16] Therefore the final frequency of occurrence is calculated by multiplying the

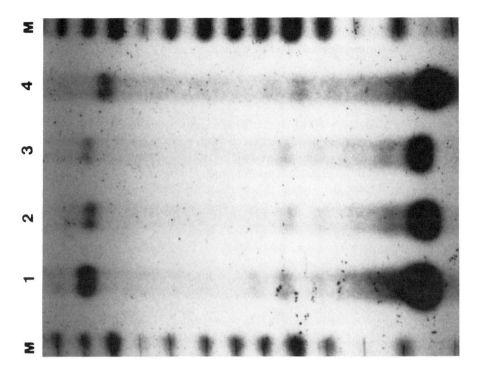

Figure 9. Results of hybridization of nylon membrane from gel 1121 to DNA probe that detects the monomorphic locus DXZ1. The overall DNA-print pattern from the five highly polymorphic loci indicate that the patterns seen from the vaginal swab, semen stain, and suspect match. The semen stain DNA was partially degraded (no signal at the D2S44 locus, Figure 5). The interlane mobilities of each lane were normalized with the monomorphic probe, which shows that the semen stain DNA traveled faster than the suspect DNA.

individual frequencies of occurrence at each locus. Running the same DNA sample multiple times shows that sizes fall within three average deviations (one average deviation equals 0.6% of the fragment size) in a Gaussian fashion. When results of constant band probes are included, the visual matches are confirmed by computer-assisted sizings. Two DNA fragments are considered the same numerically if they are within 1.8% of each other after correcting for mobility differences.

The databases for each locus are generated for black, Caucasian, Hispanic, and Oriental populations.[17] There are currently between 500 and 2000 people in the databases at Lifecodes Corporation for the various ethnic groups examined. Significant racial differences are apparent in some allele frequencies, but the size ranges over which fragments can vary appear similar among all ethnic groups. Studies done at Lifecodes to compare allele frequency distribution in different geographic areas in the United States within a single ethnic group indicate no significant differences in allele frequencies.[18] Sizing of the same samples in different labs using the same conditions shows concordance in fragment sizes.

SUMMARY

Testing of DNA by RFLP analysis promises to revolutionize the identification of biological evidence recovered from a crime scene. When an adequate amount of high molecular weight DNA is available, a DNA print generated with four to six independent loci will produce a profile that can identify the person from whom that biological evidence came. This is particularly helpful in sexual assault cases and in some murder cases.

BIBLIOGRAPHY

1. Guisti, A., M. Baird, S. Pasquale, I. Balazs, and J. Glassberg "Application of Deoxyribonucleic Acid (DNA) Polymorphisms to the Analysis of DNA Recovered From Sperm," *J. Forensic Sci.* 31:409–417 (1986).
2. Kanter, E., M. Baird, R. Shaler, and I. Balazs "Analysis of Restriction Fragment Length Polymorphisms in Deoxyribonucleic Acid (DNA) Recovered From Dried Bloodstains," *J. Forensic Sci.* 31:403–408 (1986).
3. Jelinek, W., T. Toomey, L. Leinwand, C. Duncan, P. Biro, P. Choudary, and S. Weissman "Ubiquitous, Interspersed Repeated Sequences in Mammalian Genomes," *Proc. Natl. Acad. Sci., USA* 77:1398–1402 (1980).
4. Yang, T., S. Hansen, K. Oishi, O. Ryder, and B. Hamkalo "Characterization of a Cloned Repetitive DNA Sequence Concentrated on the Human X Chromosome," *Proc. Natl. Acad. Sci.* 79:6593–6597 (1982).
5. Nakahori, Y., K. Mitani, M. Yamada, and Y. Nakagome "A Human Y-Chromosome Specific Repeated DNA Family (DYZ1) Consists of a Tandem Array of Pentanucleotides," *Nucleic Acids Res.* 14:7569–7580 (1986).
6. Southern, E. "Detection of Specific Sequences Among DNA Fragments Separated by Gel Electrophoresis," *J. Mol. Biol.*, 98:503–517 (1975).
7. Nakamura, Y., M. Leppert, P. O'Connell, R. Wolff, T. Holm, M. Culver, C. Martein, E. Fujimoto, M. Hoff, E. Kumlin, and R. White "Variable Number of Tandem Repeat (VNTR) Markers for Human Gene Mapping," *Science* 235:1616–1622 (1987).
8. Nakamura, Y., M. Lathrop, P. O'Connell, M. Leppert, D. Barker, E. Wright, M. Skolnick, S. Kondoleon, M. Litt, J. Lalouel, and R. White "A Mapped Set of DNA Markers for Human Chromosome 17," *Genomics* 2:302–309 (1988).
9. Cooke, H., W. Brown, and G. Rappold "Hypervariable Telomeric

Sequences From the Human Sex Chromosomes Are Pseudoautosomal," *Nature* 317:687–692 (1985).

10. Ip, N., I. van de Stadt, Z. Loewy, S. Leary, K. Grzechik, and I. Balazs "Identification and Characterization of a Hypervariable Region [D18S27] on Chromosome 18," *Nucleic Acids Res.* 17:8404 (1989).

11. Ip, N., L. Nicholas, H. Baum, and I. Balazs "Discovery of a Novel Multilocus DNA Polymorphism (DNF24)," *Nucleic Acids Res.* 17:4427 (1989).

12. McNally, L., M. Baird, K. McElfresh, A. Eisenberg, and I. Balazs "Increased Migration Rate Observed in DNA from Evidentiary Material Precludes the Use of Sample Mixing to Resolve Forensic Cases of Identity," *Appl. Theoret. Electrophoresis* 1:267–272 (1990).

13. McNally, L., R. Shaler, M. Baird, I. Balazs, P. DeForest, and L. Kobilinsky, "Evaluation of Deoxyribonucleic Acid (DNA) Isolated from Human Bloodstains Exposed to Ultraviolet Light, Heat, Humidity, and Soil Contamination," *J. Forensic Sci.* 34:1059–1069 (1989).

14. McNally, L., R. Shaler, M. Baird, I. Balazs, L. Kobilinsky, and P. DeForest "The Effects of Environment and Substrata on Deoxyribonucleic Acid (DNA), The Use of Casework Samples From New York City," *J. Forensic Sci.* 34:1070–1077 (1989).

15. Balazs, I., M. Baird, K. McElfresh, and J. Udey "Hardy-Weinberg Equilibrium Analysis of DNA Polymorphic Loci that Exhibit a Continuous Distribution of Fragment Sizes," in H. Polesky and W. Mayr, Eds. *Advances in Forensic Haemogenetics 3* (New York: Springer-Verlag, 1990, 71–74).

16. Devlin, B., N. Risch, and K. Roeder "No Excess of Homozygosity at Loci Used for DNA Fingerprinting," *Science* in press (1990).

17. Balazs, I., M. Baird, M. Clyne, and E. Meade "Human Population Genetic Studies of Five Hypervariable DNA Loci," *Am. J. Human Genet.* 44:182–190 (1989).

18. Balazs, I., J. Chimera, A. Eisenberg, D. Endean, R. Giles, J. Kateley, S. Maguire, B. Schall, A. Turck, and R. McKee "Accuracy, Precision, and Site-to-Site Reproducibility in Analysis of DNA Polymorphisms for Identity Testing," in H. Polesky and W. Mayr, Eds. *Advances in Forensic Haemogenetics 3* (New York: Springer-Verlag, 1990, 54–59).

4. Population Genetics of Hypervariable Human DNA

LAURENCE D. MUELLER, Ph.D.

POPULATION GENETICS BACKGROUND

A number of genetically based traits may be used in identifying an individual including, for example, the individual's race, hair color, height, and/or weight. Some of these characteristics have a well-established genetic basis (e.g., race), while other characteristics, such as weight, have both a genetic and a substantial environmental contribution. The extent to which these traits are useful in identifying a particular individual depends on how common the various characteristics are in the population. Thus, for example, knowledge that an individual has brown hair may not be terribly useful in distinguishing him from other individuals in a typical population in the United States. If, however, that person had purple hair, this feature would be quite useful.

In a similar vein, the information contained in the genotype[1] of a tissue sample found at the scene of a crime will be useful in identifying the criminal only if a fairly small number of individuals in the potential suspect population have this genotype. The methods utilized for determining the frequencies of hypervariable genotypes[2] of individuals must be objective and calculable from basic principles of genetics.

The process of statistically defining the chances of finding a particular genotype in a biological population of interest falls within the discipline of population genetics. Genotype frequencies are usually calculated by the product rule.[3] The application of this rule requires that two principles of

---

[1]*Genotype* may be defined as an individual's genetic constitution at one or more gene loci. For a single gene, for instance, an individual's genotype would consist of a description of the forms of the gene inherited from that person's mother and father.

[2]A hypervariable genotype is a genotype that is highly variable in the population.

[3]The product rule specifies the calculations that are performed to estimate the probability of finding a particular genotype in a reference population of interest. It is discussed in more detail later in this chapter.

population genetics be obeyed, i.e., the Hardy-Weinberg law[4] and the condition of linkage equilibrium.[5]

Most laboratories specifically assume that both the Hardy–Weinberg Law and linkage equilibrium are obeyed when they calculate the chance of finding a particular genotype in their reference population.[6] For this reason, it is of the utmost importance that commonly accepted scientific methods for testing these assumptions be applied to databases used in forensic science. If one or more of these simplifying assumptions is not correct, the potential implications of such findings must be understood. The following sections summarize the nature of these population genetic principles.

THE HARDY–WEINBERG LAW

A particular recognizable segment of DNA is called a gene or locus.[7] In some cases, a gene will have a specific function, such as coding for the production of a protein enzyme necessary for cellular metabolism. In other cases, such as with regard to many of the genes utilized for DNA fingerprinting, the exact function of these genes is unknown.

Except for genes located on the sex chromosomes, humans have two copies of each gene, one from their mother and one from their father. It is possible, however, that the sequence of base pairs that make up the paternal and maternal copy of a gene are not exactly the same, in which case the individual is called a heterozygote. Different forms of a gene are called alleles. If an individual has two copies of the same allele, that individual is called a homozygote.

The ability to detect different alleles in humans depends on the techniques used for quantifying genetic variation. For VNTR (variable number tandem repeat) genes, commonly used in forensics, different alleles are recognized because they contain different lengths of DNA. Thus, the assay techniques simply measure the size of each allele an individual has. A homozygote is an individual who has two copies of a VNTR gene that are the same size, while a heterozygote is an individual with two copies that have measurably different sizes. One must realize that an individual who has been classified as a homozygote by these techniques may, in actuality, have two alleles that have different sequences of base pairs but are nevertheless the same size. Such variation is "invisible" with these assay techniques but

---

[4]This law provides a means for calculating genotype frequencies at a single locus under certain assumptions that are discussed *infra*.

[5]This condition will be met in a population in which there is statistical independence of an individual's genotype at different genes.

[6]There are exceptions, such as those discussed below.

[7]These terms are often used interchangeably in the genetics literature, although the word *locus* is usually used to emphasize the physical location of a particular gene.

could be uncovered if the DNA was actually sequenced. Clearly, an individual is either a homozygote or a heterozygote with respect to any gene.

An individual may have at most two different alleles for a given gene. However, in a large population there may be many different alleles for a given gene, with the maximum number possible being 2N, where N is the total number of individuals in the population. For many genes in the human population, there is only one allele. These genes are designated as monomorphic. Genes with two or more alleles are known as polymorphic genes.

The factors that determine whether genes are monomorphic or polymorphic and, if polymorphic, to what degree, are complex. For instance, some genes code for proteins (or enzymes) that catalyze important biochemical reactions. The ability to perform these chemical reactions may often depend on the exact three-dimensional structure of the protein. In such instances, there may be regions of the protein where the structure cannot be altered without complete loss of the enzymatic function. The corresponding regions of DNA are likely to be monomorphic, since all competing alternative forms of DNA result in nonfunctional enzymes.

The maintenance of two or more alleles in a given population (polymorphisms) may be controlled by the processes of random genetic drift, natural selection, or a combination of both of these forces. The extent to which these two forces maintain genetic polymorphisms in a natual population is a controversial area of research in population genetics.[8] Typical polymorphic genes that code for proteins have two to six alleles. The genes utilized for DNA fingerprinting may have 100 or more alleles. These genes are sometimes called *hypervariable*, due to the tremendous number of different alleles.

The combination of paternal and maternal alleles present in an individual comprises that individual's genotype. It is possible to refer to an individual's genotype at more than one locus at a time. In such cases, one refers to a multilocus genotype. One way to summarize population genetic information is to compute the frequency of each allele in the population. The Hardy–Weinberg law allows one to compute genotype frequencies at a single locus based only upon knowledge of allele frequencies.[9] This turns out to be a very useful way of simplifying population genetic information. The reason for this is that there are many more genotypes at a single locus

---

[8]For examples and additional references relating to research in this field, see, e.g., Mueller, L. D., B. A. Wilcox, P. R. Ehrlich, D. G. Heckel, and D. D. Murphy *Genetics* 110:495–511 (1985) and Mueller, L. D., L. G. Barr, and F. J. Ayala *Genetics* 111:517–554 (1985).

[9]If there are a total of n alleles at a single locus, $A_1, A_2, \ldots, A_n$, and the frequency of the *i*th allele is p_i, then the frequency of a homozygote, A_iA_i, is p_i^2, and the frequency of a heterozygote, A_iA_j, is $2p_ip_j$. For a general discussion, see Hartl, D. L. and A. G. Clark *Principles of Population Genetics*, (Sunderland, MA: Sinauer, 1989).

than there are alleles.[10] As a result, much less information is needed to completely describe a population.

There are many natural phenomena that may prevent genotypes in a population from being in Hardy–Weinberg frequencies. Moreover, processes such as natural selection, inbreeding and population substructuring may cause deviations from the Hardy–Weinberg equilibrium.[11] For this reason it is important to check genetic data for agreement with the Hardy–Weinberg predictions.

Linkage Equilibrium

Genes that reside physically close to each other on the same chromosome are said to be genetically linked. Thus, the two genes are joined by an intervening length of DNA. Usually, these two genes will be passed on as a unit, with the offspring receiving a pair from the mother and a pair from the father. Occasionally, during the process of gamete formation, the DNA between these genes will be broken and a hybrid chromosome will be created from the paternal and maternal chromosomes. This shuffling process is called recombination and is more likely to happen to two genes if they are far apart.

Humans have 22 pairs of chromosomes, known as autosomes, which are inherited equally from each parent and one pair of sex chromosomes. There are two forms of these chromosomes, i.e., the X and Y chromosomes. Females have two copies of the X chromosome, while males have one X and one Y chromosome. The Y chromosome has very few genes. Consequently, males usually have only a single copy of any gene carried on the X chromosome, while females will have two copies. When alleles at two different loci are statistically independent, they are said to be in linkage equilibrium.[12] Genetic linkage and linkage equilibrium are not the same concept, although they are theoretically related.

To illustrate the difference between these concepts consider the following example. Suppose a single locus controls hair color while a second locus, which is genetically unlinked to the hair color locus, controls eye color.[13] A

---

[10]If there are n alleles at a single locus, there are a total of $n(n-1)/2$ different genotypes. If n = 50, for instance, then the total number of possible genotypes is 1225.

[11]Inbreeding and population substructure will generally result in a population having more homozygotes than expected from the Hardy–Weinberg Law. Natural selection can result in more, less, or the same number of homozygotes expected from Hardy–Weinberg.

[12]Suppose locus A has two alleles, A_1 and A_2, at frequency P_1 and P_2. Likewise, locus B has two alleles, B_1, and B_2, at frequency Q_1 and Q_2. Further suppose that gametes with A_1 and B_1 alleles occur with frequency X_1. Then the linkage disequilibrium parameter, D, is given by $D = X_1 - P_1 Q_1$, when $D = 0$ the population is in linkage equilibrium. For a more detailed treatment of measures of linkage, see, e.g., Weir, B.S. and C.C. Cockerham, in *Mathematical Evolutionary Genetics*, M.W. Feldman, Ed., (1989) pp. 86–110.

[13]Although it is known that in human populations these traits are controlled by more than one locus, these simple assumptions are made here to illustrate the phenomenon of linkage equilibrium.

Scandanavian population may consist of individuals homozygous for a blond hair-color allele and a blue eye-color allele. Likewise, a population in southern Italy may be homozygous for dark eye-color and hair-color alleles. If data were collected from both of these populations and analyzed for linkage equilbrium, one would find a high statistical association between the blue eye-color and blond hair-color alleles and the dark hair- and eye-color alleles. This would be so even though the genes for eye color and hair color are on separate chromosomes and therefore are genetically unlinked.

The Product Rule

Suppose data has been collected from four genes, labeled A, B, C, and D. If an individual is a heterozygote at locus A, for example, then the Hardy–Weinberg law is used to estimate the frequency of that genotype denoted as P_A. If the individual is a homozygote, then a different procedure is generally used.

For several reasons, the observation of only a single band on an autoradiograph[14] may indicate a true homozygote. Alternately, the individual may actually be a heterozygote in which the second allele does not appear on the autorad or is obscured by the first band. In such cases, the conservative assumption is typically made that the individual may be either a homozygote or a heterozygote for the observed allele. Based upon this assumption, the frequency of the genotype is just twice the frequency of the observed allele.[15] After the frequency of genotypes at each of the four loci is determined, the final probability of finding the particular four locus genotypes is $P_A \times P_B \times P_C \times P_D$.

ANALYSIS OF POPULATION DATA

The FBI, Cellmark, and Lifecodes have assembled human population databases. These samples generally come from a limited geographic area. Each laboratory has identified subpopulations of Caucasians, blacks, and Hispanics. In addition to these racial groups, Cellmark also has a database for Orientals. The gene loci used by each laboratory are (Cellmark),[16] D7S22, D1S7, D12S11, D7S21; (FBI),[17] D14S13, D16S85, D17S79, D1S7,

---

[14]An autoradiograph (or *autorad*, as it is commonly referred to) is the x-ray film on which the DNA print is visualized.

[15]If the frequency of the observed allele is p_i, then the chance of being either a homozygote or a heterozygote is $p_i^2 + 2p_i(1 - p_i) = p_i(2 - p_i)$. When $p_i < < 2$, then the frequency of being either a homozygote or a heterozygote is approximately $2p_i$.

[16]See, e.g., Wong, Z., V. Wilson, I. Patel, S. Povey, and A. Jeffreys, *Ann. Hum. Genet.*, 51: 264–288 (1987).

[17]Budowle, B. and K. L. Monson, "A Statistical Approach For VNTR Analysis," Proceedings Symposium on the Forensic Aspects of DNA Analysis, Government Printing Office, Washington, D.C. (1990).

D2S44, D4S139; (Lifecodes),[18] D2S44, D14S13, D17S79, D18S27, DXYS14. The number following the D designation of each allele is the chromosome location of the gene. The only laboratory using genes on the same chromosome is Cellmark and these are not closely linked.[19] The alleles at these loci differ from each other in the length of the DNA of each allele. Assays for allelic variation thus consist of making measurements of the length of the paternal and maternal allele that each individual possesses.

Hardy–Weinberg

One problematic aspect of these genetic markers is that different alleles can be so similar in size that measurement error, which is inherent in these techniques, may overlap substantially with the actual size difference of neighboring alleles. This means that it is almost impossible to say which size classes belong exclusively to genetically identical alleles.

To overcome this problem, somewhat arbitrary intervals, also called bins,[20] are created. All measured bands falling within these bins are identified as the same allele. A simple result in population genetics is that if one creates classes of alleles that totally include two or more different alleles, this new allele class will be in Hardy–Weinberg equilibrium if the constituent alleles are in Hardy–Weinberg equilibrium. Thus, as a first approximation, it would seem that bining of alleles should not produce any new problems. As discussed below, however, this assumption is not entirely true.

The fit to Hardy–Weinberg depends on the size of the bin choosen. For that reason it is important to decide which bin size is appropriate for the techniques used. The most appropriate bin size will be the same one used to estimate allele frequencies. There have been very few published analyses of these databases with respect to the previously mentioned assumptions.[21] An article by Balazs et al. reports that the Lifecodes database is in Hardy–Weinberg equilibrium and shows no linkage disequilibrium but presents no analysis of these data. The report of Odelberg et al. contradicts this claim.

Currently, it is not obvious what the most appropriate test is for Hardy–Weinberg equilibrium. Since many of these hypervariable genes have 50-100 alleles, the number of possible genotypes easily exceeds the total number of individuals in the sample. Consequently, there will be many genotype classes for which no observations will be made. Even after group-

---

[18]Balazs, I., M. Baird, M. Clyne and E. Meade *Am. J. Hum. Genet.* 44:182–190 (1989).

[19]Wong, Z., V. Wilson, I. Patel, S. Povey, and A. Jeffreys, *Ann. Hum. Genet.* 51: 264–288 (1987).

[20]Budowle, B. and K. L. Monson, "A Statistical Approach For VNTR Analysis," Proceedings Symposium on the Forensic Aspects of DNA Analysis, Government Printing Office, Washington, D.C. (1990).

[21]Balazs, I., M. Baird, M. Clyne, and E. Meade, *Am. J. Hum. Genet.* 44:182–190 (1989); Odelberg, S. J., R. Plaetke, J. R. Eldridge, L. Ballard, P. O'Connell, Y. Nakamura, M. Leppert, J. M. Lalouel, and R. White *Genomics* 5:915–924 (1989).

ing genotype classes so that at least five observations occur within any group, the chance of rejecting the Hardy–Weinberg law, even when it is true, may still exceed the nominal level.

A conservative approach to testing these data sets is to simply compute the total frequency of all homozygotes and compare this to the frequency expected from Hardy–Weinberg. The possibility exists with this sort of test that many individual genotypes may deviate substantially from Hardy–Weinberg, even though their sum may be close to the expected value. Odelberg et al. describe alternative tests of the Hardy–Weinberg law.

My own analysis[22] of these data have shown consistent deviations from the Hardy–Weinberg law. The deviations have consistently shown there to be an excess of homozygotes. Recently, genotype frequencies that deviate from Hardy–Weinberg equilibrium have been observed at the D2S44, D1S74 and D14S13 loci in a Caucasian population[23] and the D2S44 locus in Hispanics[24] by independent investigators.

Failure to reject the hypothesis that genotypes are well described by the Hardy–Weinberg law does not mean large errors can not be made. As will be discussed shortly, population substructure may be capable of producing some genotypes that will be much more common or rare than predicted from the Hardy–Weinberg law, but the population may nevertheless satisfy the tests previously described.

Linkage Equilibrium

To evaluate the extent of linkage equilibrium, one looks at pairs of loci at a time. If alleles associate at random between loci, then one would expect that the frequency of any two alleles occuring at two different loci will be given by the product of the frequency of each allele.[25] Many of the same loci that have shown deviations from Hardy–Weinberg have also shown significant levels of linkage disequilibrium. Many of the same phenomena that give rise to an excess of homozygotes may also cause a statistical association to develop between loci. Next, various scientific explanations for the deviations from Hardy–Weinberg and linkage equilibrium will be examined.

---

[22]The procedure followed is to first create bins according to the procedure followed by the particular laboratory. Measured band sizes for each individual in the database are then classified into these new bin categories. Finally, genotype and allele frequencies are estimated from the resulting data and the observed genotype frequencies are compared to those calculated from the Hardy–Weinberg law.

[23]Odelberg, S. J., R. Plaetke, J. R. Eldridge, L. Ballard, P. O'Connell, Y. Nakamura, M. Leppert, J. M. Laloel, and R. White, *Genomics* 5:915–924 (1989).

[24]Lander, E. S. *Nature* 339:501–505 (1989).

[25]The actual method for testing for linkage is described in an article by B. S. Weir, *Biometrics* 235–254 (1979).

EXPLANATIONS FOR THE OBSERVED PHENOMENA

There are at least three reasonable explanations for the observed deviations from Hardy–Weinberg. In some cases these hypotheses may also explain the observed levels of linkage disequilibrium. It is worth pointing out that these explanations are not mutually exclusive. Thus, an important goal for future research needs to be both the qualitative and quantitative assessment of each of these possibilities.

Null or Small Alleles

It is possible that many of the single banding patterns found on autorads that are called homozygotes are actually heterozygotes wherein the second allele has not been observed. This may be due to the presence of very small alleles, which can run off the end of the gel and thus not be scored. Alternately, some other phenomena may prevent the second allele from being observed. These other phenomena may all be refered to as "null" alleles and their effects on the population genetics will be similar.

If this phenomena is present, then one expects to occasionally see individuals who are homozygous for these "null" alleles. These observed deviations from Hardy–Weinberg can be used to estimate the frequency of null alleles, which in turn can be used to estimate the expected number of null homozygotes that should be observed in the database. The frequency of the null allele, p_n, may be obtained as the valid root of the cubic equation,

$$0 = -2p_n^3 + (2 - H)p_n^2 + 2(1 - H)p_n + \sum_{i=1}^{k} \tilde{p}_i^2 - H,$$

where H is the total frequency of the observed homozygotes and $\tilde{p}_i$ is the observed frequency of allele i. The frequency of null homozygotes is then p_n^2. This value can be compared to the observed frequency of null homozygotes in the database. Such cases would appear as a lane on the autorad with no bands.

It is possible the laboratory personnel may interpret such a blank lane as a failed experiment. Clearly, these sort of results should be retested to verify that they are null homozygotes. Such observations would ultimately allow for a direct estimation of the frequency of null alleles.[26]

---

[26]For instance, if the frequency of null homozygous is H_n, then the frequency of the null allele can be estimated as $\sqrt{H_n}$.

Bin Boundary

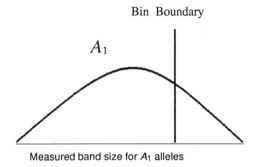

A_1

Measured band size for A_1 alleles

Figure 1. The curve above shows the distribution of measured sizes for the A_1 allele. These different measured lengths reflect experimental error. In this example all bands to the left of the vertical line will be classified as a different allele than those which fall to the right of the line even though these bands are genetically the same allele.

Arbitrary Bin Boundaries

This next problem is almost certainly present in all databases that utilize data from hypervariable gene loci. Because alleles are so numerous and close together, it is nearly impossible to determine where the bands belonging to one allele stop and where those belonging to another start. Allele frequencies are estimated by creating bins or intervals that have arbitrary end points. The boundaries of these intervals are likely to cut through the distribution of bands produced by a single allele. As a result, a population that is in Hardy–Weinberg equilibrium will show an excess of homozygotes. The general phenomena refered to is illustrated in Figure 1.

It is worth emphasizing at this point that there has been little theoretical work on this particular problem. So while my own work and that of Ellen Wijsman at the University of Washington indicates that these arbitrary bin boundaries will create an excess of homozygotes, it is not clear what the general effects of such an arbitrary determination will be on linkage. The calculations we have done presume some knowledge of where the boundaries are.[27] In general, such information will not be known. It is also not clear

---

[27]To illustrate this effect, consider a single allele, A, whose measured band sizes have a distribution similar to those in Figure 1. Assume the bin boundary falls through the middle of this distribution such that a fraction α of all A alleles fall to the left of the boundary and are classified as A_1 alleles, while the remaining A alleles $(1 - \alpha)$ fall to the right of the boundary and are classified as A_2 alleles. If the frequency of A is p, then the frequency of A_1 alleles is αp and of A_2 alleles is $(1 - \alpha)p$. In addition, assume that both alleles in a homozygous individual experience exactly the same experimental error, hence the frequency of observed homozygotes for the A_1 allele will be αp^2 and for the A_2 allele $(1 - \alpha)p^2$. However, the expected frequency of A_1 and A_2 homozygotes according to the Hardy–Weinberg law are $\alpha^2 p^2$ and $(1 - \alpha)^2 p^2$, respectively. Since $\alpha < 1$, $\alpha^2 p^2 < \alpha p^2$, and $(1 - \alpha)^2 p^2 < (1 - \alpha)p^2$, thus there is an excess of observed homozygotes. Unfortunately, the magnitude of this excess depends on α, which in general is unknown.

what methods should be used to estimate genotype frequencies in these cases. In summary, the existence of arbitrary bins may explain part or all of the excess of observed homozygotes. It would seem that the only way to demonstrate that this is the only cause of the excess of homozygotes would be to eliminate all the other possible explanations.

Wahlund Effect

A third possible explanation for the excess of homozygotes is the Wahlund effect, or more generally, population substructure. The Wahlund effect arises when genetic data from several genetically differentiated populations are collected and treated as if they have come from a single randomly mating population. The result is that the pooled population data have more homozygotes than expected from the Hardy–Weinberg law. It is perhaps easiest to explain this phenomena with reference to the previous example concerning hair and eye color. If one considers the Scandanavian population to consist of only homozygotes for blue eyes and the Italian population to consist of only homozygotes for dark eyes, then pooling these populations will result in the Wahlund effect. Thus, if one were to mistakenly treat this pooled population as a single randomly mating collection of individuals, then one would expect to see a high frequency of blue/black heterozygous individuals, when in fact none are seen. Likewise, the frequency of homozygotes for each of these alleles would be higher than expected. Pooling of populations in this manner will also lead to linkage disequilibrium between loci, even when these are located on different chromosomes.

This effect will be expected even when the pooled populations are not competely isolated, as long as there is some difference in the frequencies of the studied alleles. This possible cause of the homozygote excess is especially troubling since it is not one that can be simply corrected, nor can the potential error be easily estimated. Information concerning the genetic structure of these subpopulations would ultimately have to be obtained, and the possibility exists that the allele frequencies could be quite different between different subpopulations.

To illustrate the effects of substructure, consider the following example. Assume there are two populations wherein one is in Hardy–Weinberg equilibrium (population A), while the other contains a mixture of two subpopulations, each of which is in Hardy–Weinberg equilibrium (population B). Assume also that each population has 100 alleles, each at a frequency of 0.01. However, in population B, allele A_i and A_j only occur in a small subpopulation at a frequency of 0.5 each. This subpopulation makes up 2% of the total population (hence the frequency of the A_i and A_j allele in the whole population is $0.5 \times 0.02 = 0.01$). In population A the frequency of

A_iA_j heterozygotes is 0.0002 ($2 \times 0.01 \times 0.01$), while in population B these heterozygotes have a frequency of 0.01 ($2 \times 0.5 \times 0.5 \times 0.02$). If one had mistakenly assumed that population B was in Hardy–Weinberg equilibrium, one would have estimated the frequency of A_iA_j heterozygotes to be the same as in population A and thus have committed an error of underestimating the true frequency by a factor of 50.

The obvious question is, wouldn't population B show a deviation from the Hardy–Weinberg equilibrium? The total expected frequency of homozygotes in population B according to Hardy–Weinberg should be 0.01, while the actual observed frequency would be 0.0198. A database with greater than 800 individuals would be neccessary to determine that this small excess of homozygotes was indeed statistically significant. One conclusion from this sort of analysis is that deviations from Hardy–Weinberg are an insensitive indicator of biologically significant population substructure.

A reasonable question to ask is, why should we expect to observe population substructure for these loci when it is seldom seen at other loci in human populations? These loci have been chosen precisely because they have so much variation.[28] A primary cause of the variation is a very high rate of mutation.[29] This high mutation rate makes these loci candidates for genetic markers of more recent population subdivision. Even though populations in this country are not isolated, newly arisen alleles may take some time to equilibrate in the human population due to factors such as restricted gene flow patterns and age structure.[30]

Another way to view this process is to think of a human population as a body of water with many small eddies that represent subpopulations. If some colored dye is added to an eddy, it will discolor the local area for a while until the dye diffuses into the surrounding body of water. In a similar sense, mutations diffuse from the local population to the surrounding population. If a new colored dye is added to this one discolored eddy at very frequent intervals, the eddy will never obtain the same color as the surrounding water. Similarly, high mutation rates may prevent local populations with restricted gene flow from looking like the surrounding larger population.

---

[28]Odelberg, S. J., R. Plaetke, J. R. Eldridge, L. Ballard, P. O'Connell, Y. Nakamura, M. Leppert, J. M. Laloel, and R. White *Genomics* 5:915–924 (1989).
[29]Jeffreys, A. J., N. J. Royle, V. Wilson, and Z. Wong *Nature* 332:278–281 (1988); Smith, J. C., R. A. Anwar, J. Riley, D. Jenner, A. Alves, A. Graham, J. Morten, B. Hopkins, P. Heath, A. J. Jeffreys, and A. F. Markham, *Can. J. Forensic Sci.* (1989, in press).
[30]Li, W.-H., *Amer. Natur.* 110:841–847 (1976); Charlesworth, B., *Evolution in Age-Structured Populations* (Cambridge, U.K.: Cambridge Univ. Press, 1980)

CONCLUSIONS

The calculation of multilocus genotype frequencies in forensic science assumes that single-locus genotype frequencies are described by the Hardy–Weinberg equilibrium and that genotypes at different loci are in linkage equilibrium. Violations of these assumptions have been observed in numerous instances.[31] Three hypotheses have been offered to explain these deviations, which are certainly atypical in the human population genetics literature. To resolve these problems will require some careful study of population databases and the development of new methods for treating population data.

Work on these problems has just begun. Since the three proposed explanations are not mutually exclusive, the only way to eliminate any one explanation is to gather direct evidence against it. Merely demonstrating that one hypothesis is true does not neccessarily mean the others are false. Since the existence of substructure in racial groups may have a profound effect on the final statistics, these issues must be resolved.

It is worth mentioning that even if these data sets agreed with the Hardy–Weinberg and linkage equilibrium, problems would still remain. These problems arise from the fact that the data set and statistical tests have limited power to uncover deviations if they do exist. For instance, if one had a coin that always came up heads yet wanted to test whether the coin was fair, the following experiment could be done. The coin could be tossed twice and two heads would be observed. However, the individual conducting the experiment would conclude that the chances of observing two heads if the coin was fair is 25% and therefore one should accept the idea that the coin is fair. Clearly, this experiment does not have much power in detecting the bias present in this coin.

In a similar fashion, the mere acceptance of Hardy-Weinberg by some criteria does not mean deviations may not be present. Since it will be of interest in forensic cases to establish an upper bound on the chance of finding a particular genotype in the population, this will require developing some new statistical techniques. Such techniques would calculate the chances of finding a particular genotype while allowing for departures from Hardy–Weinberg that are consistent with the population database.

---

[31]Lander, E. S. *Nature* 339:501–505 (1989); Odelberg, S. J., R. Plaetke, J. R. Eldridge, L. Ballard, P. O'Connell, Y. Nakamura, M. Leppert, J. M. Laloel, and R. White *Genomics* 5:915–924 (1989).

5. The Polymerase Chain Reaction: Application to the Analysis of Biological Evidence

GEORGE F. SENSABAUGH, Ph.D.
CECILIA VON BEROLDINGEN, Ph.D.

INTRODUCTION

Biological evidence comes in many forms: blood stains on any imaginable surface, semen mixed with vaginal fluids, hairs, bone segments, tissue from under a victim's fingernails, etc. A major objective in the analysis of such evidence is to develop information as to the identity of the individual who left the evidence behind. The traditional approach to this problem has been to test for blood group and protein genetic markers present in the evidence samples.[1] We are now at the threshold of a new era in the genetic analysis of biological evidence — the DNA era. It has been demonstrated that informative DNA can be extracted from most types of biological evidence samples, thus allowing the analysis of genetic variation at the DNA level. Because each individual (identical siblings excepted) is genetically unique, genetic typing at the DNA level offers the promise of absolute identification, a promise that has generated considerable excitement both in the forensic community and in the public media.

There are at present two distinct approaches to the analysis of genetic variation at the DNA level: a) the detection of restriction fragment length polymorphism (RFLP) and b) the use of the polymerase chain reaction (PCR) to specifically amplify informative gene sequences. The RFLP approach is described elsewhere in this volume; the focus of this chapter is to explain the PCR approach. Although PCR is a relatively young technology — it was first described in 1985[2] — it has rapidly gained acceptance as a tool in molecular biology, population genetics, and medical diagnostics

63

(see, for example, ref. 3) and is emerging as the cornerstone technology in the human genome mapping project.

Two features of PCR are of obvious benefit to the analysis of biological evidence. First, amplification is possible from very small amounts of DNA, as little as the DNA in a single cell.[4] This allows genetic information to be obtained from evidence samples that contain insufficient cellular material for other genetic typing approaches, e.g., single shed hairs.[5] Second, amplification is possible from degraded DNA;[6] the DNA in a significant proportion of biological evidence is degraded. From an operational standpoint, PCR offers two additional benefits: it is relatively simple to perform and results can be obtained within a short time frame, usually within 24 hours.[7] These advantages ensure a prominent role for PCR in the future of forensic DNA analysis. The objective of this chapter is to describe how PCR works, how it can be used for the detection of genetic variants, and how it meets the criteria for application in the forensic context.

GENE AMPLIFICATION BY THE POLYMERASE CHAIN REACTION

PCR was conceived and first developed by Mullis et al.[2,8] at Cetus Corporation. The concept is strikingly simple (Figure 1); indeed, it is analogous to the replication process used by cells to replicate their own DNA. Two short oligonucleotides are hybridized to the opposite strands of a target DNA segment in positions flanking the sequence region of interest; these two oligonucleotides are oriented such that their 3' ends point toward each other. The two oligonucleotides prime an enzyme-mediated replication of the complementary DNA strand; they extend off their 3' end using the target sequence as the template for replication. The PCR amplification process itself consists of a three-step cycle:

1. The double-stranded template DNA is dissociated into single strands by incubation at high temperature (typically 94°C).
2. The temperature is lowered to allow the oligonucleotide primers to bind to their complementary sequences.
3. A DNA polymerase extends the primers across the region between the two primer-binding sites, using the target sequence as template.

Because the extension products of one primer bind the other primer in successive cycles, there is in principle a doubling of the target sequence in each cycle. Note that the primers become physically incorporated into the amplification products.

The amplification procedure is greatly simplified by the use of a heat-resistant DNA polymerase (Taq polymerase) isolated from the bacterium *Thermus aquaticus*.[9,10] This enzyme is stable at the elevated temperature used for strand dissociation. As a result, the reaction components — target DNA, primers, nucleotide triphosphates, and polymerase — can be mixed

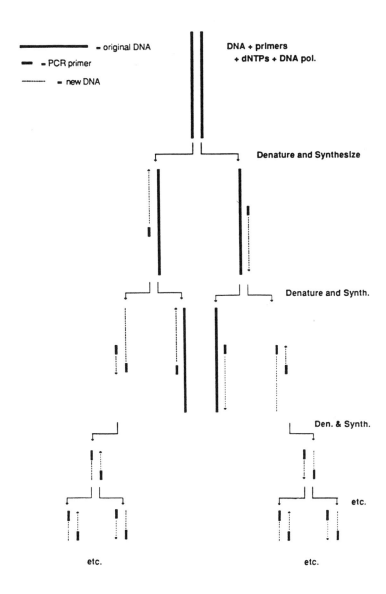

Figure 1. The PCR process. The reaction mixture contains target DNA, primer oligonucleotides, nucleotides (dNTPs), and polymerase in an appropriate buffer solution. In the first step, the reaction mix is heated to ca. 94°C to dissociate the
complementary strands of the target DNA. The temperature is lowered and the
primers, which are present at great excess, hybridize to the opposite strands of
the target DNA; the primers are oriented so that their 3′ ends are pointed toward
each other. At the third step, the primers are extended to make replicates of the
target DNA strands. The cycle is then repeated. The newly synthesized strands
add to the original target strands as templates for replication. (Drawing courtesy
of R. Higuchi, Cetus Corporation.)

and subjected to automated thermocycling for any number of cycles. The thermal stability of the Taq system also allows the annealing and extension steps to be carried out at relatively high temperatures (typically $55°$-$60°$C and $72°$C, respectively); at these temperatures, there is a marked increase in the specificity and yield of the reaction.[9]

A typical thermocycle program is $94°$C for 1 minute (strand dissociation), $55°$C for 30 seconds (primer annealing to the template strands), and $72°$C for 1 minute (primer extension) through 30–35 cycles. The efficiency of amplification is not 100%, and the yield from a 30-cycle amplification is generally about 10^6-10^7 copies of the target sequence; 10^9 would be expected with perfect doubling at each cycle. At higher cycle numbers, the polymerase becomes limiting and the amount of PCR product plateaus; further amplification offers no gain in specific product.

In principle, it should be possible to amplify DNA sequences of any length. Typically, however, sequences 100–2000 bp in length are targeted for amplification; amplifications involving sequences exceeding 5–10 kilobases (kb) are not always successful. This may be because the efficiency of amplification decreases as the length of the target sequence increases.[11] The increased amplification efficiency of short DNA segments also accounts in part for the occasional observation of "primer dimer" as a major PCR product. Primer dimers are end-to-end dimers of the primers and generally occur when the target DNA is present at low levels or is badly degraded; the amplification machinery appears to "catch" on the primer dimer, rather than on the target sequence.

DETECTION OF GENETIC VARIATION

Once PCR has been used to generate a large number of copies of a DNA segment of interest, different approaches may be taken to detect genetic variation within the segment. Because 10^6 or more copies of the target sequence can be produced, it is possible to use nonisotopic methods of detection. A number of imaginative methods for PCR product detection have been described. This section outlines some of the methods that have been used successfully for the detection of genetic variants.

Sequence Specific Probes

The use of sequence specific oligonucleotide (SSO) probes represents the most generalized approach to the detection of alleles differing in sequence.[12-13] The sequence-specific probe is usually a short oligonucleotide (15–30 nucleotides in length), with a sequence exactly matching the sequence of the target allele. The SSO probe is mixed with dissociated strands of PCR reaction product under conditions such that the SSO and a

PCR product strand will hybridize if there is perfect sequence complimentarity, but will not if there are sequence differences. The conditions defining an all-or-none hybridization system are dictated by basic chemical principles. The strength of binding between an oligonucleotide probe and its target sequence is determined by the composition of bases in the probe sequence, the number of mismatches between the probe and the target sequence, the length of the probe, the salt concentration in the hybridization reaction, and the temperature of the hybridization reaction.[14] As a general rule, for probes shorter than 20 nucleotides in length, the temperature of dissociation decreases by 3–5° for every mismatched base pair. Thus it is a fairly straightforward matter to define conditions that will allow PCR products differing by single bases to be distinguished by appropriately designed oligonucleotide probes. The greater the number of base pair differences between any two alleles, the lesser the chance of a cross-hybridization mismatch.

The classical format for the use of SSO probes is to spot dissociated PCR product strands onto a nitrocellulose or nylon membrane and to probe the membranes with labeled SSO.[13] This format is analogous to Southern blotting; because the samples are spotted as a "dot" on the membrane, this format is referred to as *dot blotting*. In this format a separate membrane must be spotted with PCR product for each probe to be used and each membrane must be individually hybridized. This process divides the amplified DNA in as many ways as there are probes and becomes labor intensive as the number of membranes to be processed increases.

To circumvent some of these problems, an alternative, reverse dot-blot format, has been recently developed by Saiki et al.[15] With this format (which has its antecedents in affinity chromatography), the SSO is immobilized on the membrane and is used to capture labeled PCR product (Figure 2). This format allows an array of SSO probes to be attached to a single membrane; this array can then be challenged by a single aliquot of PCR product. In such a system, the SSOs need to be designed to give all-or-none hybridization under a single set of hybridization conditions. A further advantage of this format is that positive and negative hybridization controls can be included in the SSO array. The application of this format to the detection of genetic variation at the DQα locus will be described in greater detail in the next section.

Allele Specific Amplification

Primers that are mismatched with the template sequence by one or more bases at the 3′ end of the primer will not extend. It is thus possible to design allele-specific primers, that is, primers having an allele-specific sequence at the 3′ end.[16] Allele-specific primers may be employed in competition or in separate reaction mixes. In either case, amplification indicates the presence

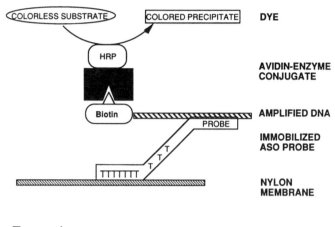

Examples:

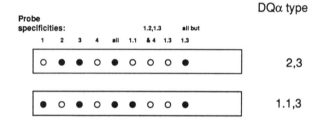

Figure 2.   Reverse dot-blot detection system. Top: Sequence-specific probes are immobilized on a nylon membrane. PCR product containing biotin label in the primers is added to the membrane; if the PCR product and the probe have complimentary sequences, the two will hybridize. Bound PCR product is detected using an avidin-horseradish peroxidase (HRP) system. Bottom: Representative presentation of a reverse dot-blot assay for genetic variants at the DQα locus. This genetic typing system is described in greater detail in the text. (Figure courtesy of Cetus Corporation.)

of the allelic sequence and lack of amplification indicates the absence of the allelic sequence. This approach is relatively straightforward when applied to biallelic systems, but can become increasingly complex as the number of alleles increases.

Variation at Restriction Sites

If the allelic variants differ in the presence of a restriction site, the PCR products representing the different alleles can be distinguished by the electrophoretic patterns produced after digestion with the appropriate restriction enzyme.[17] For example, the DNA sequence of the hemoglobin βA chain contains an *Oxa*NI site that is not present in the sickle-cell hemoglobin βS sequence. This allows the βA and βS amplification products to be distinguished by *Oxa*NI digestion; hemoglobin βA product yields two short fragments after restriction, whereas the βS product is not cut. Restriction assays allow rapid and simple detection, but are only applicable in those cases where the sequence differences between alleles results in the loss or gain of a restriction site.

Oligonucleotide Ligation Assay

This assay exploits the fact that two oligonucleotides lying end to end on a complimentary DNA strand can be ligated together by a DNA ligase. The ligation, however, requires a base pair match between the oligonucleotides and the complementary strand at the point of ligation; if there are mismatches, ligation does not occur.[18] Accordingly, oligonucleotides can be designed such that ligation will be allele specific. The ligation products can be distinguished from the nonligated oligonucleotides by electrophoresis or by attachment of different labels to each allele specific oligonucleotide.

Fragment Length Polymorphism

Amplification of DNA regions containing insertions or deletions yields products differing in size; these are readily analyzed by electrophoresis.[11,19-23] Of particular note, it has proven possible to amplify some of the DNA polymorphisms characterized by variable numbers of tandem repeats (VNTR polymorphisms);[11,20-23] these are highly polymorphic markers and offer very good discrimination potential. Unfortunately, some of the most polymorphic VNTR loci have target sequences exceeding the 5-kb practical upper limit for PCR. Moreover, as pointed out earlier, amplification efficiency decreases with increasing length of the target sequence;[11] unless the PCR conditions are carefully controlled, preferential amplification of small allelic products may overshadow large allelic products. These two factors suggest that only some VNTR polymorphisms will be amenable to practical PCR analysis. Nevertheless, it is anticipated that PCR analysis of VNTR polymorphisms offers great promise, and the next few years will see much development in this area.

Direct Sequencing

PCR provides an excellent starting point for direct DNA sequencing,[24] and some pundits see sequencing analysis as the ultimate approach to personal identification. Further development of this approach will require progress on two fronts. First, more highly variable sequence regions of the human genome will have to be discovered. At present, the D-loop region of mitochondrial DNA (mDNA) is the best-defined highly variable sequence;[25,26] although this sequence region offers great promise, more population studies are needed to fully establish the extent of variation between individuals. Additional variable sequences will no doubt be revealed in the course of the human genome sequencing project.

The second area needing development is the technology of automated sequencing. It is generally accepted that the sample throughput associated with forensic casework will require automated sequencing analysis. Although automated sequencers currently exist,[27] the rate of sequence reading ambiguity is at present unacceptably high. Clearly this level will have to be reduced well below the level of intrinsic variation between individuals.

DEVELOPMENT OF A GENETIC TYPING SYSTEM—THE DQα EXAMPLE

The development of a PCR-based genetic typing system proceeds in three steps. The first step is the generation of basic DNA sequence information about the target locus. This is needed to design the oligonucleotide primers for the PCR system. The paucity of sequence data for the human genome is at present a limiting factor for the development of new PCR test systems. The second step is the generation of sufficient sequence information to characterize the nature and extent of variation at the target locus; this defines the alleles. This sequencing is conveniently done on PCR products from the system developed at the first step. The third step is to develop a reliable assay for the detection of the variant alleles. As noted above, different approaches may be taken to the detection of variation; the choice of a detection scheme depends both on the nature of the allelic variation and on practical factors such as convenience, simplicity, and cost.

The genetic typing system for the detection of variants at the DQα locus provides a good example of this developmental process. The test system to be described was developed by the Department of Human Genetics laboratory at Cetus Corporation for use in histocompatibility testing and for research on immune diseases.[28] The discrimination power of the test and the simplicity of its use immediately suggested forensic application, and it has proven valuable in this context.[29]

Sequencing The DQα Locus

The DQα locus codes for the α subunit of the DQ protein, a class II protein of the major histocompatibility gene complex (MHC) on chromosome 6.[30] The MHC proteins are known from serological studies to be highly polymorphic; they have been implicated as major players in the immune response mechanism and the variation is believed to be important in this context. As a result, DQα and the other MHC loci have been the target of a major sequencing effort. The initial DNA sequences for DQα

Figure 3. Schematic representation of the second exon at the DQα locus. The second exon sequence region is represented by the boxed-in area; the single lines represent the adjoining introns. The constant sequence regions at the ends of the exon are stippled and are the primer binding regions. The positions containing base substitutions are represented by asterisks.

were generated both from cDNA transcripts and from genomic DNA (see, for example, ref. 31). It was found that the sequence variation is located in the second coding sequence region (the second exon); this sequence region codes for amino acids 6–87 in the protein sequence. Comparison of the DQα sequences showed: a) constant sequence segments at both ends of the exon corresponding to codon positions 12–17 and 81–86, b) a hypervariable sequence segment in the middle of the exon (codon positions 45–56), and c) lesser sequence variation on either side of the hypervariable segment. This arrangement is illustrated schematically in Figure 3.

The constant sequence segments at either end of the exon allowed the design of primers for the amplification of the exon. The DQα PCR product is approximately 242 bp in length, counting the primer sequences. The initial sequencing effort combined with the subsequent sequencing of PCR products has defined eight alleles.[32] Approximately 60 haplotype genomes have been sequenced, and it is unlikely that additional common alleles remain to be discovered. There are four major alleles defined by variation in the hypervariable segment; these have been designated A1, A2, A3, and A4. These four alleles differ from each other by at least 5-bp differences over the approximately 30-bp length of the hypervariable segment. In addition, two of the major alleles are split into subtypes by single or double base differences in the sequences flanking the hypervariable segment; the subtype alleles are designated A1.1, A1.2, A1.3, A4.1, A4.2, and A4.3. The nucleotide sequences of the eight alleles are listed in ref. 32.

Detection of DQα Alleles

The detection scheme for DQα typing is based on the use of sequence-specific oligonucleotide (SSO) probes. The typing system is directed toward detection of six alleles: A1.1, A1.2, A1.3, A2, A3, and A4; these six alleles define 21 genotypes.[15] Four probes define the major allelic types: A1, A2, A3, and A4; these probes differ substantially in sequence. The A1.1, A1.2, and A1.3 alleles are distinguished by the use of four probes: one specific for the A1.1 allelic sequence, one that recognizes a common sequence on the A1.2, A1.3, and A4.1 alleles, one specific for the A1.3 allelic sequence, and one that reacts with every allele but the A1.3 allele. Phenotypes containing the A1.2 and A1.3 alleles can be distinguished by the different reaction

Table 1.   DQα Genotype Frequencies in Caucasians (%)

	1.1	1.2	1.3	2	3	4
1.1	1.7	5.3	2.0	2.9	5.2	7.1
1.2		4.2	3.1	4.6	8.3	11.2
1.3			0.6	1.7	3.1	4.2
2				1.3	4.6	6.2
3					4.1	11.1
4						7.5

Data are from reference 33. Genotype frequencies were calculated from allele frequency estimates derived from a study on 434 Caucasian individuals. The allele frequency estimates were: A1.1—0.130; A1.2—0.205; A1.3—0.076; A2—0.113; A3—0.202; A4—0.274.

patterns with the last three probes. Each of these probes recognizes 1–2 bp differences in the target sequences.

Two detection formats have been used: the direct dot blot[13,5] and the reverse dot blot.[15] In either case, phenotypes are indicated by a pattern of labeled dots. An internal control has been built into the reverse dot-blot format in the form of a probe that reacts with all DQα PCR products. This probe is spotted at a reduced concentration relative to the typing probes; accordingly, it binds less label than the typing probes. The amount of label bound to this probe thus provides a standard of reference for the interpretation of label binding to the typing probes. The reverse dot-blot format has several additional advantages over the direct dot-blot format: It makes more efficient use of the PCR product, it removes risk of typing error due to mistakes in pipetting, and it is easier to standardize. Cetus now markets DQα reverse dot-blot typing kits.

Population Frequency Data

Population frequency data provide the basis for interpreting the significance of typing results in case work. The distribution of the 21 genotypes at the DQα locus in a Caucasian population is indicated in Table 1; less complete data are available for four other ethnic populations.[33] The distribution of homozygous and heterozygous types is close to expectation, indicating no significant population heterogeneity. What is most striking about these data is the relative evenness of the frequency values; no genotype is more frequent than about 11% in the white population. Overall, there is only about a 7% chance that two random individuals would share the same DQα type. The DQα system is thus more discriminating than any of the traditional genetic markers used in forensic work.

FORENSIC CONCERNS

With the introduction of any new genetic typing technology, questions must be asked about possible problems and potential sources of typing error. Regarding PCR, the questions fall into three categories. First, how good is the fidelity of the amplification process? Can mistakes occur during amplification that might cause one genetic type to appear as another? Second, will environmental insults typically encountered by biological evidence affect amplification fidelity? Lastly, given the great sensitivity of PCR, does incidental trace contamination by human DNA pose a serious problem?

With regard to each of these questions, it is important to emphasize that the concern is with idiosyncratic effects that do not signal their occurrence. Effects that occur in a systematic fashion or which signal themselves can be accommodated by modifications in the testing system or by placing limits on the interpretation of the typing result, depending on the level at which the effect manifests itself.

The Fidelity Question

Consequences of Nucleotide Misincorporation

It has been suggested that if the copying process is not absolutely true, then the possibility exists that one genetic type could be converted to another during amplification. This notion, however, does not stand up to a critical look. Although it is established that a low level of nucleotide misincorporation occurs during amplification,[9,34] and that therefore some proportion of PCR products will contain misincorporations, it can be demonstrated both by calculation and by experiment that this should not result in a genetic type change.[35,36]

The nucleotide misincorporation rate for *Taq* polymerase has been estimated by independent methods to be between 1 and 2 per 10^4 incorporations.[9,34] With this misincorporation rate, there is very little chance that a specific misincorporation will occur at a particular site in a DNA sequence; such a specific misincorporation would have to occur for one genetic type to be changed to another. Even were it to occur, the misincorporation would not be detectable unless it was present in a significant proportion, i.e., at least 5%, of the PCR product.

The proportion of PCR product containing any specific misincorporation depends on two factors: the number of copies of the template DNA and the PCR cycle at which the misincorporation occurs; this is demonstrated in Table 2. The worst case situation would occur if the misincorporation event was at the first cycle with an initial copy number of one (i.e., a single sperm cell). In this situation, 25% of the products would contain the misincorporation. When the initial template copy number is larger or when the misincorporation occurs at a later cycle, the proportion of product sequences containing any particular error is correspondingly decreased. Under practical testing conditions, these calculations show the proportion of product sequences containing any specific misincorporation is not high enough to significantly affect typing results.

Table 2.   Proportion of PCR Product Strands Containing an Amplification Error

Initial copies DNA	Cycle of error substitution			
	1	2	5	r
1	.25	.125	.015	$1/2^{r+1}$
10	.025	.0125	.0015	$.1/2^{r+1}$
100	.0025	.00125	.00015	$.01/2^{r+1}$

The misincorporation question has also been put to experimental test using a portion of the human hemoglobin HbβA chain sequence as the test system. This sequence contains a *Dde*I restriction site that overlaps the site at which the HbβA sequence differs from the HbβS sequence. The HbβA sequence was amplified from human genomic DNA through 30 cycles, interrupting the process every 5 cycles to restrict the accumulated product with *Dde*I; the amplification process was then continued through another 20 cycles. This test scheme thus selects for misincorporations occurring at the *Dde*I site. Of the 12 possible single-base misincorporations at this site, one gives rise to the HbβS sequence. Analysis of the PCR product, however, showed no significant HbβS sequence. Thus, even under conditions designed to generate a typing error by misincorporation, none could be produced.

Differential Amplification

Were two allelic sequences to be differentially amplified, then it is possible that the PCR product of one would overshadow the other. This drop out of an allelic product, if unrecognized, could lead to the mistyping of a heterozygote type as a homozygote. Some examples of differential amplification have been observed and others can be hypothesized; these can be generally divided into two categories, each with its own remedies.

Sequence-based differential amplification effects.—The preferential amplification of short PCR products compared to long products has already been noted;[11] this is a concern in the application of PCR to the detection of alleles varying substantially in length. A second possible sequence based cause of differential amplification is base-pair mismatching in the primer binding regions. Mismatches in the interior of the primer binding region reduce the efficiency of primer annealing, which in turn affects the amplification efficiency. Accordingly, if two alleles differ by as little as a single base in their primer binding regions, differential amplification is possible. Because primer annealing is temperature dependent, idiosyncratic effects can be avoided by using standardized conditions for the annealing and extension steps in the PCR cycle.

A third sequence-based problem can occur if alleles differ significantly in their base composition; allelic sequences containing higher GC contents may require higher temperatures for strand dissociation at the first step of the PCR cycle.[37] This, in fact, has been observed with the DQα system; the melting temperature for the A1 alleles is about 1°C higher than for the A2, A3, and A4 alleles. The remedy is to be certain that the denaturation step in the PCR cycle achieves a temperature promoting full-strand dissociation. A fourth possibility is that the alleles at a locus might be differentially susceptible to environmentally induced damage; this could be significant if the damage blocks or impairs amplification. This possibility can be tested in artificial damage studies and by evaluating casework samples that have been exposed to different environmental conditions. As a last example, one could conceive that some allelic sequences at a locus might contain runs of bases that slow the progress of the DNA polymerase; no example of this is currently known.

For the most part, the problems in this category can be avoided by gaining a thorough knowledge of the amplification properties of each allele in the typing system; this knowledge provides the base for establishing appropriate PCR conditions and controls.

Stochastic effects.—Samples containing very low numbers of starting templates, due either to small cell numbers or to sample degradation, could be subject to a "founder" effect, in which one allele of a pair begins to amplify before the other; it can gain an exponential head start on the second allele, with the result that the second allele is not seen. On statistical grounds, the possibility of such a "founder" effect diminishes as the number of starting templates increases. On statistical grounds, there should be negligible chance of a "founder" effect on samples containing 100 or more copies of starting template. In practical terms, this corresponds to about 0.3 ng of human genomic DNA.

The Environmental Insult Question

The Consequences of Environmental Insult

Biological evidence has a history prior to its entry into the laboratory. This history includes contact with a surface (e.g., a fabric, flooring, soil, etc.) and exposure to the lighting, temperature, and humidity conditions of the surrounding environment. The evidence samples may also have been exposed to any of a variety of chemical and biological contaminants, e.g., detergents, solvents, bacteria, dust, insects, etc. These various environmental exposures may have an impact on DNA analysis at three levels.

1. There may be interference with the extraction process such that the yield of DNA is reduced; this limits the analysis that can be done.
2. An environmental agent coextracting with the DNA may interfere with the enzymes or reagents used in the DNA analysis. For example, both the

restriction enzymes used in RFLP analysis and the *Taq* polymerase used in PCR have been observed to be inhibited with some evidence samples; this appears to be due to a coextracting chemical, since in some instances the inhibition can be removed by repeated DNA isolation or by modifications in extraction procedures. The result of this sort of interference is to limit the analysis that can be done.

3. The environmental exposure may damage the DNA in a way that affects the quality and/or outcome of the DNA typing analysis. In this case, the nature and the amount of damage are the relevant factors; the exposure is significant only in that it determines the nature and extent of damage.

We have focused much of our research attention upon investigating the effects of DNA damage on PCR analysis. There exists a body of knowledge linking environmental insults to specific forms of DNA damage;[38,39] some of these are outlined in Table 3. Although there are a variety of environmental conditions to which evidence samples might be exposed, the actual chemical consequences are limited; the nature of the damage is constrained by the basic chemistry of DNA. Each type of damage has predictable and measurable consequences for PCR analysis.

Degradation

Degradation — the fragmentation of DNA into smaller pieces — limits PCR only when the degraded fragments become too small to serve as templates.[40] The capacity of PCR to amplify degraded DNA has been established on forensic samples,[30] formalin fixed tissue sections,[41] and samples of paleontological and archeological interest.[6,42]

Chemical Modification of Nucleotides

The greatest variety of DNA damage is in the form of chemical modification to nucleotides.[38,39] With regard to PCR, the central question is how the polymerase responds when it encounters a damage site on the template strand: Does *Taq* polymerase read through damage sites, and, if so, does it insert a correct or incorrect nucleotide?

We have investigated this question using template DNA damaged by ultraviolet radiation.[43] We find that *Taq* polymerase stops short at UV damage sites; this is typical of the behavior of DNA polymerases at damage sites.[44] As expected, PCR product yields are reduced as the dose of UV exposure is increased; at very high UV doses, PCR appears completely inhibited. Thus the available evidence suggests that DNA damage poses little risk of introducing misincorporations that could lead to a typing error. We are continuing our studies on this matter.

Table 3. Environmental Factors Causing DNA Damage

Environmental Factor	Possible Form of DNA Damage	Comments
Microbial contamination	Strand scission	Microbial growth requires warm and moist conditions; strand scission is contingent on the release of nucleases from microbes
Light	Base modification, cross-linking between strands and to protein	Contingent on exposure to short-wave UV
Oxidizing agents	Base modification, strand scission	
Organic solvents (e.g., alcohol, gasoline, cleaning fluids)	Generally no effect	Note that DNA extraction typically includes exposure to phenol, chloroform, and alcohols
Acids	Base modification, strand scission, depurination	Damage required strong acid and/or elevated temperatures
Bases	Strand dissociation, strand scission at apurinic sites	Damage requires strong base ($>$ pH 12)
Temperature	Low—no effect; high—strand dissociation	Spontaneous damage rates increase with temperature
Time	Spontaneous base modification, strand scission, depurination	Spontaneous rates slow in solution, very low in dry state

Contamination

The exquisite sensitivity of PCR makes it susceptible to problems arising from contamination of samples by extraneous human DNA. Three sorts of contamination problems can be anticipated. The first is a familiar concern in forensic science: sample mixing in the field. There is nothing one can do to prevent this; it is forensic reality. Rather, one has to remain open minded about the possibility of mixtures and incorporate appropriate caveats into the interpretation of the typing result.

The second sort of contamination problem is reflected in the concern that dandruff, sloughed skin, or hair from investigators and laboratory personnel might fall into an evidence sample and be amplified. Since the DNA in mixed samples amplifies in proportion to the starting proportions of the mixture, this kind of contamination is likely to be a problem only with evidence samples containing very small amounts of DNA. In any case, the risk of this kind of contamination is reduced by good laboratory practice, e.g., maintenance of clean work areas, handling of samples with gloved hands, changing gloves between samples, etc.

The third kind of contamination problem is the most serious; this is contamination occurring in the laboratory by the PCR products of other amplification reactions.[45] The potential seriousness of this problem is indicated by the following consideration. A PCR reaction mixture can contain 10^{12} copies of PCR product/ml; an aerosol droplet of 0.1 μl volume deriving from this mixture would accordingly contain 10^8 copies. Should this aerosol drop find its way into a sample to be amplified that contains only 10^5 copies of target DNA, it is the contaminant that will amplify. The risk of PCR product carry-over contamination can be greatly diminished by several precautions, many of which are analogous to the precautions taken to inhibit contamination in infectious disease laboratories.[45] The major precautions include: a) separation of the area of sample preparation from the area where PCR is done and where the products are analyzed, b) use of separate reagents and tools in the different areas, c) use of aliquoted and/or premixed reagents, and d) use of appropriate positive and negative controls. The latter indicate whether contamination has occurred in a particular set of assays.

The occurrence of carry-over contamination in a set of genetic typing tests may show itself in several ways: the negative control samples (which should show nothing) may show a type; one type may show up persistently in many or all samples; and a sample may appear to contain supernumerary types, i.e., as if the sample contained the types of several different individuals. Thus, should contamination occur, it can be recognized.

CONCLUSION

Although PCR-based genetic typing does not at present have the power of RFLP analysis to distinguish between individuals, it offers many advantages for the analysis of biological evidence: sensitivity, capacity to be used on degraded samples, rapid analysis time, and ease of use. As more typing systems are developed, PCR will fully come into its own as a tool in the forensic armamentarium.

ACKNOWLEDGMENTS

We thank the Human Genetics Laboratory at Cetus—H. Erlich, R. Higuchi, R. Saiki, S. Scharf, and S. Walsh—for continuing discussion and collaboration; E. Blake of Forensic Science Associates for keeping us abreast of his research and casework efforts; and our colleagues in the laboratory at Berkeley—R. Reynolds and M. Buoncristiani—for their always helpful input. Portions of the work described in this report were supported by National Institute of Justice grant 86-IJ-CX-0044 to George F. Sensabaugh.

REFERENCES

1. Sensabaugh, G. F. "Biochemical Markers of Individuality," in *Forensic Science Handbook*, R. Saferstein, Ed. (Englewood Cliffs, NJ: Prentice Hall, 1982), 338.
2. Saiki, R. K., S. Scharf, F. Faloona, K. B. Mullis, G. T. Horn, H. A. Erlich, and N. Arnheim. "Enzymatic Amplification of β Globin Genomic Sequences and Restriction Site Analysis for Diagnosis of Sickle Cell Anemia," *Science* 230:1350–1354 (1985).
3. Erlich, H., Ed. *PCR Technology: Principles & Applications for DNA Amplification*, (New York: Stockton Press, 1988).
4. Li, H., U. B. Gyllensten, X. Cui, R. K. Saiki, H. A. Erlich, and N. Arnheim. "Amplification and Analysis of DNA Sequences in Single Human Sperm and Diploid Cells," *Nature* 335:414–417 (1988).
5. Higuchi, R., C. H. von Beroldingen, G. F. Sensabaugh, and H. A. Erlich. "DNA Typing from Single Hairs," *Nature* 332:543–546 (1988).
6. Paabo, S. "Ancient DNA: Extraction, Characterization, Molecular Cloning, and Enzymatic Amplification," *Proc. Natl. Acad. Sci. USA* 86:1939–1943 (1989).
7. Kazazian, H. H. and C. E. Dowling. "Laboratory Implications of Automated Polymerase Chain Reaction," *Am. Biotechnol. Lab.* Aug.:23 (1988).
8. Mullis, K. B. and F. A. Faloona. "Specific Synthesis of DNA In Vitro via a Polymerase Catalysed Chain Reaction," *Methods Enzymol.* 155:335–350 (1987).
9. Saiki, R. K., D. H. Gelfand, S. Stoffel, S. J. Scharf, R. Higuchi, G. T. Horn, K. B. Mullis, and H. A. Erlich. "Primer Directed Enzymatic Amplification of DNA with a Thermostable DNA Polymerase. *Science* 239:487–491 (1988).
10. Gelfand, D. H. "Taq DNA Polymerase," in *PCR Technology: Principles & Applications for DNA Amplification*, H. Erlich, Ed. (New York, Stockton Press, 1988), 17–22.
11. Jeffreys, A. J., V. Wilson, R. Neumann, and J. Keyte. "Amplification of Human Minisatellites by the Polymerase Chain Reaction: Towards DNA Fingerprinting of Single Cells," *Nucleic Acids Res.* 16:10953–10971 (1988).
12. Connor, B. J., A. A. Reyes, C. Morin, K. Itakura, R. L. Teplitz, and R. B. Wallace. "Detection of Sickle Cell βS-Globin Allele by Hybridization with Synthetic Oligonucleotides," *Proc. Natl. Acad. Sci. USA* 80:278–282 (1983).
13. Saiki, R. K., T. L. Bugawan, G. T. Horn, K. B. Mullis, and H. A. Erlich. "Analysis of Enzymatically Amplified β-globin and HLA-DQα with Allele Specific Oligonucleotide Probes." *Nature* 324:163–166 (1986).
14. Wahl, G. M., S. L. Berger, and A. R. Kimmel "Molecular Hybridization of Immobilized Nucleic Acids: Theoretical Concepts and Practical Considerations," in *Methods Enzymol.* 152:399–407 (1987).
15. Saiki, R. K., P. S. Walsh, C. H. Levenson, and H. A. Erlich "Genetic

Analysis of Amplified DNA with Immobilized Sequence-specific Oligonucleotide Probes," *Proc. Natl. Acad. Sci. USA* 86:6230–6234 (1989).

16. Okayama H., D. T. Curiel, M. L. Brantly, M. D. Holmes, and R. G. Crystal "Rapid, Nonradioactive Detection of Mutations in the Human Genome by Allele-Specific Amplification," *J. Lab. Clin. Med.* 114:105–113 (1989).

17. Chehab, F. F., M. Doherty, S. Cai, Y. W. Kan, S. Cooper, and E. M. Rubin. "Detection of Sickle Cell Anemia and Thalassaemias," *Nature* 329:294–295 (1987).

18. Landegren, U., R. Kaiser, J. Sanders, and L. Hood. "A Ligase Mediated Gene Detection Technique," *Science* 241:1077–1080 (1988).

19. Wrischnik, L. A., R. G. Higuchi, M. Stoneking, H. A. Erlich, N. Arnheim, and A. C. Wilson. "Length Mutations in Human Mitochondrial DNAS: Direct Sequencing of Enzymatically Amplified DNA," *Nucleic Acids Res.* 15:529–542 (1987).

20. Boerwinkle, E., W. Xiong, E. Fourest, and L. Chan. "Rapid Typing of Tandemly Repeated Hypervariable Loci by the Polymerase Chain Reaction: Application to the Apolipoprotein B 3′ Hypervariable Region," *Proc. Natl. Acad. Sci. USA* 86:212–216 (1989).

21. Horn, G. T., B. Richards, and K. W. Klinger. "Amplification of a Highly Polymorphic VNTR Segment by the Polymerase Chain Reaction," *Nucleic Acids Res.* 17:2140 (1989).

22. Weber, J. L., and P. E. May. "Abundant Class of Human DNA Polymorphisms Which can be Typed Using the Polymerase Chain Reaction," *Am. J. Human Genet.* 44:388–396 (1989).

23. Litt, M. and J. A. Luty. "A Hypervariable Microsatellite Revealed by In Vitro Amplification of a Dinucleotide Repeat within the Cardiac Muscle Actin Gene," *Am. J. Human Genet.* 44:397–401 (1989).

24. Gyllensten, U. B. "PCR and DNA Sequencing," *BioTechniques* 7:700–708 (1989).

25. Cann, R. L., M. Stoneking, and A. C. Wilson "Mitochondrial DNA and Human Evolution," *Nature* 325:31–36 (1987).

26. Orrego, C., A. C. Wilson, and M. C. King. "Identification of Maternally Related Individuals by Amplification and Direct Sequencing of a Highly Polymorphic, Noncoding Region of Mitochondrial DNA," *Am. J. Human Genet.* 43:A219 (1988).

27. Prober, J. M., G. L. Trainor, R. J. Dam, F. W. Hobbs, C. W. Robertson, R. J. Zagursky, A. J. Cocuzza, M. A. Jensen, and K. Baumeister. "A System for Rapid DNA Sequencing With Fluorescent Chain-Terminating Dideoxynucleotides," *Science* 238:336–341 (1987).

28. Erlich, H. A. and T. L. Bugawan. "HLA Class II Gene Polymorphism: DNA Typing, Evolution, and Relationship to Disease Susceptibility," in *PCR Technology: Principles & Applications for DNA Amplification*, H. Erlich, Ed. (New York: Stockton Press, 1988), 193–208.

29. von Beroldingen, C. H., E. T. Blake, R. Higuchi, G. F. Sensabaugh, and H. Erlich. "Applications of PCR to the Analysis of Biological Evidence," in *PCR Technology: Principles & Applications for DNA*

Amplification, H. Erlich, Ed. (New York: Stockton Press, 1988), 209–223.

30. Moller, G., Ed. *Molecular Genetics of Class I and II MHC Antigens (Immunological Reviews, Vols. 84–85)*. (Copenhagen: Munksgaard International, 1985).

31. Horn, G. T., T. L. Bugawan, C. M. Long, M. M. Manos, and H. A. Erlich. "Sequence Analysis of HLA Class II Genes from Insulin-Dependent Diabetic Individuals," *Human Immunology 21*, 249–263 (1988).

32. Gyllensten, U. B., and H. A. Erlich. "Generation of Single-Stranded DNA by the Polymerase Chain Reaction and its Application to Direct Sequencing of the HLA-DQα Locus," *Proc. Natl. Acad. Sci. USA* 85:7652–7656 (1988).

33. Madej, R, R. Helmuth, P. Louie, G. Horn, E. T. Blake, and H. A. Erlich. "HLA DQα Allele Frequencies Determined by PCR and Nonradioisotopic Dot-Blot ASO Analysis," poster presented at An International Symposium on the Forensic Aspects of DNA Analysis, F.B.I. Academy, Quantico, VA, June 18–23, 1989.

34. Tindall, K. R. and T. A. Kunkel. "Fidelity of DNA Synthesis by *Thermas aquaticus* DNA Polymerase," *Biochemistry* 27:6008–6013 (1988).

35. Sensabaugh, G. F. "Consequences of Nucleotide Misincorporation During the Polymerase Chain Reaction," poster presented at An International Symposium on the Forensic Aspects of DNA Analysis, F.B.I. Academy, Quantico, VA, June 18–23, 1989.

36. Krawczak, M., J. Reiss, J. Schmidtke, and U. Rosler "Polymerase Chain Reaction: Replication Errors and Reliability of Gene Diagnosis," *Nucleic Acids Res.* 17(6):2197–2201 (1989).

37. Higuchi, R., personal communication, 1989.

38. Friedberg, E. C. *DNA Repair* (New York: W. H. Freeman, 1985), chap. 1.

39. Imlay, J. A. and S. Linn. "DNA Damage and Oxygen Radical Toxicity," *Science* 240:1302–1309 (1988).

40. Reynolds, R., C. Von Beroldingen, and G. F. Sensabaugh. "Effects of DNA Degradation on Amplification by the Polymerase Chain Reaction," poster presented at An International Symposium on the Forensic Aspects of DNA Analysis, F.B.I. Academy, Quantico, VA, June 18–23, 1989.

41. Shibata, D. K., N. Arnheim, and W. J. Martin. "Detection of Human Papilloma Virus in Paraffin Embedded Tissue Using the Polymerase Chain Reaction," *J. Experimental Med.* 167:225–230 (1988).

42. Paabo, S., R. G. Higuchi, and A. C. Wilson. "Ancient DNA and the Polymerase Chain Reaction," *J. Biol. Chem.* 264:9709–9712 (1989).

43. Buoncristiani, M., C. von Beroldingen, and G. F. Sensabaugh. "Effects of UV Damage on DNA Amplification by the Polymerase Chain Reaction," poster presented at An International Symposium on the Forensic Aspects of DNA Analysis, F.B.I. Academy, Quantico, VA, June 18–23, 1989.

44. Clark, J. M. and G. P. Beardsley. "Functional Effects of Cis-Thymine

Glycol Lesions on DNA Synthesis In Vitro," *Biochemistry* 26:5398–5404 (1987).

45. Higuchi, R. and S. Kwok. "Avoiding False Positives With PCR," *Nature* 339:237–238 (1989).

6. Validation with Regard to Environmental Insults of the RFLP Procedure for Forensic Purposes

BRUCE BUDOWLE, Ph.D.
F. SAMUEL BAECHTEL, Ph.D.
DWIGHT E. ADAMS, Ph.D.

INTRODUCTION

Genetic marker typing to characterize body fluid stains has become a mainstay of serology sections of crime laboratories. Although the polymorphic protein genetic markers employed by forensic serology laboratories provide the potential for a high degree of discrimination among different individuals, this upper limit is attained infrequently because of the instability of some of these markers in dried stains. Moreover, of the markers that retain their structure and activity in the dried state, the number of expressed or observed forms is limited. Thus, in practice, the individualization of many evidentiary stains could not be carried out to any great extent.

Advances in recombinant DNA technology have provided techniques that enable scientists to detect the extraordinary variability that exists among individuals at the level of their DNA. This technology holds the promise of affording the forensic serologist the ultimate in discrimination power, i.e., the potential to identify a body fluid/tissue donor to the exclusion of all other individuals (except for identical twins).

One approach already gaining widespread utilization for the genetic characterization of evidentiary materials is restriction fragment length polymorphism (RFLP) technology. The RFLP technique is relatively simple. Briefly, restriction endonuclease digested DNA is subjected to agarose gel electro-

This is a publication of the Laboratory Division of the Federal Bureau of Investigation. Names of commercial manufacturers are provided for identification only and inclusion does not imply endorsement by the Federal Bureau of Investigation.

phoresis, which fractionates the DNA fragments according to their size. While still residing in the gel, the separated double-stranded DNA fragments are denatured by exposure of the gel to alkali. The denatured DNA is then transferred out of the gel by capillary action onto a membrane support, where it is immobilized.[1] Finally, specific fragments on the membrane are detected through hybridization with labeled DNA or RNA probes.

One of the most important aspects of the RFLP methodology for characterization is the polymorphic probes applied for analysis. Observations by Wyman and White[2] revealed that between restriction sites and within noncoding regions of human genomic DNA were multiple repeats of nucleotide sequences. Moreover, the number of repeats of these core sequences was shown to be highly variable within the human population and to be inherited in a Mendelian fashion. Some variable number of tandem repeats (VNTR) sequences have been reported to exhibit a high degree of polymorphism, such that analysis of a specimen with three-to five-probe systems can provide individualization.[3-13]

Extremely polymorphic systems, such as RFLP analysis of VNTRs, are the most desirable for forensic analyses. In fact, the more informative (i.e., the more polymorphic) the system, the more likely a falsely associated individual can be excluded from a particular forensic biospecimen found at a crime scene. Presently, the RFLP method is the best effort a forensic scientist can make to exclude a falsely associated individual with an evidentiary sample. When employing a technique that affords the potential of individualization, the likelihood that an individual would be falsely associated with a sample approaches zero.

The RFLP method developed by the FBI has been described elsewhere.[14] Of particular importance for the validation of a DNA typing method is the analysis of human tissue and fluid specimens that were removed from the body in an uncontrolled manner and that might have been contaminated and/or deteriorated prior to collection. It is the responsibility of those engaged in research directed at the application of DNA typing methods of forensic specimens to ensure that the methods have been comprehensively validated and can be applied legitimately to the types of specimens encountered in the crime laboratory. It is difficult to envision scientifically a false-positive occurring due to the RFLP methodology, especially when a battery of three to five VNTR probes is employed. However, a false-negative obtained as a result of this methodology had to be addressed. Validation studies will provide data regarding whether or not RFLP bands will change their relative positions in the gel and/or spurious bands will appear (due to environmental insults) and, thus, produce false-negative (as well as false-positive) results. In addition, validation data will provide the analyst with confidence that the results obtained by the technology are reliable, fill in the gaps for scientists from disciplines other than forensic science employing molecular biology techniques, and permit the courts to assess the weight of the data derived from an analysis.

Forensic evidence is often subjected to a variety of external influences prior to examination. Much effort has been dedicated to study the effects of environmental insults on DNA derived from body fluid stains. Experiments were designed to determine the effects of environmental influences on the quality and quantitative recovery of DNA in biospecimen stains. The insults included biological contaminants, chemical contaminants, sunlight, temperature, substrate effects, and stability over time. Finally, because all possible environmental adversities cannot be addressed experimentally, the remnants of adjudicated and nonprobative case samples, previously submitted to the FBI laboratory for traditional examination, were analyzed as examples of extremes to which evidence is subjected.

The design and the results of the validation study will be the subject of an extensive publication (manuscript in preparation). Therefore, the data only will be briefly discussed in this chapter.

ENVIRONMENT

Bloodstains from known donors were maintained at ambient outdoor temperatures from March through May, 1988. The stains were divided into two equal portions: One set was maintained in the dark and the other set was exposed to the natural diurnal cycle of sunlight and darkness. Both sets of specimens were subjected to identical temperatures (approximately 21°C for the daily high temperature). These samples were analyzed biweekly. After 8 weeks of exposure to sunlight, extracted DNA was degraded to a point where no RFLP patterns could be obtained. However, the samples maintained in the dark provided sufficient high molecular weight DNA for analysis for the entire period of study.

A similar experiment was performed in July 1988. The difference in this study was that the average daily high temperature was 41°C and the samples were analyzed daily for a 12-day period. The stains maintained in the sunlight yielded no results after 10 days, whereas the stains maintained in the dark provided RFLP patterns for all 12 days (Figure 1).

In an additional evaluation, blood from known donors was prepared as stains on a variety of substrates, which included cotton, nylon, denim, glass, wood, and aluminum. All samples were prepared as four replicate sets and each set was subjected to one of four temperatures: 4°C, 22°C, 37°C, and ambient outdoor temperature (maintained in the dark; daily high temperature ranged from 23°C to 41°C). Samples were harvested at 2 days and 1, 3, and 5 months. Conclusive results consistent with control samples were obtained from all specimens, even under the most adverse conditions (five months at 37°C). However, it should be noted that 4-year-old blood-

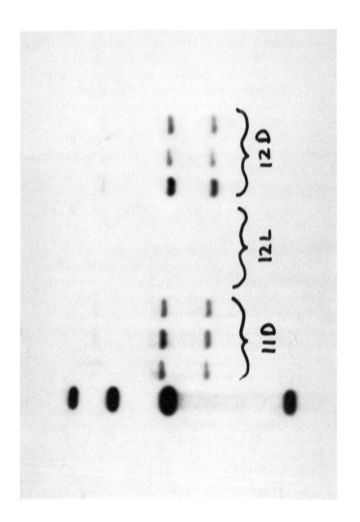

Figure 1. RFLP data on bloodstains maintained in the light or dark where the average daily high temperature was 41°C; 11D = maintained 11 days in the dark; 12L = maintained 12 days in the light; 12D = maintained twelve days in the dark.

stains maintained at 37°C yielded only low molecular weight DNA (less than 100 base pairs). Thus, DNA is not stable indefinitely.

CHEMICAL CONTAMINATION

The study was designed to determine the influence of a set of chemical substances on the recovery of DNA from bloodstained material and subsequent analysis for RFLP. The study was similar in design to the approach described by Budowle and Allen.[15] The chemicals used were representative of a variety of commonly encountered substances, which included unleaded gasoline, motor oil, detergent, acid, base, salt, bleach, and soil. After 5 days, the contaminated bloodstains were analyzed. High molecular weight DNA was recovered from all contaminated bloodstains, with the exception of soil. In the case of soil no result was obtained. In all other samples RFLP patterns were produced that were identical to uncontaminated control samples (Figure 2).

BACTERIAL AND YEAST CONTAMINATION

Two microorganisms commonly found in the vaginal vault are *Staphylococcus epidermidis* and *Candida valida* (personal communication, Brian Parkin, Metropolitan Police Laboratory, London, England). These two organisms and the ubiquitous *Escherichia coli* and *Bacillus subtilis* (personal communication, Brian Parkin) were used to study the effects of microorganisms on DNA derived from semen stains and bloodstains. Mixtures of each of the four microorganisms were made with blood or semen, and stains were prepared. The stains (maintained at ambient temperatures of the laboratory) were analyzed after 5 days. All stains produced RFLP patterns identical to uncontaminated controls. Also, DNA isolated from purified cultures of the microorganisms themselves yielded no RFLP patterns (i.e., no cross-reactivity with probes).

MIXED BODY FLUIDS

This study addressed whether or not RFLP profiles could be detected from different body fluid sources (from different individuals). An array of mixed body fluid stains were prepared from different donors. The fluids analyzed were semen, blood, urine, saliva, and vaginal secretions. Each stain consisted of two body fluids from separate donors in all possible combinations. RFLP patterns were obtained from almost all samples containing vaginal secretions, semen, and blood. The only exception was

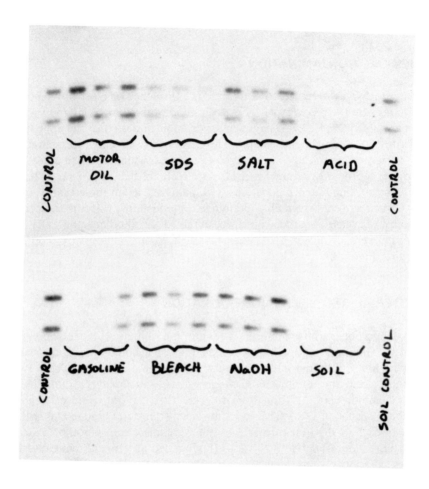

Figure 2.   RFLP data on bloodstains exposed to a variety of chemical substances.

samples containing 1 µl of blood in the mixture; in this case the blood contribution could not be detected. Saliva profiles were detected only in a few cases and the quantity of urine in stains was insufficient to yield analytical quantities of DNA. The study demonstrated that mixing of body fluids does not alter RFLP band positions compared with control samples.

CROSS-REACTIVITY WITH NONHUMAN SOURCES

The previous bacterial and yeast study demonstrated that the probes employed in the experiments do not hybridize to DNA derived from micro-

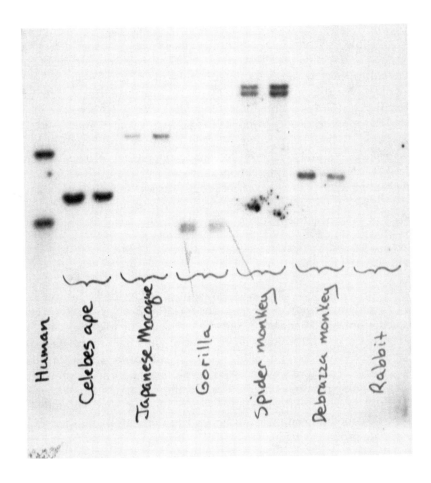

Figure 3.   RFLP data demonstrating cross-reactivity of a VNTR probe (YNH24) with higher primates. The probe does not hybridize to rabbit DNA.

organisms. The analysis was extended to nonhuman primates and domestic and wild game animals. These included cockatoo, scarlet macaw, ferret, dog, cat, rabbit, cow, horse, goat, burrow, pig, chicken, sheep, gorilla, Japanese macaque, spider monkey, celebes ape, and debrazza monkey. The probes used for RFLP-VNTR analysis in our laboratory cross-react only with DNA from primates (Figure 3).

EVIDENTIARY STAINED MATERIAL

All possible environmental adversities can not be addressed experimentally; therefore remnants (429 stains) from 122 different adjudicated cases submitted to the FBI laboratory were analyzed. These samples were 1–2 years old and had been maintained at -20°C in our laboratory. Interpretable RFLP profiles were obtained for approximately 60% of the stains. That 40% of stains produced no RFLP pattern was attributed to sample degradation or insufficient quantity. The most desirable portions of the stains used in this study had been consumed by previous serological examination; therefore, after implementation, the conclusive call rate for RFLP analysis is expected to increase. (More recent casework evaluation data with regard to victim's DNA on the substrata provided no evidence of false-positive or false-negative results).

CONCLUSION

DNA from more than 2000 samples was analyzed by the RFLP technique in this validation study. The data support the conclusion that results obtained from RFLP analysis from contaminated samples are valid and reliable. As expected, there was no evidence of any false positive due to the methodology. Expectations are that the occurrence of false-negative results for the RFLP procedure approaches zero. The legitimate application of the RFLP technology to the analysis of evidentiary materials is evident. The analyst should have confidence in the results and with proper training can and should proceed to apply the technology to the analysis of specimens of appropriate probative value.

REFERENCES

1. Southern, E. M., "Detection of Specific Sequences Among DNA Fragments Separated by Gel Electrophoresis," *J. Mol. Biol.* 98:503–517 (1975).
2. Wymann, A. R. and R. White "A Highly Polymorphic Locus in Human DNA," *Proc. Natl. Acad. Sci. USA* 77:6754–6758 (1980).
3. Budowle, B., H. A. Deadman, R. S. Murch, and F. S. Baechtel "An Introduction to the Methods of DNA Analysis Under Investigation in the FBI Laboratory," *Crime Lab. Dig.* 15:8-21 (1988).
4. Milner, E. C., C. L. Latshaw, K. Willems van Dijk, P. Charmley, P. Concannon, and H. W. Schroeder, *Nucleic Acids Res.* 17:400 (1989).
5. Nakamura, Y., M. Culver, J. Gill, P. O'Connell, M. Leppert, G. Lathrop, J. Lalouel, and R. White "Isolation and Mapping of a Polymorphic DNA Sequence pMLJ14 on Chromosome 14 (D14S13)," *Nucleic Acids Res.* 16:381 (1988).
6. Wong, Z., V. Wilson, A. J. Jeffreys, and TS. L. Thein "Cloning a

Selected Fragment from a Human DNA Fingerprint: Isolation of an Extremely Polymorphic Minisatellite," *Nucleic Acids Res.* 14:4005–4616 (1986).

7. Wong, Z., V. Wilson, I. Patel, S. Povey, and A. J. Jeffreys "Characterization Of a Panel of Highly Variable Minisatellites Cloned from Human DNA," *Ann. Hum. Genet.* 51:269–288 (1987).

8. Wainscoat, J. S., S. Pilkington, T. E. Peto, J. I. Bell, and D. R. Higgs "Allele-Specific DNA Identity Patterns," *Human Genet.* 75:384–387 (1987).

9. Nakamura, Y., C. Martin, R. Myers, L. Ballard, M. Leppert, P. O'Connell, G. Lathrop, J. Lalouel, and R. White "Isolation and Mapping of a Polymorphic DNA Sequence (pCMM86) on Chromosome 17q (D17S74)," *Nucleic Acids Res.* 16:5223 (1988).

10. Donnis-Keller, H., P. Green, C. Helms, S. Cartinhour, B. Weiffenback, et al. "A Genetic Linkage Map of the Human Genome," *Cell* 51:319–337 (1987).

11. Balasz, I., M. Baird, M. Clyne, and E. Meade "Human Population Genetic Studies of Five Hypervariable DNA Loci," *Am. J. Human Genet.* 44:182–190 (1989).

12. Nakamura, Y., M. Lepppert, P. O'Connell, R. Wolff, T. Holm, M. Culver, C. Martin, E. Fujimoto, M. Hoff, E. Kumlin, and R. White "Variable Number Of Tandem Repeat (VNTR) Markers for Human Genome Mapping," *Science* 235:1616–1622 (1987).

13. Nakamura, Y., S. Gillilan, P. O'Connell, M. Leppert, G. M. Lathrop, J. M. Lalouel, and R. White "Isolation and Mapping of a Polymorphic DNA Sequence pYNH24 on Chromosome 2(D2S44)," *Nucleic Acids Res.* 15:10073 (1987).

14. Budowle, B. and F. S. Baechtel "Modifications to Improve the Effectiveness of Restriction Fragment Length Polymorphism Typing," *Appl. Theor. Electrophoresis* 1:181–187 (1990).

15. Budowle, B. and R. C. Allen "Electrophoresis Reliability: I. The Contaminant Issue," *J. Forens. Sci.* 32:1537–1550 (1987).

7. The Meaning of a Match: Sources of Ambiguity in the Interpretation of DNA Prints

WILLIAM C. THOMPSON, Ph.D.
SIMON FORD, Ph.D.

INTRODUCTION

Techniques for detecting restriction fragment length polymorphisms (RFLPs) are well established in molecular biology and are beginning to be used for medical diagnosis of genetic diseases.[1] The development of probes capable of identifying "hypervariable" DNA regions[2] has also made these techniques promising for use in criminal identification. A great deal of excitement has accompanied efforts by commercial firms, such as Lifecodes Corp. and Cellmark Diagnostics, and government agencies, such as the FBI, to adapt RFLP analysis for forensic use.[3] As DNA test results have been submitted to the courts, however, concerns have surfaced about the reliability of the results reported by the forensic DNA laboratories and about the accuracy of statistics reported by DNA laboratories on the fre-

---

[1] See generally, *Nucleic Acid Probes in Diagnosis of Human Genetic Disease*. (New York: Alan R. Liss, Inc., 1988).

[2] Nakamura, Leppert, O'Connell, Wolff, Holm, Culver, Martin, Fujimoto, Hoff, Kumlin, & White "Variable Number of Tandem Repeat (VNTR) Markers For Human Gene Mapping," *Science* 235:1616 (1987); Jeffreys, Wilson, & Thein "Individual-Specific 'Fingerprints' of Human DNA," *Nature* 316:76 (1985).

[3] A number of journalistic accounts have heralded DNA typing as a "breakthrough" that "could revolutionize law enforcement." E.g., Moss, "DNA—The New Fingerprints," *A.B.A. J.*, May 1, 1988, at 66; also Lewis, "DNA Fingerprints: Witness for the Prosecution," *Discover*, June 1988, at 44; Marx, "DNA Fingerprinting Takes the Witness Stand," *Science* 240:1616 (1988).

quency of occurrence of DNA "prints."[4] Problems in casework have led to calls for additional validation research, the development of better control procedures and clearer standards for interpreting the autoradiograms produced by the technique, and for more extensive proficiency testing.[5]

The need for validation and for strict standards for interpretation arises from two unique features of forensic DNA tests. First, DNA identification tests are far more likely than DNA diagnostic tests to be rendered ambiguous by variability or "slop" in the results of RFLP analysis.[6] Under the best of conditions, DNA prints of the same individual often vary slightly in the position and appearance of their bands due to inevitable inconsistencies in reagents, gels, sample quality, and so on. Variability is likely to be even greater when dealing with the sort of degraded and contaminated samples that are commonly encountered in forensic applications.[7] Although some experts have denied that such variability is possible,[8] data from casework indicates DNA prints of the same individual may not appear identical. Bands are sometimes shifted up or down in their lanes relative to standard markers, bands sometimes are not visible, extra bands sometimes appear, and bands are sometimes indistinct, smeared, or smudged, making it diffi-

---

[4]Thompson & Ford "DNA Typing: Promising Technique Needs Additional Validation," *Trial* (Sept. 1988); Thompson & Ford, "DNA Typing: Acceptance and Weight of the New Genetic Identification Tests," 75 U.Va.L.R. 45 (1989) (hereafter Thompson & Ford); Thompson "Misprint," *The New Republic*, April 3, 1989; Lander "DNA Fingerprinting On Trial" *Nature* 339:501 (1989); Sherman "DNA Tests Unravel?" *National Law J.*, Dec. 18 (1989); Anderson "DNA Fingerprinting On Trial," *Nature* 342:844 (1989); Norman "Maine Case Deals Blow to DNA Fingerprinting," *Science* 246:1556 (1989); Kolata "Some Scientists Doubt the Value of 'Genetic Fingerprint' Evidence," *New York Times*, Jan. 29, 1990, p. 1; Thompson & Ford "Is DNA Fingerprinting Ready for the Courts," *New Scientist* 125:38 (1990).

[5]Lander, supra note 4; Sherman, supra note 4; Anderson, supra note 4; Norman, supra note 4; Kolata, supra note 4.

[6]The term *slop* is one we coined earlier to refer to the inevitable variability in the appearance of DNA prints caused by minor variations in procedures, reagents, samples, and the like. See Thompson & Ford, 1988, supra note 4; Thompson & Ford, 1989, supra note 4, at 87. In using the term *slop* we do not mean to suggest or imply that forensic analysts are necessarily sloppy or negligent. Although poor laboratory procedure may increase the amount of "slop" by inducing greater variability in results, "slop" will occur in the best of laboratories due to the inherent variability of the analytical systems used to produce DNA prints.

[7]Thompson & Ford, supra note 4, at 64–76, 87–91, n. 188.

[8]Some promoters of forensic DNA testing have suggested that RFLP autoradiographs (autorads) are as clear as supermarket bar codes, that each autorad is unique, and that the fragment pattern (print) on the autorad containing DNA from one individual is readily and absolutely distinguishable from all others. The potential for variability in the results of RFLP analysis has sometimes been denied by experts in testimony with a tone of absolute certainty, as in this passage from a deposition in State v. Hopkins, Ft. Wayne, Ind. No. CCR-86–428, September 26, 1988; RT 39:13–21):

Q: [Defense Attorney]: If we were to test two different samples from the same individual and come up with a DNA fingerprint, is there any variability between the test result in sample one and sample two? Might we expect there might be some variability in the two?
A: [Prosecution expert]: I wouldn't expect there to be any.
Q: They would be exactly the same?
A: Yep.

cult to determine their true position. Some of the interpretational difficulties that may arise from these problems are illustrated in Figure 1.

"Slop" in the procedure is of little consequence for most research and diagnostic applications of RFLP analysis because there is typically no need in such applications to precisely measure the position of bands,[9] and there are built-in controls to account for artifacts such as extra bands and missing bands.[10] When RFLP analysis is used for individual identification, however, precise measurement of bands is essential[11] and artifacts such as missing bands and extra bands are potentially misleading.

These problems require careful consideration due to the need, in forensic DNA typing, to make decisions of critical importance on the basis of a single result. In research and medical diagnostics, scientists have ample samples and can repeat experiments that produce equivocal results. In many instances, conclusions are based on multiple samples; an error in one observation is of little consequence because it is averaged out. In forensic DNA typing, however, limited samples often make it impossible to run a test more than once. Faced with a less-than-ideal result, the analyst must choose between making no call (thereby losing what may well be important evidence) and attempting an interpretation.

Although "slop" would seem more likely to cause false exclusions than false identifications, there is always a danger that an analyst will mistakenly attribute true genetic differences between samples to the slop effects.

---

[9]Consider, for example, this testimony by a prominent human geneticist who testified in the Frye hearing in *People v. Axell*, Ventura, Ca. No. CR 23911, the first California case in which DNA typing based on RFLP analysis was admitted:
Q: [Prosecutor] Incidentally, do population geneticists engage in the type of precise band measurements that we see in the forensic cases?
A: No, they — we do not.
Q: Why is that?
A: Because . . . . we work with probes that only have a few bands and they are so far apart, these bands, they are so different in size that . . . when you see a band you know it's either a, b, or c. You know which it is. (RT 1735:2–17)
Another human geneticist who testified in the case also acknowledged this point. He stated that in the majority of his work, he needs to distinguish and classify individuals as having only 1 of 3–10 phenotypes (RT 326:7–9) and noted "if one has only three [patterns to distinguish] one doesn't do measurement. One does qualitative evaluation of the pattern." (RT 326:20–22.)
[10]See Lander, supra note 4; also note 11, infra.
[11]This point is emphasized in Eric Lander's article in *Nature*:
DNA fingerprinting is far more technically demanding than DNA diagnostics . . . DNA diagnostics requires simply identifying whether each parent has passed to a child the RFLP pattern inherited from his or her mother or father. Because the four discrete patterns are known in advance, these investigations have built-in consistency checks which guard against many errors and artifacts.
DNA fingerprinting, by contrast, is more like analytical biochemistry: One must determine whether two completely unknown samples are identical. Because hypervariable RFLP loci often involve 50–100 alleles yielding restriction fragments of very similar lengths, reliably recognizing a match is technically demanding. Lander, supra note 4, at 501.

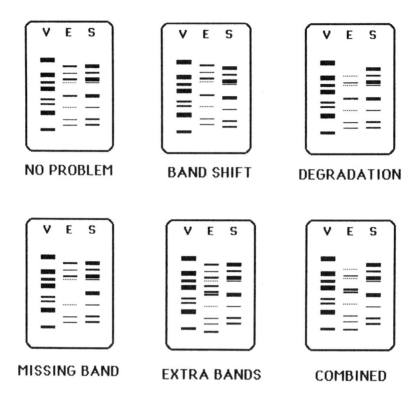

PROBLEMS WITH DNA TYPING

Figure 1.   Interpretational problems that can arise in DNA typing. The diagram illustrates ambiguities that may arise in DNA typing due to several technical problems that affect the appearance of DNA prints. Prints of a victim (V) and suspect (S) bracket a print from evidentiary material (E). Prints of this type could be produced with a cocktail of four single-locus probes. In the absence of technical problems, the comparison is straightforward. Comparison with other samples is more problematic when one sample (E) is affected by band shift (causing misalignment of bands), degradation (causing loss of upper bands), loss of bands in other parts of the print, or the presence of extra bands. When two or more of these problems occur simultaneously, or when both prints are affected by problems, the ambiguity becomes more severe. The dilemma faced by the analyst is how to distinguish differences induced by technical problems and artifacts from true genetic differences between samples.

In a number of cases we have reviewed, analysts have declared a match between two DNA prints that differ with regard to the number or position of bands, attributing the differences to experimental artifacts. In some instances, "slop" is invoked as an explanation in the absence of supporting experimental evidence. Although this practice has been criticized by some commentators,[12] it has been common and has gone unchallenged in many cases.

A second unique feature of forensic DNA typing is the need to estimate the frequency with which matching DNA prints will be found by chance in order to determine the probative value of a "match". Even when the match between two prints is perfect, such estimates may be problematic due to their reliance on "simplifying assumptions about population genetics whose accuracy has not yet been rigorously tested for highly polymorphic RFLP loci."[13] The matter is further complicated when "slop" is a factor. If an analyst can call two prints a "match" when they do not match perfectly, the probative value of the evidence is best gauged not by the frequency of prints that would match perfectly, but by the frequency of prints that would match under the looser standards actually used by the analyst. Such estimates may be difficult to make, particularly where the analyst relies upon subjective judgment to distinguish true genetic variation from "slop". There is no other application of RFLP analysis for which such frequency estimates are necessary. Hence, the issues that have arisen recently in legal proceedings concerning the appropriateness of various approaches for estimating allele frequencies and computing the frequency of sets of alleles are unique to forensic DNA typing and have not arisen elsewhere in science.

This chapter discusses the potential for ambiguity in forensic DNA typing and the problems facing an analyst when attempting to interpret DNA prints in the absence of adequate standards. It identifies areas in which additional validation research is needed and proposes conservative controls and standards for assistance in interpreting DNA test results. We base our conclusions and recommendations in part on technical literature in molecular biology and on validation research conducted by forensic scientists. To illustrate interpretive problems, however, we have, of necessity, relied primarily on the testimony of a number of scientists who have participated in admissibility hearings as expert witnesses and upon laboratory notes,

---

[12]Lander, supra note 4, at 502 argues that this practice "is inappropriate in DNA fingerprinting analysis of unknown samples — as one runs the risk of discounting precisely those differences that would exonerate an innocent defendant." He suggests forensic laboratories "should be required to use experiments to rule out proposed artefacts." Id.; see also Thompson & Ford, supra note 4 at 91 (arguing that this practice undermines the probative value of DNA evidence).

[13]Lander, supra note 4, at 50.

reports, and autoradiograms from actual casework.[14] Casework is the primary source of data regarding potential ambiguities in forensic DNA typing; most of the issues we discuss here have not yet been addressed in the scientific or medical literature. In addition, we have drawn upon results of proficiency tests that have become available to the courts in the course of the admissibility hearings.

SOURCES OF AMBIGUITY AND THEIR IMPLICATIONS FOR INTERPRETATION OF FORENSIC DNA PRINTS

A DNA "print" is composed of a set of bands on an autoradiogram (autorad). To determine whether two samples could have a common source, an analyst must compare their DNA prints. Whether the analyst declares the prints a "match" (inclusion), not a match (exclusion), or inconclusive depends on how closely the bands of one print appear to align with corresponding bands in the other (i.e., whether corresponding bands appear to have the same molecular weight). Consequently, the position of the bands within a DNA print, relative to other bands and relative to the position of reference bands known as molecular weight markers, is of paramount importance in determining identity. Any factor that is likely to affect the position or number of bands in a DNA print will affect the confidence with which a determination of identity can be made. In this section we will review a number of factors that can alter the appearance of DNA prints, grouping them into three categories: those that cause the position of the bands to shift up or down relative to standard markers and other prints, those that cause the appearance of extra bands, and those that cause the disappearance of bands (i.e., "allelic dropout").

Band Shift

In forensic RFLP analysis, bands from the same source but in different tracks on a gel are sometimes misaligned (Figure 2); the banding patterns may be displaced up or down relative to each other or relative to marker DNA patterns. The resulting shifts were described in recent testimony in a California case: "In general, what you see — I have seen exceptions, but in general . . . the whole pattern has shifted, usually upwards, so that you have

---

[14]The cases we reviewed in preparation of this chapter are listed in Table 1. We examined autorads, laboratory notes, and laboratory reports of these cases.

From this casework we draw a number of examples that we believe illustrate ambiguity or the potential for ambiguity in forensic DNA analysis. By singling out specific cases to illustrate problems, however, we do not necessarily mean to imply that the laboratory reached a wrong conclusion or that any injustice was done. Those interested in a broader evaluation of these cases should examine the original case materials and court transcripts, rather than relying on the limited examples we have chosen to present here. Our goal is to illustrate sources of ambiguity and the potential for errors and problems, not to challenge the results of cases already adjudicated.

MASSACHUSETTS vs ROBERT CURNIN

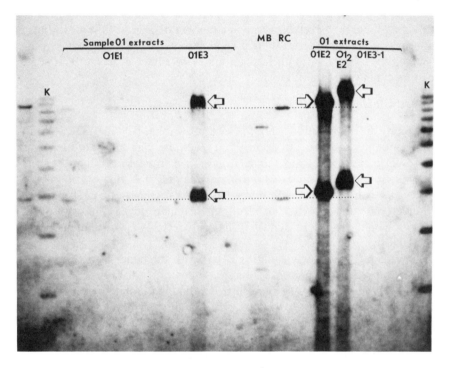

Figure 2. Band shift. Cellmark autoradiograph from Commonwealth of Massachusetts v. Robert Curnin (Worcester, MA) showing several prints, all derived from the same evidentiary stain (Sample 01), and prints of defendant (RC) and victim (MB). A comparison across lanes reveals upward band shift in samples 01E3, 01E2, and 01_2E2 in comparison with 01E1, RC, and 01E3–1. We have added a dotted line between samples 01E1 and 01E3–1 to illustrate the mobility shift (shifted bands marked with arrows). Also evident are marked differences in the darkness of bands, indicating significant variation in the amount of DNA applied to various lanes.

Lanes RC and MB are *Hin*fl–digested DNA extracted from blood samples. Lanes marked "01 extracts" are all derived from a stain on a nightgown, prepared through a series of differential extractions and washes. The 12 resulting DNA fractions were digested with *Hin*fl. Cellmark declared that the DNA print of the semen stain matched the defendant's DNA print based on a comparison of samples 01E1 and 01E3–1 to RC. Differences between samples 01E3, 01E2, 01_2E2, and RC were attributed to band shift, although no experimental confirmation of differential mobility in those lanes was produced.

Lane K shows molecular weight markers (1 kb DNA ladder BRL Life Technologies, Inc. Gaithersburg, MD. Fragment sizes kb: 12.2, 11.2, 10.2, 9.2, 8.1, 7.1, 6.1, 5.1, 4.1, 3.1, 2.0, 1.6, and 1.0. BRL Life Technologies, Inc. 1989 Catalogue & Reference Guide). Hybridization was performed with the single-locus probe MS43. Cellmark declared a match based on hybridization with three additional single-locus probes—MS1, MS31, and g3 (not shown). Only samples RC, 01E1, and 01E3–1 were sized. No attempt was made to size bands in lanes exhibiting shifted patterns, but the shift is apparent for all four probes by visual inspection.

a hint that they are from the same source because the relative distances from one band to the next has [sic] remained the same."[15]

Although the possibility of "band shift" was initially denied by some experts,[16] it has now been observed in a number of cases.[17] In some instances the shifts observed have been great enough to exceed the standard criterion used by the laboratory in declaring a match. We have observed band shifts of this magnitude in a number of cases.[18]

Causes of Band Shift

Among molecular biologists, it is well known that lane-to-lane variations in the mobility of DNA can occur,[19] but the underlying causes of band shift in forensic cases are poorly understood. In courtroom testimony experts have attributed band shift to a variety of factors, including overloading of gel tracks with excessive amounts of DNA, the presence of contaminants in samples, and the presence of ethidium bromide during electrophoresis. Research on the causes of band shift has only recently begun and has not yet resolved the issue.

Overloading was the explanation offered for the band shifts observed in the Curnin case (see Figure 2). In experimental studies, overloading has indeed been shown to cause band shift,[20] although the shifts observed in the experiments are downward, while in Curnin and some other forensic cases overloading has been invoked to explain upward shifts. Band shift is sometimes observed on autorads that have marked lane-to-lane variations in the intensity of bands, but this is not always the case (Figure 3).

---

[15]*People v. Barney*, Oakland, Calif. No. H 10291, June 28, 1989; RT665:4–9

[16]Bruce Budowle of the FBI at one point noted that he had been unable to produce band shift during the FBI's extensive validation studies, that his bands were "steady as a rock . . . nothing makes them move." Quoted in Thompson & Ford, 1989, supra note 4, at 70. But the FBI no longer takes that position. See also the expert testimony quoted in note 8, supra.

[17]Band shift has also been observed in other applications of Southern blot analysis involving contaminated samples. See, e.g., Goelz, Hamilton, & Vogelstein "Purification of DNA from Formaldehyde Fixed and Paraffin Embedded Human Tissue," *Biochem. Biophys. Res. Commun.* 130:118–125 (1985); Dubeau, Chandler, Gralow, Nichols, & Jones "Southern Blot Analysis of DNA Extracted from Formalin-Fixed Pathology Specimens," *Cancer Res.* 46:2964 (1986).

[18]See listing in Table 1.

[19]Grossman, "Gel Electrophoresis of DNA," presented at An International Symposium on the Forensic Aspects of DNA Analysis, FBI Academy, Quantico, VA.

[20]Grossman, supra note 17; Johnson, Miller, & Grossman, "Electrophoresis of DNA in Agarose Gels: II. Effects of Loading Mass and Electroendosmosis on Electrophoretic Mobilities," *Analyt. Biochem.* 102:159 (1980); Waye & Fourney, "Agarose Gel Electrophoresis of Linear Genomic DNA in the Presence of Ethidium Bromide: Band Shifting and Implications for Forensic Identity Testing," *Appl. Theor. Electrophoresis* (in press) (suggesting that the amount of shift may be dependent on the DNA concentration applied to the gel when electrophoresis is performed in the presence of ethidium bromide). See also, Myers, Sanchez, Elwell, & Falkow, "Simple Electrophoretic Method for the Identification and Characterization of Plasmid Deoxyribonucleic Acid," *J.Bacteriol.* 127:1529 (1976).

DELAWARE vs STEVEN PENNELL

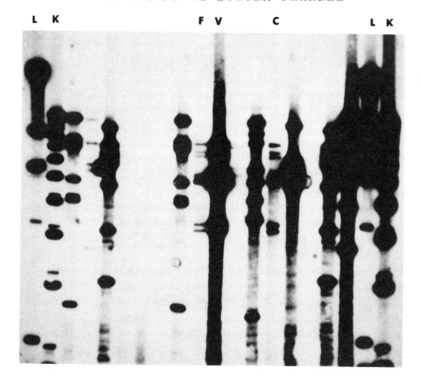

Figure 3. Lane-to-lane variation in band intensity. The autorad from Commonwealth of Delaware v. Pennell, No. IN88–12–0051–3, Wilmington, DE shows marked variation across lanes in band intensity. The laboratory declared a match between the print of the victim (V) and prints obtained from evidentiary blood stains from a piece of carpet (C) and the underlying foam rubber (F). Overexposure of V makes it difficult to compare V directly with F and C on this autorad. Fortunately, shorter exposures were also available, although the bands in F and C were difficult to visualize on these. The wide discrepancy in the amount of DNA loaded in lanes F and V does not appear to have produced band shift. Had the comparison of F and V been the only one available, concerns might have arisen that the matching DNA print in F was the result of contamination of the F gel well with trace amounts of DNA from V. Because cross-contamination of adjacent gel wells is always possible, an evidentiary sample should not be run in the lane adjacent to the sample to which it will be compared. Lane L contains molecular weight markers (lambda digested with HindIII). Lane K also contains markers (1 kb DNA ladder, see Figure 2).

There are two types of control procedures that can be used to minimize lane-to-lane discrepancies in band intensity and to reduce the likelihood of overloading.[21] One approach, currently used by all forensic DNA laboratories, is simply to quantify the DNA in each sample before electrophoresis to assure that roughly equal amounts are added to each gel well. The problem with this approach is that current methods of quantitation[22] do not appear to be sufficiently accurate to prevent marked differences in the amount of DNA loaded in lanes on the same gel, as evidenced by the striking differences in the intensities of DNA bands across lanes observed in many forensic cases.

An alternative way to deal with the problem of overloading, which has been suggested by some experts,[23] is serial dilution. To assure accurate comparison of unknown DNA samples to standards, a number of standard DNA samples are applied in a dilution range. In the absence of reliable methods for quantitation, the use of serial dilution would appear to be a highly desirable control procedure. To date it has not been adopted by the forensic DNA laboratories.

Band shift may also be caused by the presence in forensic samples of contaminating materials (e.g., soil, clothing dyes, foreign proteins) that survive the DNA extraction and purification process or to the introduction of contaminating materials during the extraction process (e.g., NaCl, solvents, detergents, dyes) that are not successfully removed.[24] Contaminants

---

[21]Overloading is a problem not only because it may induce band shift, but also because it can obscure the possibility of cross-contamination and render estimates of band position less precise (see Figure 3). It can also cause other problems. Where two samples being compared are of different intensity, it is always possible that some bands in the fainter sample are too faint to visualize (see section on faint bands, infra).

[22]Spectroscopy (optical density at 260 nm) is widely accepted as the preferred method for quantifying DNA in research laboratories, see Maniatis, T., E. Fritsch, & J. Sambrook *Molecular Cloning, A Laboratory Manual* (1982)[hereinafter, Maniatis], but appears to be unreliable on forensic samples where DNA solutions are often contaminated with proteins, solvents, dyes, or other materials that interfere with absorbance. RNA, bacterial, and other nonhuman DNAs may also be present in forensic samples, producing an overestimation in readings for human DNA content. Because of these problems, forensic DNA laboratories rely heavily on "yield" gels—in which a small amount of the DNA solution is run on an agarose gel alongside one or more known standard DNA solutions. The gel is treated with ethidium bromide, which stains DNA, and the amount of DNA present in each sample is estimated by comparison with the standards. Quantitation by this visual method is very inaccurate, however, and may still be compromised by the presence of bacterial DNA and other nonhuman DNAs. The reliability of this method is also dependent on its correct implementation. Recent developments in the quantitation of DNA are likely to enable forensic DNA laboratories to use more reliable methods for accurately quantitating the amount of DNA to apply to each gel track. Waye, Presley, Budowle, Shutler & Fourney, "A Simple and Sensitive Method for Quantifying Human Genomic DNA in Forensic Specimen Extracts," *Biotechniques* 17:852 (1989).

[23]See testimony of Richard Roberts in *People v. Castro*, Bronx, NY, No. 1508/87, RT 4267–68.

[24]In November 1988 a telephone survey, designed by the authors, was administered to 215 Ph.D.-level molecular biologists and geneticists randomly selected from the membership of the American Society for Microbiology. The survey was conducted by the University of

may induce band shift in two ways. First, they may perturb conditions in an agarose gel lane, altering the rate at which DNA can migrate in one lane relative to the other lanes. Just as a horse may be faster on a dry track than a wet track, DNA may move more quickly under some conditions than under others.[25] Second, contaminants may actually bind to the DNA in a given lane, altering the rate at which the DNA can migrate. DNA bound with protein, for example, may move more slowly than unbound DNA, just as a horse with a heavy rider will move more slowly than the same horse with a light rider.

Forensic samples may contain a number of types of molecules known to bind to DNA. It is well established that proteins will bind to DNA under some conditions and, as a result, retard the mobility of DNA during electrophoresis.[26] Indeed, scientists often rely on this phenomenon to study the interaction of protein and DNA, identifying DNA sequences at which a protein might bind by looking for a characteristic "gel retardation" of restriction fragments.[27] Although protocols for forensic DNA testing typically include an enzymatic digestion stage to remove proteins, and the kind of binding that proteins exhibit can be dissociated by heat treatment of the DNA sample before loading it on the gel,[28] under some circumstances proteins may escape digestion or become irreversibly bound to DNA (for example, cross-linking may occur due to exposure to ultraviolet light) such that heat denaturation would be ineffective.[29]

Dyes may also interact with DNA in a manner that can cause band shift. It is known that some dyes interact with the DNA molecule by a process

---

Kentucky Survey Research Center. When asked whether the mobility of bands during electrophoresis could be affected by residual contaminants that survive a DNA extraction procedure, 69% of these scientists responded "yes". Seventy-two percent said they had encountered aberrant mobility of bands during electrophoresis in their own labs, although only 15% labeled this phenomenon "common". Thompson & Ford, "Survey of Molecular Biologists Concerning Acceptance of Forensic DNA Typing Procedures," (unpublished manuscript, 1989).

[25]It is commonly observed, for example, that restriction digests of DNA digested in buffers with differing salt concentrations display "shifts" relative to each other.

[26]Crothers, "Gel Electrophoresis of Protein-DNA Complexes," Nature 325:464 (1987); Revzin, "Gel Electrophoresis Assays for DNA Protein Interactions," Biotechniques 7:346 (1989).

[27]See, e.g., Garner & Revzin "A Gel Electrophoresis Method for Quantifying the Binding of Proteins to Specific DNA Regions," Nucleic Acids Res. 9:3047 (1981). Some proteins bind selectively to specific DNA sequences, causing selective retardation of some bands but not others. S. Ford "Gene Expression in the Mercury Resistance Transposon Tn501," Unpublished dissertation, University of Bristol at 82.

[28]Heating the sample to 65°C for 5 minutes is standard practice in many research laboratories and has the added advantage that it leads to a sharpening of the bands. Fuchs & Blakesley "Guide to the Use of Type II Restriction Endonucleases," in 100 Methods in Enzymology 3 (1983), but this procedure has not always been employed in forensic laboratories.

[29]See generally, Shetlar chapter in Smith, K., Ed. Photochemical and Photobiological Reviews, (1980) 105–197.

known as "intercalation".[30] Recently, ethidium bromide, a dye commonly used to stain DNA, has been shown to cause band shift.[31] The degree of shift occurring in the presence of ethidium bromide appears to vary depending on the concentration of DNA loaded in the gel lane. Thus, the interaction of DNA with ethidium bromide may account for some instances in which marked lane-to-lane variations in band intensity are associated with band shift.[32] There have also been reports that some clothing dyes cause band shift,[33] but this problem has not been systematically studied.

Humic acid, which is found in soil, may also contribute to band shift[34] and poses special problems, because it is similar in structure and properties to DNA. As such it copurifies with DNA. The DNA extraction and purification procedures used by the forensic DNA laboratories do not include any stages known to separate DNA from humic materials. The mechanism by which humic acid leads to band shift is not known; one possibility is that it contributes to the overloading problem by interfering with accurate quantitation of DNA.[35]

Although the list of factors that may cause band shift is long, the precise conditions under which the phenomenon will occur are poorly understood. After a recent study on the effects of contaminants on band shift, Cellmark concluded that "with the possible exception of [the detergent] SDS, the components normally used in the extraction of DNA from stains presented as evidence are not likely to cause the type of band shifting observed in casework;" further, Cellmark reported that "it has not yet been possible to induce such band shifting with substances extracted from two common substrate materials encountered in casework."[36] Cellmark's failure to produce band shift in these experimental studies may undermine some of the explanations offered for the phenomenon and indicates that a full explanation of band shift has yet to be found.

One control procedure that has been proposed for dealing with band shift

---

[30]Maniatis, supra note 22 at 161. Intercalation is best described by analogy. The flat, plate-like molecules of the dye load onto the DNA double helix as if they were plates being loaded into a plate rack.

[31]Waye & Fourney, supra note 20; Fourney, Shutler, Monteith, Bishop, Gaudette, & Waye, "DNA Typing In the Royal Canadian Mounted Police," Proceedings of An International Symposium on the Forensic Aspects of DNA Analysis (in press).

[32]Waye and Fourney suggest that the concentration-dependent shift in band position observed in their research "could complicate the task of comparing restriction fragment length polymorphism profiles and introduce a degree of uncertainty to allele frequency population databases." Supra note 20 (abstract).

[33]Robin Cotton of Cellmark notes that samples extracted from certain dyed fabrics tend to produce shifted patterns. People v. Barney, supra note 15; RT 658–59.

[34]S. Ford and B. Olson, unpublished observation.

[35]Because humic materials absorb light in a range similar to that absorbed by DNA, their presence may interfere with accurate quantitation of DNA by optical densitometry.

[36]"Summary of Experiments Studying Contamination Effects on Band Migration," Unpublished manuscript, Cellmark Diagnostics (December, 1989).

is the use of a "mixing experiment". Expert testimony in *People v. Castro* convinced the court that this control is essential:

> "Because lanes of DNA may not run exactly the same during electrophoresis, a mixing experiment should be conducted when there is sufficient quantity of DNA available. The technique is simple and scientifically accepted. A sample (x) is placed in lane A, a 50–50 mixture of sample (x) and sample (y) is run in lane B and sample (y) is run in lane C. The fragments should give identical patterns on a Southern blot on all three lanes."[37]

The theory behind this control is that band shift may cause a lack of alignment between the prints in lanes A and C, but that there should be perfect alignment in the mixed lane where lane-to-lane variation is not a factor. Accordingly, under this analysis, a superimposed or double print in the mixed lane indicates a true genetic difference between the samples. The problem with this control, however, is that it may be fooled in instances where a band shift is caused by the binding of contaminants to the DNA in one of the two samples. In such instances the contaminant-bound sample may have different mobility than the other sample and form a distinct pattern, even if the two samples are from the same source. By analogy, two identical horses may run at different speeds on the same track if one is carrying a heavier rider. The mixing experiment controls for track conditions (putting both horses on the same track), but not for the load the horses are carrying. Thus, if the mixing control is interpreted in the manner the Castro opinion suggests, it could contribute to an erroneous exclusion.[38]

Problems of Interpretation Raised by Band Shift

The possibility of band shift adds an element of ambiguity to the interpretation of DNA prints. An analyst will sometimes need to distinguish band shift from an exclusion in cases where the bands of two DNA prints do not align but the patterns are similar. While such distinctions may be straightforward in some instances, they are likely to be more difficult where bands in different regions of the gel shift in an inconsistent manner (Figure 4) or where band shift occurs in conjuction with other problems that make some bands impossible to visualize or cause the appearance of extra bands (see Figure 1).

Band shift may also increase the likelihood of false positives. There is a possibility, albeit remote, that band shift will bring nonmatching bands into alignment. More important, however, is the danger that analysts, knowing band shift may occur, will relax their standards for declaring a match in

---

[37] *People v. Castro*, supra note 23, at 23.
[38] Mixing experiments may nevertheless be a useful control for ruling out the possibility that an apparent match between two DNA prints (run separately) is due to an adventitious band shift. If the two samples produce a single print when run together, the match cannot be due to lane-to-lane variation in DNA mobility.

GEORGIA vs CALDWELL

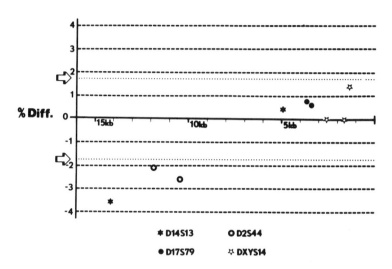

Figure 4. Inconsistent band shift. Figure shows the direction and degree of shift of bands in an evidentiary stain relative to bands in the blood standard to which it was declared to match in a Lifecodes report. The horizontal axis shows the average size of corresponding bands in the two DNA prints. The vertical axis shows the direction and degree of deviation of the bands in the evidentiary stain from corresponding bands in the blood standard (deviation is expressed as a percent of the average size of the two bands). Arrows on the vertical axis show the upper and lower boundaries of Lifecodes' formal "window" for declaring a match between samples (± 1.8%). For high molecular weight bands (between 15 kb and 10 kb) the bands in the evidentiary stain appear to be 2–4% smaller than corresponding bands in the blood standard. For low molecular weight bands (less than 5 kb) the bands in the evidentiary stain appear to be up to 1.4% larger. Data in the chart is taken from Lifecodes report no. FB20590, dated July 27, 1989, and accompanying DNA fragment size sheets in *Georgia v. Caldwell*. The blood standard is sample #FB20590; the evidentiary stain is sample #FI13554.

order to avoid falsely exonerating a guilty suspect, and in doing so will undermine the power of the test to exclude nonmatching samples.

One approach for dealing with apparent band shift has been reliance on simple visual comparisons to determine whether two prints match. Measurements of band position may indicate a lack of alignment, but, as Kevin McElfresh, now Director of Forensics and Paternity of Lifecodes Corp., explains, there may be "a consistent non-alignment of the bands throughout the test, telling us there's a match."[39] There are, however, two serious problems with visual matching. First, it is subjective. In several

---

[39]Quoted in Lander, supra note 4.

recent cases, experts testifying for the defense have disputed such calls. In each instance, the laboratory, relying apparently on visual comparisons, declared a match in instances in which the bands being compared differed by more than three standard deviations. The defense experts examined the same materials but considered the results inconclusive. As Eric Lander notes "[w]hen a result is reported to have an error rate of 1 in 100,000,000, it seems essential that the underlying data are not left as a matter of subjective opinion."[40]

Visual matching also renders problematic efforts to use statistics to gauge the probative value of the "match". This point is illustrated by casework in *State v. Caldwell*,[41] a Georgia case. Figure 4 shows the relative positions of bands in an evidentiary stain and a blood standard. The two prints were declared a visual match by the analyst, even though the misalignment of the bands is not consistent. The bands of the evidentiary stain appear to have shifted down at the top of the gel and up at the bottom of the gel relative to the markers. Assuming the two samples are from the same individual, as the analyst maintained, then this configuration may be the result of some problem that caused the evidentiary sample to run faster than the blood standard at the top of the gel and slower at the bottom relative to the markers.

To estimate the likelihood that a "visual match" of this type might occur by chance, one must weigh the likelihood that this particular misalignment of bands could be a result of problems in electrophoresis, a problematic endeavor at best. More importantly, one must realize that if a pattern as discrepant from the blood standard as that of the evidentiary stain appears to match it, then a great many other patterns would be called a match as well. It is the cumulative frequency of such patterns that must be estimated to determine the likelihood of a coincidental match using a "visual matching" approach. However, as Lander notes, "without an objective definition of a match, there is no meaningful way to determine the probability that a declared match might have arisen by chance." [42]

A second possible method for distinguishing band shift from true genetic differences in the DNA samples being tested is the use of a "constant band" or monomorphic probe. Such a probe would always identify DNA fragments of a known length and thus would produce a band at a known position. This "constant band" would serve as a benchmark for determining the direction and degree of shift in each gel track. Lifecodes recently began

---

[40]Lander, supra note 4 at 502.
[41]Marietta, Georgia. Lifecodes case No. FB13551; final report dated 11/88.
[42]Lander, supra note 4, at 502–503.

using a constant band probe,[43] and similar probes are being utilized by Cellmark and the FBI.

To be useful for forensic casework, these probes must meet several criteria. First, research must demonstrate that the probe is actually monomorphic.[44] As Robin Cotton of Cellmark notes, "you don't want to have a probe that is 98 percent of the time monomorphic and 2 percent of the time shows a slightly higher or lower band . . . "[45] To eliminate the possibility that the probe produces different bands in a small percentage of individuals or in some population subgroups, research should be conducted in which a sizable number of samples from a variety of population subgroups are hybridized with the probe.

Second, probes must be used that would produce several bands falling in different regions of the gel. Because band shift is sometimes nonlinear, as shown in Figure 4, the use of probes producing bands in only one region of the gel may be misleading. Note in Figure 4 that a single monomorphic band in the 9–15 kb region would indicate that the evidentiary sample had shifted down by approximately 3%; a monomorphic band at 1.4 kb would indicate an upward shift of about 1.4%; a band between 2 and 5 kb would indicate no shift. DXZ1, a probe currently being used by at least one forensic laboratory, produces bands at approximately 4.1 and 2.1 kb. These bands would not be "high" enough on the gel to verify that the displacement in the three upper bands of Figure 4 is, in fact, due to band shift.

Third, the bands produced by the benchmark monomorphic probes must be tight and distinct, that is, they should not produce wide smudge-type bands or it will be too difficult to measure the band shift they indicate. The monomorphic probe bands shown in Figure 5, which were used to adjust for band shift and were offered as evidence in *People v. Davis*,[46] cover a

---

[43]Lifecodes first attempted to use such a probe to account for band shift in *People v. Davis*, Queens, NY, No. 6870–87, June, 1989 (See Figure 5), but it was not admitted in evidence because the judge determined that the defense had not had an adequate opportunity to review it. Testimony about such a probe was allowed in *Georgia v. Caldwell*, supra note 41, and *Oregon v. Futch*, Astoria, Oregon. In all three cases the band shift probe was introduced after defense experts pointed out that bands Lifecodes had declared a match were misaligned by more than three standard deviations. In a recent case in Maine, however, the prosecution chose to withdraw DNA evidence after Lifecodes' Michael Baird admitted that two different monomorphic probes used to account for a purported band shift, DXZ1 and DYZ1, had produced inconsistent results. *Maine v. McLeod*, CR 89–62, Cumberland Superior Court, Portland, December, 1989. See, Anderson "DNA Fingerprinting On Trial," *Nature* 342:844 (1989); Norman "Maine Case Deals Blow to DNA Fingerprinting," *Science* 246:1556 (1989); Kolata "Some Scientists Doubt the Value of 'Genetic Fingerprint' Evidence," *New York Times*, Jan. 29, 1990, p. 1.

[44]In *State v. Caldwell*, supra note 41, an expert argued that Lifecodes' use of DXZ1 as a monomorphic probe is accepted by the scientific community, basing this claim, in part, on the fact that the probe is listed by the Human Gene Mapping Workshop. It is worth noting that such a listing, though perhaps important for other reasons, does not constitute evidence that the probe is monomorphic or is suitable for the purpose for which it is used.

[45]Testimony in *People v. Barney*, supra note 15, RT 712–13.

[46]Supra note 43.

Figure 5. Bands produced by monomorphic probe. Lifecodes autorad offered in evidence in *New York v. Davis* (Queens, NY), which was reported to show the result of hybridization with the monomorphic probe DXZ1. Lifecodes reports that this probe detects bands at aproximately 2.1 and 4.1 kb. The arrows indicate the signal detected by the probe.

region of several kilobases. In cases where the bands are as broad and blurry as this, it is a matter of subjective judgment as to where they fall. Hence, subjective visual estimation remains an important element of interpretation, even when such probes are used. Given that these probes were introduced to avoid the need to rely on subjective visual matching, this is a serious shortcoming.

As yet, no monomorphic probes have been shown to meet these three criteria, hence the use of monomorphic probes to establish benchmarks for the analysis of band shift remains questionable at this time. There is currently no acceptable quantitative method for determining whether a misalignment in bands is due to band shift or whether it is due to true genetic differences in the DNA samples being analyzed. In the absence of such a method, experts may disagree about whether band shift has occurred. We agree with Lander that such a potential for subjectivity is unacceptable in a test that purports to identify individuals with a specificity near uniqueness. Until adequate probes for detecting band shift are identified and validated, it would be advisable to declare the results inconclusive where two DNA patterns appear visually to match but are so badly aligned that corresponding bands do not meet the laboratory's quantitative standards for calling a match.

Extra Bands

When comparing two DNA prints (A and B), analysts sometimes find that all of the bands in print A align with corresponding bands in print B, but that print B also contains "extra bands" not appearing in A. The appearance of extra bands has been a common event in recent casework.[47] Extra bands create ambiguity in the interpretation of DNA prints because they have a number of possible explanations. The simplest explanation is that there is a genetic difference between the two samples, i.e., the samples do not match. However, extra bands may also appear for a variety of other reasons, including mixing of samples at the crime scene, cross-contamination of samples (at the crime scene or in the laboratory), problems in restriction digestion, problems in hybridization, or the presence of nonhuman DNA (e.g., from bacteria) in a sample. The various possible explanations may have dramatically different implications for the interpretation of a DNA print. Mere examination of the print, however, often provides an inadequate basis for deciding which explanation is correct. Hence, there is a danger that an analyst will seriously misinterpret a DNA print by attributing extra bands to the wrong cause.

In the following sections, we will discuss various causes of extra bands and comment on the difficulty of distinguishing among them. We also discuss control procedures for dealing with these problems.

---

[47]See cases with extra bands listed in Table 1.

Sample Cross-Contamination

Cross-contamination of samples is a constant danger in molecular biology. DNA from one sample may inadvertently be mixed with another sample at a number of stages: when the samples are collected, during DNA extraction procedures, when enzymes and buffers are added to samples for restriction digestion, or when samples are placed in the well of the gel (due to failure to use a fresh micropipet tip, spillage, or inaccurate sample placement).[48]

Cross-contamination may also result from lateral movement of DNA across the gel (from one lane to adjacent lanes). Lateral movement may occur during electrophoresis due to defects in the gel (although this probably occurs only rarely), during Southern blotting (as a result of capillary action when the nylon membrane is placed in contact with the gel or removed by dragging it across the gel), or during drying (if the membrane is placed on a blotter contaminated with DNA). Lateral movement is sometimes apparent on examination of the autorads due to the presence of dark streaks connecting bands in adjacent lanes (Figure 6). Autorads in three recent cases have shown evidence of lateral DNA movement.[49]

Cross-contamination has been documented in forensic applications of RFLP analysis. One instance involves research to establish allele frequencies for probes. Cellmark analyzed a number of blood samples from blood banks; each sample from a single individual produces one or two bands when hybridized with a single-locus probe. Sample 2417 showed four bands in a single-locus hybridization with MS-1, two of them are faint and appear to align with those of sample 2416, which was run on the same autorad. The most logical explanation for this result is that DNA in sample 2416 was inadvertently allowed to cross-contaminate sample 2417 (Figure 7). Cross-contamination is dangerous because it can produce false matches between samples from different individuals, as illustrated by an error one laboratory made during a proficiency test sponsored by the California Association of Crime Laboratory Directors.[50] Cellmark declared that the DNA band pat-

---

[48]Cross-contamination is a problem in any DNA lab, but is more serious in forensic laboratories for two reasons. First, in nonforensic laboratories, analyses that reveal extra bands or other evidence of contamination can be repeated, with care to avoid the handling errors that can lead to cross-contamination. Given the very small amounts of DNA often retrieved from a crime scene, there may be insufficient DNA to repeat procedures in a forensic laboratory. Second, forensic DNA procedures are designed to be extremely sensitive in order to allow forensic analysts to work with samples at the threshold of detectability. The extreme sensitivity of these systems makes it possible for cross-contamination of even tiny amounts of sample to produce misleading extra bands. Therefore the procedures used to avoid cross-contamination in many research laboratories may not be adequate for avoiding problems in forensic laboratories.

[49]See cases listed in Table 1: *Texas v. Hicks*; *Wash v. Cauthron*; *Vir. v. Johnson*.

[50]Graves & Kuo, "DNA: A Blind Trial Study of Three Commerical Testing Laboratories," Presented at the Meeting of the American Academy of Forensic Sciences, Las Vegas, February 1989.

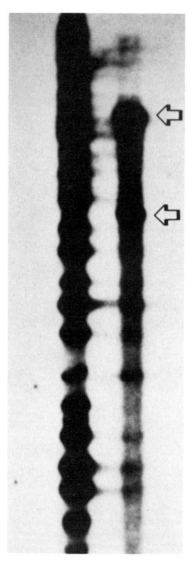

Figure 6. Lateral movement of DNA. Detail from Lifecodes autoradiograph—*State of Texas v. David Hicks* (Fairfield, TX). Lane M—molecular weight markers (Lifecodes Corp. Valhalla, NY). Lane S—*Pst*I digested DNA sample.

Lifecodes hybridized this membrane with the single-locus probe D2S44 and probe DXYS14, which identifies multiple alleles. Two bands from the probe D2S44 are visible in lane S (marked with arrows). The DXYS14 bands are not shown. Additional "pseudo-bands" in lane S have apparently resulted from lateral movement of DNA from the adjacent molecular weight markers.

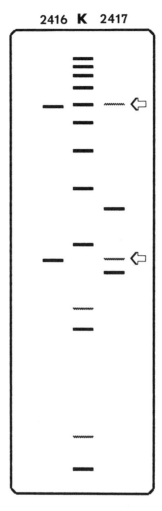

Figure 7. Possible instance of cross-contamination. Diagramatic representation of position of bands in two lanes of an autoradiograph from Cellmark's black database (Gel 1005887A). Each sample in the database is believed to be from a different individual. The samples are digested with *Hinf*1 and hybridized with a series of single-locus probes. This figure depicts the hybridization with MS-1. Sample 2417 shows two intense bands and two faint bands. The faint bands appear to align with the bands in sample 2416, which was run on the same gel. This finding could have arisen due to cross-contamination of 2417 with DNA from 2416.

terns obtained for three samples (numbers 57, 58, 59) were the same; in fact, while samples 57 and 58 had a common source, sample 59 was from a different individual (Figure 8). The error was attributed to cross-contamination of sample 59 with DNA from sample 57 due to a sample handling error during the DNA extraction process; the DNA from sample 59 was either lost or degraded (no bands were produced indicating its presence), and the DNA from sample 57 was thus the only visible DNA in the sample 59 autorad, producing an exact match, erroneously.[51]

Possible instances of cross-contamination have also appeared in casework. In the case of *State of Washington v. Cauthron*,[52] for example, one autorad showed a DNA pattern in a gel lane in which it was recorded that no DNA had been loaded.[53] On another autorad there had been apparent cross-contamination of two molecular weight markers, with bands from lambda *Hind*III and the 1 kb ladder appearing in the same lane, although the laboratory notes indicated they had been loaded separately.[54] Cross-contamination is relatively easy to detect when it produces bands where none should appear or affects known DNA patterns; it is more difficult to detect when working with unknown DNAs.

Whenever extra bands appear in a sample, the analyst must be alert to the possibility that cross-contamination has occurred. The major danger is that cross-contamination will occur in a manner that falsely incriminates an innocent suspect. The only clue that such a problem has occurred may be the appearance of extra bands in one of the samples. In a rape case, for example, a semen sample may contain DNA from the rapist as well as contaminating DNA from an innocent suspect. The resulting print would contain a number of bands matching the suspect as well as some "extra" bands (those of the rapist). Similarly, in a case where a bloodstain from the perpetrator is compared to that of an innocent suspect, the stain may contain contaminating DNA from the suspect as well as DNA from the perpetrator. Although the extra bands should alert the analyst that there is a problem, the ability of analysts to correctly diagnose such problems and thereby reach a correct interpretation has not been demonstrated. Thus, there is a danger that the extra bands that should flag the problem will be ignored because the analyst assumes (without evidence) that they are the DNA of an individual other than the perpetrator or mistakenly attributes the extra bands to bacterial contamination or to problems with restriction digestion. There is also a danger that the "extra" bands that should flag the problem will be too faint to visualize, as happened in the case of the false positive on the CACLD proficiency test.

---

[51]Steps have reportedly been taken by the laboratory to reduce the likelihood of such errors in the future.
[52]Snohomish County, Case #88–1-01253–3, March 1989.
[53]Cellmark Gel # F11188813A.
[54]Cellmark Gel # F1117885B.

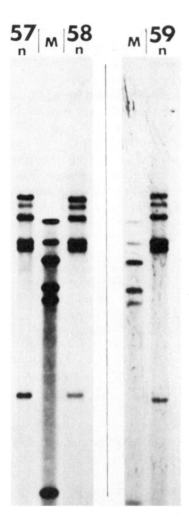

Figure 8. False positive. Cellmark autorad from the California Association of Crime Laboratory Directors (CACLD) "Blind" Trial Study. Lane 57n—*Hinf*1-digested DNA (first extract) from CACLD sample 57, a 1987 semen stain. Lane 58n—*Hinf*1 digested DNA (first extract) from CACLD sample 58, also a 1987 semen stain from the same individual as sample 57. Lane 59n—*Hinf*1 digested DNA (first extract) from CACLD sample 59, a 1980 semen stain from a different individual than the donor of 57 and 58. Lane M—known human control DNA. Cellmark reported that it hybridized this membrane with a single-locus probe cocktail consisting of MS1, MS31, MS43, and g3. The erroneous match between samples 57 and 59 and samples 58 and 59 occurred due to two problems: the DNA in sample 59 was either completely degraded or lost and a sample–handling error caused DNA to be transferred from sample 57 into sample 59. The mishandling of the sample apparently arose due to an error in tube labeling. Cellmark has reportedly revised its procedures to reduce the likelihood of this latter problem.

Evidence of lateral movement of DNA should invalidate any comparison of the lanes involved. The movement means that DNA from the two or more lanes may have mixed, making it impossible to determine the origin of the bands in those lanes. An interesting example arose in *Commonwealth v. Lonnie Johnson*,[55] where unexplained lateral movement of DNA, combined with degradation of the samples, made it impossible for one laboratory to verify a previous determination by another laboratory that the defendant matched an evidentiary stain (Figure 9).[56] If only a tiny fraction of the DNA in one lane moves laterally into the adjacent lane, an erroneous "match" could occur. The appearance of such a match might be similar to the match shown in Figure 3. Leaving an empty lane between any two samples to be compared can reduce the likelihood of such a problem.

Mixed Stains

Mixed stains are common in forensic casework. In rape cases, it is normal for vaginal swabs to contain DNA from the semen of the rapist and from the epithelial cells of the victim. In addition the swab may contain semen from other sexual partners of the victim (husband, boyfriend). The DNA extraction procedures used by forensic DNA laboratories take advantage of unique biological properties of the sperm cell to separate male and female DNA in such samples. Compared to epithelial cells, sperm cells are more resistant to lysis. It is therefore possible to fractionate a vaginal swab sample to produce a sperm (or male) DNA print of the rapist and a non-sperm (or female) DNA print of the victim.[57] However, the separation is not always perfect: The sperm DNA print may show extra bands from the victim and the nonsperm DNA print may show extra bands from the sperm.[58]

In the case of mixed bloodstains, the DNA of the contributors cannot be separated. The resulting DNA prints are superimposed, but the intensity of the bands from each individual will vary depending on the relative amount of DNA from each contributor to the mix. Thus, the appearance of two or three times the usual number of bands, coupled with a variation in intensity among the bands, should alert the analyst to the possibility of a mixed stain. However, as noted, similar patterns can result from digestion problems, cross-contamination of samples, or bacterial contamination, leaving an element of ambiguity.

This element of ambiguity makes it crucial that all observed bands be

---

[55]Charlottesville, VA. Lifecodes Case No. FI06761, final report issued 4/29/88.

[56]This case never came to trial because the defendant accepted a plea bargain offered by the state.

[57]The first extract is most likely to contain female DNA and later extracts are more likely to contain male DNA.

[58]See, for example, Figure 12, infra, which shows band patterns produced by the first extract of semen stains.

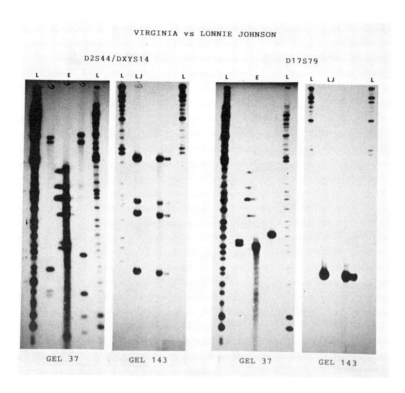

Figure 9. Multiple sources of ambiguity affect quality of match. Based on these autorads from *Commonwealth of Virginia v. Johnson*, Lifecodes case no. FI06761, Lifecodes declared a match between evidentiary sample (E) and the blood standard from the defendant (LJ). All samples were digested with *Pst*1 and hybridized with a cocktail of D2S44 and DXYS14 (left panel) and with D17S79 (right panel). The comparison is problematic for several reasons. First, samples from the defendant and the evidentiary sample were run on different gels. Second, dark extra bands from an unknown source are superimposed on lane E and the adjacent lane to the left; additional faint bands, possibly from bacterial contamination also appear in E. Third, degradation produced a dark background in E, possibly obscuring other bands. The bands in E that Lifecodes scored as matching bands in LJ are indicated by Lifecodes' pencil marks on the autorad.

reported in the written report issued by a forensic laboratory. When an analyst fails to report extra bands on the assumption that they are artifacts, crucial information can be lost. This point is illustrated by the case of *Mississippi v. Parker*.[59] Blood samples from Parker, a rape-murder suspect, were compared with a vaginal swab from the victim. The laboratory reported a match but failed to report the presence of extra bands in the vaginal swab. (Figure 10; extra bands indicated by arrows). After a consul-

---

[59] Tried in Philadelphia, MS in November 1989.

MISSISSIPPI vs MICHAEL PARKER

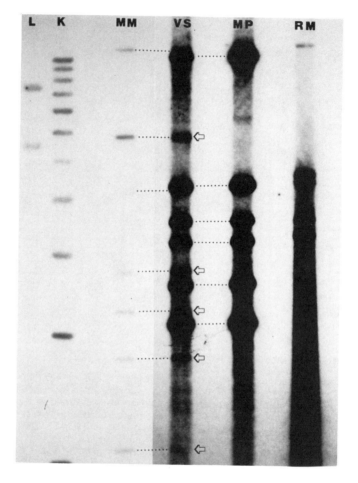

Figure 10. Previously unreported "extra" bands are found to match second individual. In this autorad from *Mississippi v. Michael Parker* (Philadelphia, MS) lanes L and K contain molecular weight markers (lambda digested with *Hind*III and 1 kb ladder, respectively, see legend to Figure 2). The other lanes contain *Hin*f1–digested DNA extracted from blood samples of the victim (RM), defendant (MP), and a second man (MM), as well as DNA extracted from a vaginal swab (VS). This membrane was hybridized with a single-locus probe cocktail consisting of MS1, MS31, MS43, and g3.

Previously samples from the defendant, the victim and a vaginal swab (but not MM) had been tested and a match between the vaginal swab and defendant had been reported. The vaginal swab contained other bands, also visible here, which could be attributed to neither defendant nor the victim, but the report made no mention of these additional bands. At the request of the defense, another individual, MM, was tested and, as shown in this figure, was found to have bands that appear to align with the previously unreported "extra" bands in the swab.

tant retained by the defense noted the extra bands in the autorad, the defense insisted that a second individual, MM, be tested.[60] As Figure 10 shows, and the laboratory acknowledged, MM appeared to match the unreported "extra" bands. Had the attorneys relied solely on the initial written report, a crucial piece of evidence would have been missed, i.e., that semen matching MM's pattern was also present in the victim.

Where mixed stains may be encountered, the laboratory should, whenever possible, run as controls the DNA of any individual whose biological material might be part of the "mix". This control may help to distinguish mixed stains from stains that have been cross-contaminated by the samples to which they are being compared. When comparing DNA prints of a rape suspect and of a vaginal swab from the victim, for example, an analyst may assume that any "extra" bands in the swab (beyond those that match the suspect) are those of the victim or a sexual partner (husband or boyfriend). If the "extra" bands are not accounted for by running samples from these individuals as controls, however, the possibility that the "extra" bands are those of the rapist and that the suspect's bands appear in the sample due to cross-contamination cannot be ruled out. Failure to account for extra bands may also hide other problems (e.g., star activity, partial digestion), which could invalidate the comparison of two samples. Finally, running samples of the victim in rape cases helps to assure that any female cells found in evidentiary samples (e.g., from a stain on a bedsheet) are in fact from the alleged victim rather than another sexual partner of the defendant.[61]

The importance of accounting for all bands in a mixed stain is illustrated by a recent case in which the defendant was charged with committing incest with his daughter.[62] The primary physical evidence was a stain on a washcloth, which was alleged to be the product of the defendant's intercourse with his daughter. According to the defense counsel, the defendant claimed the stain was the product of intercourse with his wife, the mother of the alleged victim. The stain was fractionated when sent for analysis. The extract that normally shows male bands produced a DNA pattern matching the defendant's DNA print, seemingly verifying the defendant's guilt. However, the extract that normally shows female bands produced a pattern that, according to the laboratory, matched neither the father nor the daughter.

---

[60]The defense theory was that MM committed the rape and murder, but according to defense counsel MM was not taken seriously as a suspect in the investigation and trial in light of the report that appeared to link the semen from the victim only to Parker.

[61]In several rape cases that we have reviewed recently, one laboratory has failed to run samples from the victim as a control, typing only the suspect and an evidentiary sample. We view this as a bad practice, because it requires the analyst to engage in guesswork, subtracting the bands that do not line up with the suspect's on the assumption that they are the victim's. As noted in text, this procedure fails to control for several potentially serious problems.

[62]Those interested in technical details of the case may contact the authors. The name of the case is not reported here in order to protect the privacy of the parties.

One analyst attributed this pattern to DNA from "an unknown source" and suggested that the daughter's pattern failed to appear in the female extract because too little of her DNA had been present in the stain.[63] The prosecution chose to withdraw the DNA evidence after an expert retained by the defendant pointed out that the "unknown" pattern shared half its bands with the daughter and therefore was consistent with the expected pattern for the girl's mother (defendant's wife). Although the mother was not tested, an inference about her DNA pattern could be made based on the prints of the father and daughter. As shown in Figure 11, for each of four single-locus probes, one of the daughter's bands appears to match one of the bands in the unknown pattern, and the other matched one of the father's bands. By inference, the "unknown" print would match the mother's on at least four bands (those that also appeared in the daughter's print) and hence could have come from the mother, as the defendant had claimed.

Altered Enzyme Specificity

The number of bands in a DNA print and their position depends on the way in which the DNA in the sample is cut by a restriction enzyme. Restriction enzymes are known to cut the DNA chain wherever they find a specific sequence of bases, known as a restriction site.[64] However, restriction enzymes sometimes cut at the wrong sites, due to an alteration in their "specificity",[65] thereby changing the position and/or the number of bands in the resulting DNA print. Alterations in enzyme specificity fall into two categories. Where the alteration results in incomplete cleavage of the DNA, it is known as partial digestion; where the alteration produces cuts at too many sites, it is known as star activity.[66] Alterations in specificity may arise from a variety of causes. According to Fuchs and Blakesley, the most important factors affecting the performance of restriction enzymes are: "(a) the purity and physical characteristics of the substrate DNA; (b) the reagents used in the reaction; (c) the assay volume and associated errors; and (d) the time and temperature of incubation."[67]

---

[63]According to the analyst, the "unknown" pattern might have come from another male or a female. Although the stain appeared in the extract that normally shows female bands, the separation by sex is not perfect. The laboratory does not employ a male-specific DNA probe, which might have resolved this ambiguity.

[64]See generally, Brooks "Properties and Uses of Restriction Endonucleases," *Methods in Enzymol.* 152:113 (1987). There are hundreds of different restriction enzymes available that recognize and cut at different restriction sites.

[65]Fuchs & Blakesley, supra note 28. The ability of a restriction enzyme to cut at a particular restriction site is referred to as its *specificity*. Changes in the specificity of a restriction enzyme will cause the enzyme to cut the DNA at the wrong sites and will change the position and number of bands in a DNA print. Id.

[66]"Secondary (star) activity of a restriction endonuclease refers to the relaxation of the strict canonical recognition sequence specificity resulting in the production of additional cleavages within a DNA." Id. at 30.

[67]Id. at 5.

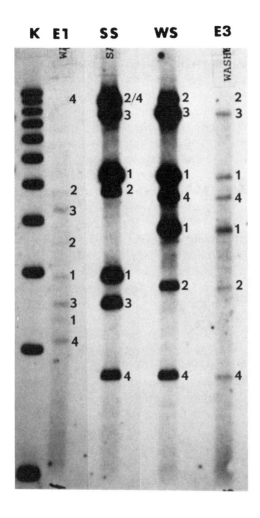

Figure 11. Female fraction of evidentiary stain fails to match alleged victim. Autoradiographs from a case in which defendant was charged with committing incest with his daughter. Lane K contains molecular weight markers (1 kb DNA ladder BRL Life Technologies, Inc, see legend to Figure 2). The other lanes contain *Hinf*1–digested DNA from blood samples of the alleged victim (SS) and the defendant (WS) and DNA extracted from a washcloth reportedly containing the product of intercourse between WS and SS—Lane E1 contains extract 1 (female fraction); Lane E3 contains extract 3 (male fraction). This membrane was hybridized with probes MS1, MS31, MS43, and g3. Individual single-locus probe autoradiographs have been superimposed to produce this figure; the autoradiographs were aligned using the molecular weight markers. The bands identified by each probe are indicated by the numbers: (1)MS1, (2)MS31, (3)MS43, (4)g3.

Sample E3 was relied upon to declare a match between the stain on the washcloth and the defendant WS. No explanation was offered for the differences between the expected pattern for the female fraction of the stain (E1) and the observed pattern of the alleged victim (SS), other than to suggest E1 may be theDNA of an individual other than SS (possibly another male). Notice, however, that for each probe, SS appears to share one band with WS and the other with E1. Based on this it is impossible to exclude the possibility that the banding pattern in sample E1 is that of SS's mother, the defendant's wife.

Partial Digestion. Failure of the restriction enzyme to completely digest DNA results in "fragments of higher molecular weight than the final cleavage products"[68] and typically causes extra bands to appear in the upper region of the gel (as the partially digested fragments will be longer than anticipated). Partial digestion may occur in one sample and not in another,

---

[68]Id. at 32.

causing two samples containing identical DNA to have different DNA prints (Figure 12).

Partial digestion can result from a number of technical problems. The enzyme can lose activity during storage, inhibitors (such as the plasticizer present in a bad batch of tubes) may affect the enzyme, trace contaminants present in a DNA preparation can inhibit enzyme activity, and methylation or other forms of DNA modification are known to lead to partial digestion.[69] Human error is also a major contributer to partial digestion, which can arise when reaction conditions are not properly implemented or when tubes are not properly mixed (for example, if a portion of the reaction volume is left unreacted on the side or lid of the tube), when errors occur in pipetting of reagents, when the wrong amount of enzyme is used, or when the enzyme is mishandled.[70]

With so many factors that can inhibit the activity of the restriction enzyme, it is essential to use good control procedures to monitor the completeness of restriction reactions. In research laboratories using small bacterial DNA molecules, a simple control, known as a test gel, has become widely used. Following digestion, a sample of the restriction reaction is drawn off and subjected to gel electrophoresis and stained with ethidium bromide. The size of the DNA fragments resulting from digestion is typically known and any difference between the observed pattern and what was expected indicates a problem. Partial digestion is generally evident by the appearance of multiple large bands where only one band might be expected. The use of test gels has been widely adopted by the forensic DNA laboratories, even though it loses its critical edge because restricted human DNA is far too complicated to be visualized with ethidium bromide. In order to reliably detect complete digestion, proper discrimination between fragments of partial digestion and fragments attributed to the final pattern is an essential prerequisite that cannot be achieved by an ethidium-bromide-stained test gel of human DNA.

Laboratories that use RFLP analysis in medical diagnostics often make use of a far more critical control for determining the completeness of restriction digestion. "Since partial digestion can cause alleles to be misread, we have found it very helpful to remove an aliquot of the digestion reaction mixture from each specimen and add purified lambda phage DNA in a parallel reaction."[71] This "parallel reaction" control[72] is a simple and sensitive control procedure that has been widely used in research laboratories

---

[69]Id. at 34–37.
[70]Id. at 34–37.
[71]Simon "Establishment of an Approved Clinical Laboratory Based on the Analysis of Restriction Fragment Length Polymorphisms," in *Nucleic Acid Probes in Diagnosis of Human Genetic Diseases*, supra note 1, at 195–216.
[72]For description see Id. and Thompson & Ford, supra note 4, at n. 215.

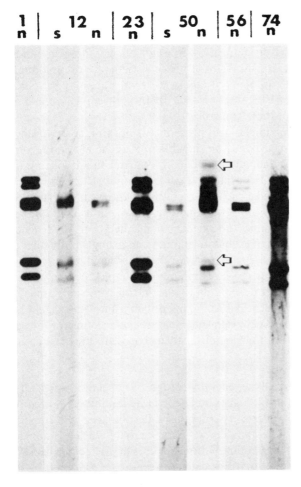

Figure 12. "Extra" bands apparently mistaken for DNA of second individual. This figure shows a set of DNA prints of the same individual produced by Cellmark during the CACLD "Blind" Trial Study. The prints are from different autorads; all are of *Hinf*1-digested DNA of the same individual hybridized with a single-locus probe cocktail consisting of MS1, MS31, MS43, and g3. Lane 1n—*Hinf*1 digested DNA (first extract) from a 1987 blood stain. Lane 12s—*Hinf*1-digested DNA (second extract) from CACLD sample 12, a 1987 semen stain. Lane 12n—*Hinf*1 digested DNA (first extract) from the same semen stain. Lane 23n—*Hinf*1-digested DNA (first extract) from a 1987 blood stain. Lane 50s—*Hinf*1 digested DNA (second extract) from a 1987 semen stain. Lane 50n—*Hinf*1 digested DNA (first extract) from the same semen stain. Lane 56n—*Hinf*1 digested DNA (first extract) a 1987 blood stain. Lane 74n—*Hinf*1 digested DNA (female extract) from a 1987 semen stain.

Cellmark reported its findings with respect to sample 50 differently in its first and second report. In the first report, sample 50 was reported as matching 1, 12, 23, 56, and 74, and as also having a "DNA Fingerprint . . . [with which] . . . no pattern matches were identified." In the second report, sample 50 was still said to match samples 1, 12, 23, 56, and 74, however, there was no report of the additional pattern. The arrow indicates the position of extra bands present in lane 50n, which probably arose from partial digestion of the DNA. The presence of these artifacts apparently misled the interpreter of the first report to describe this sample as containing the DNA of two different individuals.

working with human and mammalian DNA for almost 10 years and that we have previously recommended for forensic use.[73]

Control procedures also depend on there being adequate DNA for use in test-gel or parallel–reaction controls. Although the parallel-reaction only uses the same amount of DNA as the test–gel method, forensic analysts working with very small amounts of DNA, less than 1 μg, may be reluctant to risk failure of the RFLP analysis due to insufficient DNA and may therefore neglect to run these controls.

When the parallel reaction control procedure is not run, correct interpretation of the DNA print depends on the ability of the analyst to recognize partial digestion, if it occurs, and to distinguish partial digestion from other phenomena that generate extra bands. There is no published research that tests analysts' ability to make such distinctions on the basis of visual comparisons. It seems unlikely, however, that such distinctions could be made reliably. Thus, on one hand, undetected partial digestion might lead an analyst mistakenly to conclude that a sample from a single individual contains DNA from two or more sources.[74] On the other hand, an analyst may fail to recognize a mixed or cross-contaminated sample because he or she mistakenly attributes the extra bands to partial digestion or some other phenomenon producing extra bands.[75] This possible ambiguity again highlights the importance of taking rigorous measures to account for any extra bands that appear, rather than ignoring them based on untested assumptions about their source.

Star Activity. Star activity is a generally recognized phenomenon.[76] Of 215 Ph.D. research molecular biologists and geneticists randomly selected from the membership of the American Society for Microbiology who responded to a 1988 survey, 169 were familiar with star activity. 70% of those who responded believed that contamination of a sample could cause the phenomenon, and 89% felt that star activity would alter the resulting band pattern on the autorad.[77]

Whether the particular restriction enzymes used in forensic DNA typing are susceptible to star activity has been a hotly debated issue at admissibility hearings. The issue is important not only because star activity may contribute to "slop", but also because some experts question the wisdom of using an enzyme susceptible to star activity in forensic work. Richard Roberts, a widely recognized authority on restriction enzymes noted: "[I]f

---

[73]Thompson & Ford, supra note 4, at n. 215.

[74]The authors believe this is what happened when Cellmark initially interpreted sample 50 in the CACLD "Blind" Trial Experiment. See Figure 12.

[75]This is apparently what happened with the initial interpretation of the autorads in *Mississippi v. Parker.* See note 59 supra and accompanying text; also Figure 11.

[76]See notes 64–66, supra.

[77]Thompson & Ford, "Survey of Molecular Biologists Concerning Acceptance of Forensic DNA Typing Procedures," supra note 24.

in fact *Hin*f-1 showed a star activity, I think it would be very unwise on [Cellmark's] part to choose that as an enzyme for fingerprinting. I don't think it would cause problems that would not be recognizable. It would just mean that on many occasions you would get an uninterpretable result. And so it would just be — it would be a stupid choice."[78]

Scientists at Cellmark initially maintained that *Hin*f1 does not show star activity,[79] but they recently reversed their position.[80] Evidence of aberrant enzyme activity with *Hin*f1 was reported by researchers at the FBI, who found that methylation and varying the concentration of interacting reagents could cause aberrations in restriction digestion. They noted "one additional band could be generated for a profile by changing the concentrations of DNA and *Hin*f1, although the ratio of enzyme units to DNA was maintained. Thus, a normal two-banded pattern could be induced to become a three-banded pattern."[81] George Herrin of Cellmark recently acknowledged the possibility of star activity with *Hin*f1, saying "I have [always] said we can induce star activity with *Hin*f-1 . . . and one of the primary ways that you would recognize star activity is that you get . . . additional bands which you are not expecting to get."[82] There is ample evidence of star activity with *Pst*1[83] and *Hae*III[84] as well, notwithstanding some expert testimony to the contrary.[85]

---

[78]Testimony by Roberts in *People v. Axell*, supra note 9, April 12, 1989, RT 407–408.

[79]Testimony by Robin Cotton of Cellmark and Bonnie Blomberg of U. Miami was sufficient to convince District Court Judge Michael J. Davis of Minneapolis that "Hinf-1 does not result in star activity as evidenced by research." (Memorandum Opinion, *Minnesota v. Schwartz*, D.C. File No,: 97549–1, February 17, 1989). However, when Cellmark was ordered, during a subsequent admissibility hearing, to produce, *inter alia*, records of "all validation studies, in house or otherwise, relating to star activity [with *Hin*f–1] . . . " the company responded that no such studies existed. See pretrial motions, declarations, and court orders, *Washington v. Cauthron*, Snohomish County Superior Court, No. 88–1-01253–3. Richard Roberts, widely recognized as an authority on restriction enzymes, testified on Cellmark's behalf that he had conducted an exhaustive search of the scientific literature and had found no support for the claim of star activity in *Hin*f1. *People v. Axell*, supra note 9, RT 73:27. However, at least one reference apparently escaped his notice. Perbal, B. *A Practical Guide to Molecular Cloning*. (New York: John Wiley, 1988) 327–329.; see also New England Biolabs 1989 Catalog, p 20; Promega 1989 Catalog (warning of star activity with *Hin*f1).

[80]Kriss, Herrin, Forman, & Cotton "Perturbation in Digestion Conditions Which Result in Altered Cut Site Specificity for HINF I," paper presented at the International Symposium on Human Identification, Promega Corporation, Minneapolis, MN, November 30, 1989.

[81]Budowle, Waye, Shutler, & Baechtel, in press. This result is attributed to a "type of partial digestion," but may be akin to star activity. As Richard Roberts notes, "star activity just gives you a different kind of partial digestion . . . instead of giving you a lot of fragments larger than the ones that you expect, star activity gives you fragments that are smaller than the ones you expect." *People v. Axell*, supra note 9, RT 413: 18–24.

[82]Testimony in *People v. Davis*, Ventura, California, RT 3197:7-12.

[83]Fuchs & Blakesley, supra note 28, at 31; BRL 1989 Catalog, p. 160.

[84]Fuchs & Blakesley, supra note 28, at 31; BRL 1989 Catalog, p. 159.

[85]See testimony of Richard Roberts in *People v. Castro*, supra note 23.

Because the occurrence of star activity is not necessarily apparent from an examination of the autorads,[86] it is essential that restriction digestion be conducted under carefully controlled conditions. To avoid star activity, Brooks recommends "keeping glycerol and endonuclease concentrations low, ionic strength high, and digestion times as short as possible."[87] The three enzymes currently used in forensic work (*Hin*f1, *Hae*III, and *PST*1) have all been reported to show star activity with glycerol concentrations of 12–20% or with enzyme/DNA concentrations greater than 25 units/μg.[88] Maniatis et al. recommend keeping glycerol concentrations below 5%.[89] This has not always been done. Court testimony in several cases shows that Cellmark has used the enzyme *Hin*f1 to digest DNA in glycerol concentrations exceeding 5% and often as high as 14%.[90] To Cellmark's credit, the company has recently revised its standard operating protocol to limit glycerol concentrations to 5%, but validation studies to test the reliability of the revised procedure are not complete. Additionally, Cellmark and other laboratories sometimes fail to record the volume of reactions, the lot number (concentration) of the restriction enzyme, and the concentration of the DNA, which makes it impossible to calculate the enzyme/DNA ratio for a particular sample.

The interpretation problems potentially caused by star activity are similar to those for partial digestion. Extra bands produced by star activity may be mistakenly attributed to genetic differences between two samples or to the presence of another individual's DNA. Extra bands reflecting true genetic differences or cross-contamination may mistakenly be attributed to star activity. The only way to avoid these ambiguities is to declare inconclusive any comparison in which one of the samples contains extra bands that cannot be accounted for with rigorous scientific evidence.

An ambiguity possibly arising from star activity occurred in the CACLD "Blind" Proficiency Study. Figure 13 shows DNA patterns of two samples (nos. 30 and 36) that came from the same individual. Sample 30 was a bloodstain, 36 was semen. In a report of its findings, filed March 24, 1988, Cellmark reported a "match" between 30 and 36 but stated that sample 36 also "yielded additional DNA patterns unique to that sample." Cellmark's erroneous assumption that sample 36 was a "mixed" stain is not surprising,

---

[86]Based on her research on star activity with *Hin*f1, Robin Cotton reported "[y]ou cannot tell in a normal run of the mill gel whether it has occurred. What you're depending on is that you've done your digestion under conditions that should not elicit any star activity." *People v. Barney,* supra note 15, RT 801:19–22.

[87]Brooks, supra note 64, at 118.

[88]See BRL Life Technologies, Inc. 1989 Catalog at 25; New England Biolabs 1989 Catalog at 20.

[89]Maniatis, supra note 22 at 105.

[90]Among those cases are *Indiana v. Hopkins,* supra note 8; *Del. v. Pennell,* and *Calif. v. Marlow* (see Table 1).

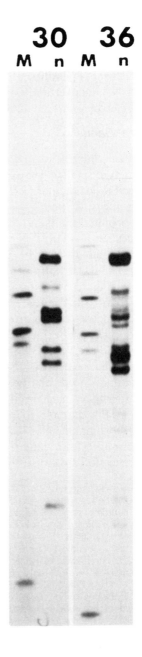

Figure 13. Extra bands again apparently mistaken for DNA of second individual. Two DNA prints of the same individual produced by Cellmark during the CACLD "Blind" Trial Study. Lane 30n—*Hin*f1-digested DNA (first extract) from CACLD sample 30, a 1987 bloodstain. Lane 36n—*Hin*f1-digested DNA (first extract) from CACLD sample 36, a 1987 semen stain from the same individual. Lane M—known human control DNA. Samples 30 and 36 were run on different gels under different electrophoresis conditions. Cellmark hybridized these membranes with a single-locus probe cocktail consisting of MS1, MS31, MS43, and g3. In the first report Cellmark reported samples 30 and 36 as matching. Sample 36 was also described as having an "additional DNA pattern . . . [which was] . . . unique to that sample." In the second report samples 30 and 36 were reported as matching and there was no mention of the additional bands. Although the origin of the extra bands (marked with arrow) is unknown, it appears that, as in the case of sample 50 in Figure 12, they were mistaken for the DNA of an additional person.

given the presence of additional bands in 36. The extra bands might be due to partial digestion, although they appear to represent smaller fragments (rather than the larger fragments usually seen where digestion is incomplete). It is also possible, of course, that the extra bands are due to additional DNA inadvertently mixed into sample 36 as a result of a sample handling error or sloppy laboratory procedure.[91]

Bacterial Bands

Another source of extra bands in DNA prints is bacterial contamination, which may occur frequently in forensic work due to the sources of these samples: blood, vaginal secretions, hair, scrapings of skin, vomit, and similar substances. Cellmark and the FBI maintain that bacterial contaminants do not produce bands in their systems, but in a number of forensic cases, Lifecodes has attributed extra bands on its autorads to this problem. These "bacterial" bands may be indistinguishable from bands resulting from human DNA. The "extra band" in the blood sample from the victim in *State v. Hicks* (Figure 14) is an example, although in general these bands are fainter than "true" bands.

Lifecodes uses a two-probe system for identifying bacterial bands. A vector-specific probe (blue scribe) is used to identify vector DNA that might contaminate the VNTR probes, producing extra bands. A ribosomal gene probe is used to identify DNA of bacteria that might contaminate evidentiary samples, producing extra bands.

The sensitivity and specificity of this system has yet to be rigorously evaluated. For example, there are as yet no published studies on the efficacy of the ribosomal gene probe for detecting the sorts of bacteria capable of giving rise to a false band that may be found in evidentiary samples. The effectiveness of the bluescribe probe was questioned in *People v. Castro,*[92]

---

[91]We have shown Figure 13 to a number of molecular biologists, including several who are authorities on restriction digestion. These scientists have expressed conflicting opinions on the source of the extra bands in sample 36.

It should be noted that Cellmark's mistaken call on sample 36 appeared only in its first report of its findings. The CACLD DNA Committee allowed Cellmark to file a revised report after meeting with Dan Garner of Cellmark, reviewing the autorads, and discussing with Garner problems in the first report. According to testimony by Margaret Kuo, Chair of the Committee: "we look[ed] at the results, and . . . [said] here we have noted one error, or why is it that your report did not exactly reflect what the autorads really meant." *People v. Axell*, supra note 9, RT 874:1–4. After this meeting, which arguably undermined the blindness of the proficiency test, Cellmark issued a second report in which sample 36 is correctly reported to match 30 and no mention is made of additional DNA in 36. (The CACLD based its formal conclusions concerning Cellmark's performance on the "blind" test only on the second report). Our feeling is that Cellmark's first call on sample 36 better reflects the way such a pattern would normally be interpreted. In any case, the fact that the same pattern can on one occasion be said to contain multiple DNAs and on another to contain a single DNA print nicely illustrates the point we are making here, which is that phenomena that produce extra bands can create ambiguity in the interpretation of DNA prints. In our opinion, such results should properly be called inconclusive.
[92]Supra note 21.

Figure 14. Faint Bands and Extra Bands. Autorads from *Texas v. Hicks*, a rape-murder case. Samples from victim (OH), a vaginal swab (VS), and four suspects (RP, DH, LB, and ES) were digested with *Pst*1 and hybridized with D2S44 and DXYS14 to produce prints shown here. Lanes marked L contain molecular weight markers. Dotted arrows mark the positions on the vaginal swab where Lifecodes scored bands. Lifecodes declared a match with defendant (DH) and excluded other suspects. Note that two of defendant's four bands align with bands of victim (who was his grandmother). Defendant and victim also had matching bands on probe D17S79 (not shown). Hence, there are only two bands in the vaginal swab that align with those of defendant and that could not have come from the victim. These bands, indicated by the upper and lower dotted arrows, are extremely faint — so faint that they cannot be seen on a copy of the autorad. In the trial, prosecution and defense experts differed over whether the upper band was dark enough to be scored.

Although the third band (from the top) in the vaginal swab does not match any of defendant's bands, it does align with one of victim's bands and therefore was attributed to the victim's DNA. There is no visible band in the vaginal swab that corresponds to the third band in the victim's print (marked with dark arrow). This band was attributed to bacterial contamination based on a subsequent hybridization (not shown) in which a bacterial probe produced a band in this location. The bacterial probe also produced a band in approximately the same position as one of the victim's upper bands, but only the band marked with the dark arrow was scored as a bacterial artifact.

TEXAS vs DAVID HICKS

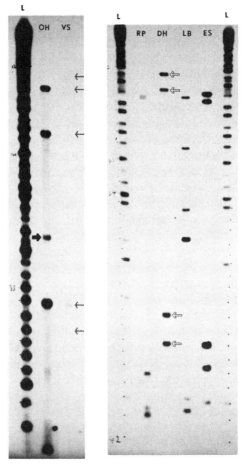

in which there was a retroactive attempt to use the probe to demonstrate that a band at 6.0 kb was bacterial in origin. As Eric Lander pointed out, however, the probe bound to approximately 20 bands in a control lane that contained only human DNA, indicating a lack of the required specificity for a definitive test for the presence of bacterial DNA contamination.[93] Whether this failure of the probe as a control was an isolated problem in Castro[94] or a more systematic deficiency in the system is an issue requiring further examination.

Cellmark's literature and testimony indicates that its polymorphic probes do not produce bands from bacterial contamination. Validation of this assertion would require tests with a variety of common bacteria using Cellmark's normal laboratory procedures. In addition, while Cellmark's polymorphic probes may not hybridize with bacterial DNA, both Cellmark and Lifecodes use radioactively labeled markers in their hybridizations, which use DNAs closely related to bacterial DNA, including bacteriophage lambda and phi X174. These markers probes may hybridize to bacterial DNA, even if the polymorphic probes do not.

Although Cellmark asserts that its probes do not identify nonprimate DNA, faint "extra" bands have been identified on their autorads in several recent cases (Table 1). These bands pose an interpretation problem for the analyst, who cannot, under Cellmark's protocol, explore the potential that they are due to bacterial contamination. Without the ability to check for contamination, the analyst has no satisfactory way to account for these additional bands.

The possibility of bacterial bands is another complication in the analysis of the autorad. Extra bands resulting from cross-contamination, mixing, or true genetic differences between samples may be indistinguishable from bacterial bands. Hence, an analyst should not attribute extra bands to bacteria in the absence of experimental confirmation. Extra bands that cannot be accounted for in this rigorous manner should invalidate a "match" between two prints.

Hybridization of Probes to Closely Related Sequences

Extra bands may also appear due to hybridization of VNTR probes to DNA sequences that are similar to (but not the same as) their complements. It is well known that probes can hybridize to DNA sequences that are closely homologous to the sequences that are the "targets" of the probe. The ability of a probe to hybridize with such homologous sequences depends on the stringency of the hybridization reaction. Under high stringency (e.g., low salt, high temperature), a probe requires sequences that are perfect or near-perfect complements in order to hybridize. As stringency is reduced, however, the probe is able to hybridize with more distantly related targets, producing "secondary bands", which are typically fainter than the "true bands" produced by the primary target sequence.

---

[93] Lander, "Expert's Report in *People v. Castro*," (1989) 13; unpublished manuscript.
[94] It might have been due, for example, to inadvertant contamination of the probe—a problem that could be prevented with rigorous quality control procedures.

The presence of "secondary bands" in forensic casework may contribute to ambiguity in two ways. First, because the "secondary bands" are not necessarily polymorphic, hybridization to homologous sequences may produce common false bands in the same position in several samples. The possibility that the presence of such bands in an evidentiary sample and a sample from a suspect could contribute to a false positive is an issue worthy of consideration. Second, as with other sources of extra bands, there is a danger that analysts may mistakenly attribute faint extra bands that provide a clue to cross-contamination or mixing of samples to hybridization of the probes with homologous sequences, thereby ignoring information of crucial importance.

The tendency of probes to produce "secondary bands" under the hybridization conditions used in forensic work might be checked by observing the number of secondary bands that appear in population databases. Our observation is that "secondary bands" appear far more common with some probes than others. Given that a number of probes are available, not all of which produce secondary bands, it would appear advisable for laboratories simply to avoid the use of probes that have this problem.

Incomplete Stripping

When using multiple probes, it is necessary to strip off one probe prior to the application of the next.[95] In some instances, this stripping is incomplete and the first probe produces "extra bands" during the second hybridization.

Extra bands caused by incomplete stripping can usually be detected by careful comparison of the successive hybridizations. However, such bands have created confusion in at least one case.[96] Extra bands on an autorad appeared to exclude a suspect until it was determined that the apparent mismatch was due to incomplete stripping of an experimental probe applied on a previous hybridization. It is very important that independent experts asked to evaluate forensic DNA evidence have access to all autorads in the case in order to avoid ambiguity of this sort.

One control procedure to check that stripping is complete is to run a test autorad after each probe is stripped. If the test autorad is blank, the possibility of any carryover from one hybridization to the next is ruled out. The exposure time on the test autorad should, of course, be comparable to that of the other autorads exposed to the membrane.

---

[95]See generally, Maniatis, supra note 22.
[96]*State v. Caldwell*, supra note 41.

Missing Bands

One or more bands in a DNA print sometimes fail to appear in another print of the same individual. This section describes various phenomena that cause the disappearance of bands (sometimes called band loss or "allelic dropout") and discusses the interpretive difficulties that result. As with other phenomena that change the appearance of a DNA print, the challenge for the analyst is to distinguish instances in which an apparent difference between prints is due to band loss from instances in which there are true genetic differences.

Degradation

The most common cause of band loss is degradation of the DNA in a sample. As degradation progresses, high molecular weight DNA fragments are lost first, hence bands at the top of the gel are the first to disappear. The degraded DNA from the lost fragment sometimes appears as "background" in the print, but often is not detectable.

One of Cellmark's errors on the CACLD proficiency test illustrates the potential for degradation to be mistaken for a true genetic difference between samples. In Cellmark's first report, samples 18 and 25 (Figure 15), which are from the same individual, were erroneously classified as prints for which "no pattern matches were identified." The reasons for this error can readily be seen. In sample 25, degradation has caused the loss of a band at the top of the print; moreover, the "background" produced by the degraded product has created what appear to be smudgy extra bands at the bottom (a bubble during transfer may have further contributed to the appearance of these extra bands).

After a Cellmark official met with the individuals who administered the proficiency test,[97] Cellmark issued a second report in which samples 18 and 25 are listed as matching. This call illustrates a second danger created by degradation—that analysts faced with a degraded sample will lower their standards for declaring a match in ways that undermine the power of the test to exclude nonmatching samples. If a pattern as discrepant from sample 18 as that of sample 25 can be declared a match, then a great many other patterns would "match" as well. Hence, statistics on the frequency of prints that precisely match sample 18 may greatly underestimate the probability of a coincidental match.

Because partial degradation results in a loss of information about the

---

[97]See note 91, supra.

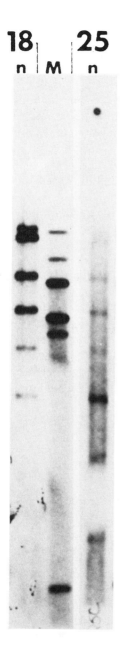

Figure 15. Ambiguity created by degradation. This figure shows DNA prints of two samples from the CACLD "Blind" Trial Study. Lane 18n—*Hinf*1 digested DNA (first extract) from CACLD sample 18, a 1987 bloodstain. Lane 25n—*Hinf*1 digested DNA (first extract) from CACLD sample 25, a 1982 bloodstain. Samples 18 and 25 are from the same person. Lane M—known human control DNA. Cellmark hybridized this membrane with a single-locus probe cocktail consisting of MS1, MS31, MS43, and g3. In its first report Cellmark listed samples 18 and 25 as being suitable for comparison but not matching. In the second report, filed after a Cellmark official met with the CACLD committee to discuss problems in the first report, samples 18 and 25 were reported as matching. Degradation of the high molecular weight DNA is visible in sample 25 and may explain Cellmark's initial failure to detect the match.

upper portion of the gel (i.e., about the existence and position of unseen bands), it has the potential to hide information that would produce an exclusion. Where a single locus hybridization produces an apparent "match" between two samples that appear to be homozygous, for example, the analyst must always consider the possibility that one or both of the samples has a second band that was obscured by degradation.[98] For this reason, it is dangerous for an analyst to draw conclusions from a match between apparent homozygotes where there is evidence (e.g., from other hybridizations) that degradation may have occurred.[99] It is also dangerous, of course, for an analyst to attribute a missing band to degradation in the absence of evidence that degradation has occurred.

Forensic DNA laboratories typically check for degradation only by the use of ethidium bromide staining of minigels. This is an unreliable method, because samples are sometimes contaminated with nonhuman DNA, which cannot be distinguished from human DNA with this technique. Hence, contamination may hide degradation. Determining the degree of degradation and whether it is sufficient to cause the disappearance of high molecular weight bands is, to some extent, a matter of subjective judgment. A better approach would be the use of a high molecular weight monomorphic probe. If the probe produced a band high on the gel, the analyst would know that sufficient high molecular weight DNA was present to produce bands and would know not to attribute a missing band to degradation. If the probe did not produce a band in the expected place, it would support the conclusion that degradation had occurred.

---

[98]A problem of this type arose during an open proficiency test conducted by the FBI at its DNA testing facility. Degradation caused the loss of a high molecular weight band in four samples (all from the same individual) run on a gel and probed with D1S7. As a result, the heterozygous individual was mistyped as a homozygote. This problem did not result in a mismatch of samples, because all four samples from the individuals were mistyped in the same manner. See testimony of Harold Deadman and Bruce Budowle in *New Mexico v. Anderson*, No. CR 46255, Albuquerque, NM (January-February, 1990). In a case where the missing upper bands were not the same, however, such a problem could lead to a false positive; the degradation might obscure the very information that would exclude a nonmatching sample. Hence, it is very important that the possibility of degradation be considered. A match between two samples on a single band should be viewed with suspicion where degradation may have obscured a second band. An excellent control for dealing with this problem would be the use of a monomorphic probe producing a high molecular weight band. See Lander, supra note 4, at 503.

[99]By the same reasoning, it is dangerous to draw conclusions from a match between prints produced by a probe capable of showing variable numbers of bands where degradation or another phenomenon may have obscured additional bands in one of the prints.

Loss of Middle and Lower Bands

Bands in the middle and lower portions of a print are sometimes lost as well.[100] While the reasons for this are difficult to determine in a given instance, there are a number of potential causes. There may be no DNA on the portion of the membrane where a band should appear due to problems in the Southern transfer process or loss of the DNA during stripping of probes from previous hybridizations.[101] The probes may fail to adhere to some portion of the membrane due to problems in hybridization (e.g., bubbles). Bands may be lost due to selective protein binding during electrophoresis.[102] Finally, middle and lower bands may be lost due to underexposure of the autorad in instances in which the bands of the print are of uneven intensity.

Missing bands may pose a difficult dilemma for an analyst. In instances where two DNA prints, A and B, appear to match on six or seven bands, but A has one or two additional bands not found in B, an analyst may be tempted simply to assume the mismatch is due to an artifactual loss of bands in B and to call the prints a match. Under ideal conditions, a mismatch on even one band proves that the samples originated from two different people, but under the less than ideal circumstances that exist in a forensic laboratory, the analyst may reasonably believe that the mismatch is more likely due to "slop" than to true genetic differences between the samples. As we have noted elsewhere,[103] the problem with calling a match on such evidence is that it undermines the power of the test to exclude nonmatching samples.

---

[100]An interesting example is provided by an autorad produced in the case of *People v. Davis*, supra note 82. Samples from the defendant and from a semen stain were hybridized with a cocktail of four single-locus probes. Seven bands appear in the defendant's print; only four appear in the print of the semen stain. Two of the three "missing" bands are lower on the gel than a band that can be visualized, making it unlikely that their disappearance is due simply to degradation.

[101]To check for this possibility it is useful to perform a DNA stain of the membrane after the completion of autoradiography. In the absence of such a control, it would be dangerous to assume a "missing" band was caused by DNA loss on the membrane.

[102]It is known that some proteins bind selectively to specific DNA sequences and can cause selective retardation of some bands and not others. See, e.g., Ford "Gene Expression in the Mercury Resistance Transposon Tn501," Dissertation. University of Bristol, 1981, at 82. Typically, selective protein binding would produce complete loss of the band and would be evidenced by a retarded DNA-protein complex (visualizable as a smear) at the top of the gel. It might also simply retard the band, however, and thus might explain instances in which band shift causes some bands to shift more than others.

[103]Thompson & Ford, supra note 4 at 87–91.

Other Sources of Ambiguity

Faint Bands

Faint bands may occur for a variety of reasons,[104] although the instances we have observed appear to result most commonly from poor recovery of DNA from the samples, degradation of the DNA found in samples, inaccurate quantitation of the DNA (resulting in too little DNA being applied to the gel), and insufficient exposure time during autoradiography.

The interpretation problem posed by faint bands is relatively obvious. Faint bands are quite difficult to distinguish from phenomena such as smudges on the film and artifacts produced in electrophoresis and Southern transfer. In addition, given that very faint bands are known to occur, there may be a potential for an analyst to "find" a band where in fact there is no band, merely because a band "should" be in the location. For example, if there are several apparent matches of suspect and evidentiary DNA on an autorad, and a very faint band/smudge/film flaw near the appropriate place for the final, conclusive match, it is reasonable to think that the analyst will interpret this evidence as a band. An interesting example of a case in which a critical call was based on extremely faint bands is *State v. Hicks* (see Figure 14).

The difficulties that can arise when an analyst attempts to interpret faint bands are illustrated by testimony in the Castro case. Regarding locus DXYS14 on autoradiogram 5 from 6/12/87, the expert initially identified three bands, later reported two bands in his report to the District Attorney, later testified that there were two bands (but one at a different location on the autorad than previously reported), and later reconcluded that the bands identified in the official report were the correct bands. In the face of ambiguous results, which another expert stated he would be hesitant to interpret, the analyst may simply have struggled too hard to draw a conclusion; even when faced with clear inconsistency in his own analysis, the expert persisted in attempting to be definitive in this case.

Faint bands, or phenomena that look like faint bands, again place an emphasis on the subjective judgment of the analyst, who may choose to declare a band on the basis of a barely visible mark on relatively imperfect film. Given this potential, and given that declaring a very faint band to complete a match between suspect and evidentiary sample may produce a false positive, laboratories should endeavor, wherever possible, to produce autorad exposures dark enough that bands are unambiguous. Because this

---

[104]E.g., insufficient DNA in the digest, insufficient probe used or simply poorly labeled probes, problems during transfer from the gel to the Southern blot, excessive washing of the nitrocellulose blotting material following hybridization, and problems involving placement of the autorad on the nitrocellulose membrane. Those familiar with RFLP analysis in a research setting have generally encountered these laboratory problems; they are well documented in the literature. See generally Maniatis, supra note 22.

may not always be possible (due to the limited quantity or quality of DNA available for analysis), standardized criteria must be formulated for determining whether a band is present. The standards should set forth a minimum intensity of image that is needed to declare a band. The standards might also set forth a procedure for blind reading of autorads to assure that any calls made in a close case are reproducible in the absence of external clues regarding the likely band position.[105]

In some cases, laboratories have attempted to interpret extremely faint bands produced by short exposures, rather than simply producing longer exposures.[106] It is possible to expose two autorads simultaneously from the same membrane. If the first one removed is underexposed, the second can be left on for an additional period to obtain a better exposure. Given the ease with which this procedure can be implemented, it is simply unacceptable for laboratories to make judgments of critical importance based on faint bands in underexposed autorads.

Smears and Broad Bands

Broad, smeary bands can arise from such phenomena as overloading of the gel, degradation, or overexposure of the autorad (see Figures 5, 9, and 15). There are several interpretational problems caused by smears or broad bands. If a band image spans a length of the lane that represents several hundred kilobases in length, or if two bands overlap so that it is difficult to determine the exact length of the fragment that they represent, then measurement errors may exceed the standards for declaring a match. This leaves analysis to "visual matching" again, introducing subjective judgment into yet another aspect of the analysis.

THE CUMULATIVE EFFECT OF AMBIGUITY AND TECHNICAL PROBLEMS ON INTERPRETATION OF DNA PRINTS

The examples discussed thus far illustrate the ways in which "slop" in the RFLP procedure can create ambiguity and subjectivity in the interpretation of forensic DNA prints. Band shift, extra bands, missing bands, faint

---

[105]A more practical problem posed by faint bands is that they do not reproduce well when copies are made of the original autorad. This is a special problem in forensic work because the experts retained by various parties in a legal proceeding often must work from copies. Misunderstandings sometimes arise because the various experts are, quite literally, trying to draw conclusions based on different information. In a number of cases, e.g., *N.Y. v. Golub* and *State v. Hicks*, (see Figure 14) forensic DNA laboratories have based important conclusions on bands that cannot be seen on copies of the autorads and experts have disagreed as to whether or not the bands could be seen on the original.
[106]For example, in *New York v. Golub* (See Table 1) experts called by the prosecution and defense disagreed over the reliability of a call made by Lifecodes due, in part, to the faintness of several critical bands. This avoidable conflict arose because the Lifecodes autorad in question was a short exposure and no longer exposures were available.

bands, and smeary bands can each cause ambiguity. Where two or more of these problems occur simultaneously, the ambiguity and concomitant need for subjective interpretation increase (see Figure 1).

These problems were quite common in the forensic casework we reviewed in preparing this chapter. We reviewed autorads, reports, and laboratory notes associated with 20 forensic DNA cases, 8 involving the Lifecodes test and 12 involving Cellmark Diagnostics. A list of the problems observed in each of those cases appears in Table 1. Table 1 shows that one or more problems were observed in nearly every case, although the problems did not always affect the specific prints that were relied upon to incriminate the suspect. The problems in the evidence in *People v. Castro*, which Eric Lander has documented,[107] appear to have been frequent.[108]

The high frequency of these problems in forensic casework is undoubtedly due, in part, to the difficulty of dealing with forensic samples. Unlike the samples normally encountered in research applications of RFLP analysis, or in medical diagnostics, forensic samples may contain any number of unknown contaminants, some of which clearly can affect the results of the procedure. It is not surprising, then, that "slop" is a greater problem with forensic samples than it is in research laboratories.[109] Given the greater technical demands and higher precision required for individual identification than for other applications of RFLP analysis,[110] however, and the frequent need to rely on the results of a single test, the high rate of these problems in forensic work is particularly problematic.

In some instances there may be no reliable and relatively simple method of determining the cause of an anomalous result or an imperfect match. The appearance of an extra band, for example, may be the result of true genetic differences between samples, but may also be caused by the presence of other human DNA, cross-contamination, bacterial DNA, digestion problems, and so on. The analyst is thus faced with having to interpret in a very complex environment, with a range of potential (and reasonable) interpretations and little guidance in how to choose among them.

In such an environment, it should not be surprising that misinterpretations occur or that different analysts reach different conclusions based on the same evidence. In Castro, for example, a distinguished group of experts called by the defense repeatedly disagreed with Lifecodes' Dr. Michael Baird. In this case alone, there were disagreements not only about the

---

[107]Lander, supra note 108. See also, Lander, "Experts Report," in *People v. Castro*, supra note 93.

[108]It is important to note, of course, that the techniques used by forensic DNA laboratories are constantly changing as this new technology evolves. We are confident that many of the problems discussed here will be resolved through further research.

[109]Those experts who denied the existence of "slop" in DNA typing, see note 8, *supra*, may simply be unfamiliar with forensic casework or with samples exposed to heavy environmental contamination.

[110]See discussion of this point supra at notes 9–11.

Table 1.   Sources of Ambiguity Observed in Forensic Casework

| | Potential source of ambiguity | | | | |
	Band shift	Missing bands	Faint bands	Extra bands	Other
Tex. v. Hicks LC FB10942 12/10/88 (Fairfield, 1/89)		*	*	*	1, 2, 4, 5, 12
Vir. v. Johnson LC FI06761 4/29/88 (Charlottesville, Plea)	*	*		*	1, 3, 4, 6, 12
N.Y. v. Castro No. 1508-87 (Bronx, 5–8/89)	*	*	*	*	4
N.Y. v. Davis No. 6870-87 (Queens, 6/89)	*				5, 6, 7, 12
Ga. v. Caldwell LC FB13551 11/88 (Marietta, 5/89)	*				2
Mass. v. Hill No. 066505-6 LC F13587 9/88, (Boston, withdrawn)		*	*	+	2, 7, 12
N.Y. v. Drozic LC FI9028 11/88, 9/89 (Buffalo, Plea)		*		*	2, 4, 5, 6, 7, 8, 12
N.Y. v. Golub LC FI19320 11/89 (Mineola, N.Y.)	+	*	*		5, 7, 8
Ind. v. Hopkins No. CCR-86-428 (Ft. Wayne, 12/88)					2, 6, 9, 10
Minn. v. Schwartz No. C5-89-460 (Minneapolis, 2/89)	+				9, 10
Wash. v. Cauthron No. 88-1-01253-3 (Everett, 3/89)			*	*	1, 2, 3, 9, 10
Calif. v. Axell No. CR 23911 (Ventura, 3-8/89)					2, 9, 10
Penn. v. Shorter No. 7656-88 (Media, 6/89, later withdrawn)			*		2, 3, 10

Table 1. continued.

	Potential source of ambiguity				
	Band shift	**Missing bands**	**Faint bands**	**Extra bands**	**Other**
Calif. v. Davis CM F891121 5/89, 7/89 (Ventura, 8/89)		*	*		2, 10
Del. v. Pennell No. IN88-12-0051-3 (Wilmington, 8-9/89			*	*	2, 6, 9, 10
Mass. v. Curnin (Worcester, 9/89)	+				2, 6, 9, 10
Miss. v. Parker (Philadelphia, 10/89)				*	4, 9, 10
Calif. v. Wilds No. A816963 (Van Nuys, 10/89)	+			*	2, 6, 10
Ind. v. Simpson No. 4350-88 (Michigan City, 11/89)				+	9, 10, 12
Calif. v. Marlow No. 16413 (Hollister, 11/89)	+				2, 6, 9, 10, 12

This table lists the cases reviewed by the authors while preparing this chapter and indicates what problems, if any, were observed in the autorads for each case. Cases are identified by docket number or by laboratory case number (LC = Lifecodes; CM = Cellmark) and the date of the lab report. In parentheses under each case is the city where it arose and the approximate date the evidence was first presented in court. (Some autorads were never presented in court because they were withdrawn or because the case was resolved through a plea arrangement). Instances of band shift, missing bands, faint bands, and extra bands are indicated with an asterisk where the problem affected the prints relied upon to incrimi-nate the defendant (i.e., where the best available match was affected by the problem) and with a plus where the problem affected prints other than those relied upon to incriminate the defendant (e.g., where the prints affected by the problem were not the only ones available to make the match). Other problems are designated by the following code numbers in the Other Problems column: 1. lateral movement of DNA on gel; 2. marked variation in intensity of bands; from lane to lane; 3. failure to account for bands in mixed stain; 4. failure to report extra bands; 5. error on report; 6. broad, smeary bands; 7. analyst made marks on autorad to indicate the presence of bands; 8. autorad mislabeled; 9. glycerol concentration exceeded 5% during restriction digestion; 10. no known human DNA control; 12. eviden-tiary samples and blood standards on different autorads.

interpretation of DNA prints, but also over the existence of bands, the location of bands, and the origin of bands.

A related danger is that analysts may overinterpret ambiguous autorads due to a desire to make a definitive statement. The natural desire to provide a definitive answer in order to be helpful may induce analysts to disregard ambiguities or to attribute them to artifacts in the absence of supporting evidence.

Given the significant potential for ambiguity in forensic DNA testing, and the tendency to want to draw definitive conclusions, there is also the danger of an unintentional bias toward interpretations that produce the expected or desired result.[111] The possibility that analysts will (perhaps without even realizing it) misuse the interpretational flexibility available to them in this manner argues for strict controls on laboratory procedure and for the procedure to be conducted "blind", that is, without the analyst knowing the identity of the samples. However, this is not the case. Analysts not only know which samples are expected to match, but often are familiar with details of the case wholly unrelated to the forensic samples, such as the past criminal history of the suspect and the opinions of the police regarding his or her likelihood of guilt. Where samples are submitted by a law enforcement agency, direct communication between the analyst and the detective handling the case frequently occurs. Fears have been voiced that when faced with ambiguity (whatever its technical cause), it may be difficult for the analyst not to be influenced by this type of information.

THE NEED FOR ADDITIONAL VALIDATION RESEARCH

How frequently do the sorts of problems discussed here lead to erroneous results? The answer to this crucial question is, at this point, unknown. The question cannot be answered based on scientific experience with nonforensic applications of RFLP analysis. In nonforensic applications, there is less potential for "slop" to occur, less potential for "slop" to create ambiguity and error, greater potential for retesting in the event any ambiguity arises, and generally much less at stake should an error occur.[112] Consequently, acceptance of RFLP analysis for use in other contexts for other purposes does not necessarily imply that it is reliable for criminal identification based on samples from crime scenes.[113] In addition, questions concerning the reliability of forensic DNA typing cannot be answered based on experience with forensic casework. Analysts will never learn of some errors and, given the adversarial atmosphere in which DNA

---

[111]A possible example arose in *N.Y. v. Drozic*, a Lifecodes case (Lifecodes No. FI9028, reports issued 11/88 and 9/89). An initial report indicated that Drozic's DNA print matched that of semen samples recovered from five rape victims. Drozic's sample was later reexamined and found to have a different print than initially reported (the two prints differed in the position of two bands), apparently due to a laboratory error in the initial analysis. This second print was, nevertheless, declared to match all five semen samples.

[112]See the discussion of these issues supra at notes 6–10.

[113]Analogously, the fact that a bicycle is accepted as a reliable means of transportation on streets does not necessarily imply that it is reliable for travel in other sorts of terrain, such as through a swamp.

testing has entered the courts, may be reluctant to publicize those that do come to their attention.[114]

The best way to assess the reliability of forensic DNA typing is through blind proficiency testing with samples simulating actual casework. Blind testing is viewed as an essential step in the validation of DNA-based tests both for medical diagnosis[115] and criminal identification.[116] Blind testing may be the only way to evaluate the role that "slop" and other technical problems can play in misclassification of samples, and thus is a crucial type of validation research.

To date there has been only limited blind testing of forensic DNA laboratories, and the results of this testing raise serious concerns. The most useful data currently available on this issue are from a "blind trial" sponsored by the DNA Committee of the California Association of Crime Laboratory Directors (CACLD) and administered by the Orange County, California Sheriff-Coroner's Department.[117] Figures 8, 12, 13, and 15 are drawn from that study,[118] which is the only meaningful blind trial of the proficiency of

---

[114]An interesting example of this tendency to suppress problems occurred in *Mississippi v. Parker.* The defense asked Lifecodes to perform a confirmatory test on *Hinf*1-digested DNA processed by Cellmark. Although the Lifecodes report indicated that no useful results had been obtained, an examination of Lifecodes autorads revealed a perplexing finding: A sample from the defendant produced a print that appeared to match that of a sample from the victim (see Figure 16). This spurious match may simply be due to sample mislabeling or cross-contamination. (A second sample from the defendant failed to match the first). On the other hand, it raises the intriguing possibility that Lifecodes probes may be less polymorphic on DNA digested with *Hinf*1 than *Pst*1, and thus be susceptible to producing false matches in such confirmatory testing. Our feeling is that anomalous results such as this should be brought to light and discussed openly so that the scientific community can get to the bottom of the underlying problems, whatever they may be. In this instance, the anomaly might never have come to light had the defense not asked an independent expert to examine the Lifecodes report and autorads.

[115]Klinger, Balfour, Rochelle, and Watkins "Establishment of a Centralized DNA-Based Genetic Reference Laboratory," in *Nucleic Acid Probes in Diagnosis of Human Genetic Diseases,* supra note 1, 175–193.

[116]See, e.g., the guidelines promulgated by the DNA Committee of the California Association of Crime Laboratory Directors, which state in part "(4) Methods used for typing must have been evaluated by blind trial testing on samples simulating case evidence material, and the results of such testing must be available for review." This guideline appears to be widely endorsed by the forensic science community. In a survey of the membership of the American Society of Crime Laboratory Directors in October 1988, 154 of 179 respondents (86%) agreed that a laboratory should be "required to demonstrate its proficiency in blind testing before it uses DNA typing for routine casework." Eighty percent of respondents said that the proficiency testing should "be done on samples similar to those encountered in actual forensic casework" rather than "fresh blood samples." The survey was designed by the authors and administered by the Indiana-Purdue Survey Research Center. Thompson & Ford, supra note 24.

[117]Graves & Kuo "DNA: A Blind Trial Study of Three Commercial Testing Laboratories," supra note 50.

[118]We had access only to autorads produced by Cellmark in connection with that study and did not review those produced by Lifecodes.

MISSISSIPPI vs MICHAEL PARKER

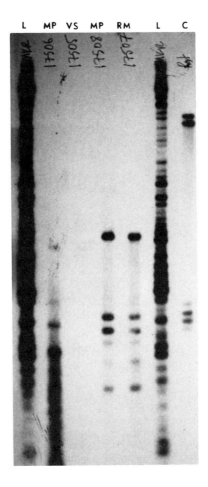

Figure 16.   Defendant matches victim: Possible instance of sample handling error? Life-codes autorad showing hybridization of *Hinf*1 digested DNA with a cocktail of D2S44 and DXYS14. The same samples were previously tested by Cellmark, which reported a match between the defendant (MP) and the sample from a vaginal swab (VS)(see Figure 10). The victim (RM) had a distinct pattern. As part of a confirmatory test requested by the defense in *Mississippi v. Parker*, Lifecodes retested four samples of digested DNA received from Cellmark—two samples from the defendant (both marked MP) and one each from the victim (RM) and the vaginal swab (VS). Lifecodes results indicate a match between the victim and one of defendant's samples, with the other defendant sample showing a distinct (and degraded) pattern. These findings could have arisen due to the victim's sample being switched with one of defendant's samples or due to cross-contamination of the two samples. Other possible explanations are mentioned at note 114.

DNA laboratories conducted to date by an independent organization.[119] A first set of approximately 50 test samples was sent to Lifecodes in August 1987 and to Cellmark in December 1987. According to the reports issued by the CACLD DNA Committee, there was only one misclassification by the two labs—Cellmark mistakenly declared a match between two samples from different individuals (see Figure 8). During discovery proceedings conducted in connection with an admissibility hearing, however, it was learned that Cellmark had produced two reports of its findings. The first report, dated March 24, 1988, contained an extraordinary number of misclassifications, including one false positive, at least three false negatives (one of which is shown in Figure 15), and at least two incorrect reports of mixed stains (see Figures 12 and 13).[120] As noted earlier,[121] the first report appears to more accurately reflect the way these autorads would normally be interpreted.[122]

A second batch of 50 test samples was sent to Cellmark and Lifecodes by the CACLD in July 1988. Lifecodes reported its results to the CACLD in January 1989 and made two errors. "[O]ne sample, a 1:1 mixture of blood from two donors and a second sample, a 1:1 mixture of semen from two donors, were not recognized as mixtures. In each case, the sample was matched to one donor only." The other samples were correctly classified, according to the CACLD DNA Committee. Cellmark reported its results to the CACLD in February, 1990 and made several errors, including falsely matching two samples from different individuals (an additional false positive), mistakenly reporting that a stain from a single individual was a mixed

---

[119]A few blind samples have also been sent to Cellmark by Collaborative Testing, but this proficiency test is not very meaningful because the samples are few in number and some samples have been analyzed using procedures more rigorous than those used in routine forensic cases, e.g., samples are split and analyzed in duplicate.

[120]It also classified a number of samples in two or more categories. Sample 36, for example (shown in Figure 13), was listed as matching sample 30, as matching no other sample, and as "unsuitable for comparison." Robin Cotton of Cellmark recently acknowledged that Cellmark's analysts may have been "hedging their bets a little" when making these inconsistent calls on the same print. Testimony in *Del. v. Pennell*, June 2, 1989 RT 44:12–15.

[121]Note 91, supra.

[122]The CACLD DNA Committee allowed Cellmark to withdraw the first report and replace it with a second report (dated May 2, 1988), but only after the committee met with Dan Garner of Cellmark, reviewed the autorads, questioned him about problems in the first report, and, as Committee Chair Margaret Kuo described it, asked Garner to explain "why is it that your report did not exactly reflect what the autorads really meant." See note 91 supra. After this meeting, which arguably undermined the "blindness" of the test, the committee based its conclusions about Cellmark's performance only on this second report and never mentioned the first report in any publication of its results. The first report came to light after defense attorneys subpoenaed the Committee's records. Disclosure of the first report was particularly embarrassing to Cellmark because the company had previously been under court order to produce all correspondence related to this proficiency study (and specifically any that occurred in March of 1988) but failed to produce the first report; when asked directly about an initial report, Cellmark officials had denied its existence.

stain, and mistakenly reporting that two mixed stains were from a single donor.[123]

The high rate of errors in the CACLD Proficiency Study suggests that the problems of "slop" discussed in this chapter can indeed produce misclassifications. In fact, it is arguable that the laboratories' performance on this study underestimated the rate of errors in actual casework because the labs knew they were being tested and that results of the test would be "available for review" (and therefore were extra careful) and because the test involved laboratory prepared blood and semen samples, which were probably a lot cleaner than many crime scene samples and therefore were less susceptible to "slop".

It appears that the only other meaningful proficiency tests of a DNA typing procedure based on RFLP analysis are the internal proficiency trials reportedly conducted by the FBI. The FBI has refused to make the results of these studies available and has vigorously sought to quash court orders to disclose any information about these studies.[124] By refusing to make this information public, the FBI is depriving the scientific community of access to what we regard as the single most important type of validation research that can be done.[125]

Beyond proficiency testing, several other types of validation research are needed. Research in the following areas should be a high priority: a) conditions giving rise to faint bands, b) reliability of DNA quantitation procedures, c) conditions giving rise to band shift, d) conditions giving rise to extra bands, e) conditions giving rise to problems in restriction digestion, and f) development of monomorphic probes capable of producing bands at several points on the gel. Particularly useful would be a probe to produce bands high on the gel, as the absence of such a band could be used as evidence of degradation.

Validation research is necessary not only to assure the reliability of the calls made on unknown samples, but also to assess the accuracy of the statistics presented in conjunction with DNA evidence. The statistics are derived from

---

[123]Cellmark's results on the second round of the CACLD proficiency test were announced as this chapter went to press in a letter from Margaret Kuo to Daniel Garner dated February 22, 1990, which was made public by Los Angeles Deputy District Attorney Lisa Kahn. Cellmark's autorads in this study will be an important new source of data on the problems discussed in this chapter.

[124]In the middle of an extensive Frye hearing in Yuma, AZ recently, *State v. Kiles*, No. CR 15444/15577, a dispute arose over the FBI's refusal to comply with a court order that the records of this proficiency testing be disclosed to the defense. After the prosecution had presented testimony by a number of experts to support the FBI's DNA test, the judge announced that he would rule the test results inadmissible unless the FBI complied with the order; the next day the DNA evidence was withdrawn.

[125]In January 1990, a judge in Albuquerque, NM ordered the FBI to produce all results of its internal proficiency trials and later refused to issue a requested protective order forbidding disclosure of that information to anyone other than defense experts in that case: *State v. Anderson*, No. CR 46255, Albuquerque, NM Copies of these materials are available from the authors.

databases consisting of DNA prints of a large sample of individuals. Estimates of the frequency in the population of specific alleles are made by determining the frequency of those alleles in the database. If DNA prints in the database are affected by "slop", the resulting variability and measurement error may cause analysts to overestimate the number of distinct alleles identified by a probe and to underestimate their frequency.[126] Band shift, problems with restriction digestion, and degradation may all introduce variability into the position of bands in databases.[127]

REDUCING POTENTIAL AMBIGUITY: PROPOSED STANDARDS FOR DNA TYPING

The potential for error in DNA typing could be reduced if laboratories used stringent controls and if analysts consistently followed a set of conservative standards for interpreting DNA prints. In this final section, we propose some standards and controls that we believe will address some, though not all, of the problems discussed herein. This is by no means a comprehensive list of necessary standards and controls. It is a partial list intended to stimulate and contribute to broader discussion of the issue in the forensic science community.

Necessary Control Procedures

Quality Control Office

Each laboratory should have a quality control office (or officer) to act as a buffer between the analyst and the party submitting the samples for testing. There should be no direct communication between the analyst and the party submitting the samples. All communication should be through the quality control office.

The analyst should never be informed of any facts of the case beyond those necessary to analyze the samples appropriately. When the analyst receives samples from the quality control office, they should be labeled

---

[126]Suppose, for example, that an allele that normally produces a band at 10 kb appears in a database four times but "slop" in the procedure causes the position of the four bands to be at 9.8, 9.9, 10.1, and 10.2 kb. Analysts relying on the database may think they are seeing four distinct alleles that each occur only once. Depending on the setting of bin boundaries, some of the bands produced by an allele may fall out of the bin, resulting in underestimation of allele frequency.

[127]Additionally, there has been testimony in several Frye hearings about a problem affecting the position of the size markers on some of the autorads in Cellmark's database. Cellmark failed to heat its lambda markers to the standard 65°C before applying them to gels, causing broad, smeary bands, some of which were in the wrong position due to a "sticky ends" problem. To its credit, Cellmark has remedied this deficiency in its laboratory protocol, so the problem should no longer affect casework. Cellmark is reportedly in the process of rescoring autorads in its database that may have been affected by this problem.

according to their nature (e.g., blood standard #1, blood standard #2; questioned stain) and, if necessary, the conditions under which they were obtained or stored (e.g., 3-month-old semen stain from bedsheet stored at room temperature). Information needed to link the samples to particular individuals should be kept in the quality control office and related back to the samples only after the analysis is completed and all calls are made.

At least one known human blood standard should be submitted to the analyst and run on each autorad as a control. This known human control should be labeled in a manner that makes it indistinguishable from the other blood standards. The quality control office should check to determine that the known human DNAs produced the expected pattern and that the bands on the known print are in the correct position with respect to the markers. The quality control office should keep a number of control samples on hand and use them in random or rotating order.

Sample Portion Saved For PCR

Where possible, a portion of each sample processed for RFLP analysis should be saved for future confirmatory analysis with PCR.[128] The sample portion saved for PCR should be removed from the original sample material, not from DNA extracted from the sample, and ideally should be removed before the sample enters the laboratory where the RFLP analysis will be performed. Extreme caution in handling samples saved for later analysis with PCR is warranted due to the danger that cross-contamination of even minute amounts of material between samples could produce an erroneous result with the highly sensitive PCR technique.

Sample Splitting

Where enough material is available, samples should always be split and analyzed in duplicate by independent analysts. Splitting samples and processing them independently, in duplicate, is a procedure viewed as essential by some laboratories that use RFLP analysis for medical diagnostics.[129] We believe that forensic DNA laboratories should be at least as careful in this regard as their medical counterparts where sufficient sample is available.

---

[128]*PCR* stands for polymerase chain reaction, a technique for "amplifying" DNA. For a discussion of the use of PCR for analysis of forensic samples, see Thompson & Ford, 1989, supra note 4, at 76–81, 96–100.

[129]Consider, for example, this description of procedures in a medical diagnostics laboratory:

Most importantly, two laboratory technicians, well trained in molecular biology, perform

Separate Processing of Suspect and Evidentiary Samples

Given the potential for cross-contamination of evidentiary samples with a suspect's DNA to cause tragic results, a prudent procedure would be to process the suspect's blood standard separately from any evidentiary materials to which it will be compared, perhaps in a different part of the laboratory, to avoid inadvertent mixing.[130]

Blank Control Lanes

Samples to be compared should never be run in adjacent lanes. A blank control lane should always exist between two samples to be compared so that spill-over and lateral movement of DNA is likely to be detected.[131]

Controls for Mixed Stains

Where a mixed stain is suspected, the laboratory should, wherever possible, run samples from all individuals whose DNA might be part of the "mix" as controls. In rape cases, a sample from the victim (and, where relevant, her husband or boyfriend) should always be run as a control.

Routine Blind Testing

Blind proficiency tests should be conducted on a regular basis by an entity that is not affiliated with the laboratory; all results of this testing should be open to review by any interested party.

---

the tests independently from DNA extraction through the final results. This approach is considered to have a number of advantages: 1. It minimizes the chance of mixing of samples . . . 4. Operating the test in duplicate reduces the chance of undetected laboratory error . . . The individual results are compared to determine concurrence and checked by a third party prior to a laboratory report being filed.

Klinger, Balfour, Rochelle, & Watkins, "Establishment of a Centralized DNA-Based Genetic Reference Laboratory," in *Nucleic Acid Probe in Diagnosis of Human Genetic Diseases*, supra note 1, at 175, 188.

[130] This procedure would not eliminate the possibility of cross-contamination among different evidentiary samples, which could also produce a false positive, but would be a significant advance over the procedures currently in use.

[131] The importance of this control has been recognized for some nonforensic applications of these techniques. A recent article discussing techniques for analyzing distributions of DNA on agarose gels, for example, declares "[l]anes containing samples should be separated by at least one empty lane. This prevents any "spillover" of fluorescence from one lane to another . . . " Ribeiro, Larcom & Miller "Quantitative Fluorescence of DNA-Intercalated Ethidium Bromide on Agarose Gels," *Analyt. Biochem.* 181:197 (1989).

No Marks on Autorads

In several forensic cases we reviewed, analysts made pencil or felt pen marks directly on the autorads to indicate the position of faint bands. This practice precludes the possibility of an independent second assessment of the presence and location of the band. Any marks necessary for band measurement should be made on transparent overlays, not on the autorads.

Equal Intensity of Bands

DNA prints to be compared should have bands of approximately equal intensity. If a laboratory cannot achieve this through DNA quantitation, it should be done through serial dilution of blood standards.

Monomorphic Probes

An array of monomorphic probes should be used as a control to check for band shift and loss of high molecular weight DNA. Constant band probes would also help control, to some extent, for lane-to-lane variation in band intensity.

Reporting Procedures

To deal with the problem of faint bands, standards must be developed for what constitutes a band. A requirement that bands achieve a defined minimum density before being declared to be bands would be appropriate. Once the standard is developed, all bands passing the standard must be reported and no band that fails to pass the standard should be reported or relied upon for any purpose.

In the absence of standards for whether a band is present, the analyst must determine the number and position of bands in each print while blind to the number and position of bands in any print to which it will be compared. Other prints on the same autorad should be shielded during this procedure to prevent the analyst from comparing across lanes when determining whether a band is present or absent.[132]

All bands relied upon for declaring a match must be sized, and the molecular weight (sizing) of each band should be reported separately. Reporting the average size of two bands that are thought to match is unacceptable.

---

[132]This procedure would require two or more analysts, each of whom would size the bands on one print, while blind to the print being sized by the other.

Standards for Interpretation

In an earlier publication we called for the development of clearer standards for interpreting DNA prints,[133] a call recently echoed by others.[134] Here we propose a few minimal standards that we believe are necessary (though perhaps not sufficient) for avoiding the sort of interpretive errors discussed in this chapter.

1. Any difference between two prints is presumptively a genetic difference between the samples unless proved otherwise by research.[135] Missing bands may not be attributed to degradation without a convincing showing that degradation occurred. Misalignment may not be attributed to band shift without a convincing showing band shift occurring. Extra bands may not be attributed to any phenomenon other than a genetic difference without a convincing showing that the phenomenon occurred.

2. The existence of a phenomenon used to explain an imperfect match must be proved entirely by evidence independent of the problem it is invoked to explain. For example, the misalignment of bands in two DNA prints cannot be cited as evidence of the band shift that purportedly produced the misalignment. The absence of a band where expected cannot be used as proof of the degradation that purportedly explains its absence.

3. Analysts may not draw conclusions about the probable source of a band based on band morphology or appearance without a convincing demonstration that bands from different sources can reliably be distinguished using that criterion. If band morphology or appearance is used as a criterion for distinguishing true bands from artifactual bands, it must be used consistently. All bands having the appearance of artifactual bands must be ignored and no band not having that appearance may be ignored. Furthermore, the analyst must make a "call" on each band separately (as either true or artifactual) while blind to whether the call helps make the match.[136]

4. Results should be declared inconclusive if there is evidence of partial digestion, star activity, cross-contamination, or lateral movement of DNA in the lanes being compared.

CONCLUSIONS

The problems discussed in this chapter do not indicate that RFLP analysis is inappropriate for forensic use. They are largely problems arising from

---

[133]Thompson & Ford, supra note 4, at 88.

[134]Lander, supra note 4.

[135]This standard was first articulated by the defense attorneys and defense experts in the Castro case and should be the cornerstone of any set of standards for interpreting DNA prints.

[136]The analyst should be unaware of the position of bands in the print to which a sample will be compared while determining whether bands are true or artifactual. The autorad should be shielded to prevent cross-lane comparisons during this procedure.

the transfer of a technology developed in another context and used for different purposes to forensic science.[137] Although problems of technology transfer can generally be resolved by developing standards and controls appropriate for the new situation and by conducting validation research to ensure that the new procedure is reliable, it appears that DNA testing was placed in routine use before these steps were completed. Hence, current laboratory procedures are not adequately stringent and interpretive standards either do not exist or are not consistently followed. This situation has probably occurred at least in part as a result of genuine enthusiasm for the technique, which has the potential to advance forensic science significantly. Premature introduction may also have been a result of problems inherent in the commercial application of any complex technique when demand for its application is high; in the rush to get the product on the market, the laboratories may simply have made too many simplifying assumptions about the technique.

In an ideal world, the necessary validation research would have been completed by the forensic DNA laboratories before they began accepting casework. It is generally accepted scientific practice to conduct validation studies of innovations before implementing them in situations where their validity may be critical.[138] Such work should now be completed as quickly as possible, and arguably should be done by organizations independent of the forensic laboratories, as some have expressed fears that retrospective validation by a laboratory already heavily invested in a particular technology or procedure will be half-hearted, goal-directed, self-congratulatory, or even deceitful.[139]

The development of standards for conducting and interpreting DNA tests is also an urgent priority. To develop adequate standards one must be familiar with the sort of problems that may arise in DNA testing. Our hope is that this chapter will provide some guidance in that area. Discussions of problems in forensic DNA typing have been surprisingly scarce in the forensic science literature; greater scholarly attention to these problems is surely needed.[140]

---

[137]See notes 6–10 supra, and accompanying text.

[138]Extensive tests are required before the release of pharmaceuticals, for example, to ensure that they are safe and effective. Tests used in medical diagnosis undergo extensive validation, including blind trials of their accuracy, before they are placed in routine use, and laboratories performing those tests undergo routine proficiency testing thereafter.

[139]Independent validation would eliminate any appearance of a conflict of interest and help restore public confidence in DNA typing procedures.

[140]Scientific debate in this area may have arisen first in the courts, rather than traditional scientific fora, because forensic DNA typing procedures were first implemented by commercial laboratories whose procedures are proprietary, whose work product is generally not available for examination by outsiders (except when used as evidence in a court hearing), who have little incentive to discuss problems, and whose laboratory protocols until recently were available only by court order.

Finally, there is a need to ensure that standards developed and endorsed by the scientific community are actually followed by the laboratories. As Lander notes, "forensic science is vitually unregulated — with the paradoxical result that clinical laboratories must meet higher standards to be allowed to diagnose strep throat than forensic labs must meet to put a defendant on death row."[141] Whether compliance is best assured through promulgation of voluntary guidelines,[142] through making compliance a condition for the admissibility of test results,[143] or through legislative enactment[144] is an issue beyond the scope of this chapter, but one deserving careful consideration in both the legal and scientific communities.

---

[141]Lander, supra note 4, at 505.

[142]E.g., guidelines by the CACLD DNA Committee, supra note 115, and guidelines recently issued by the Technical Working Group on DNA Analysis Methods (TWGDAM).

[143]See *Minnesota v. Schwartz*, C5–89–460, November 3, 1989, where the Minnesota Supreme Court unanimously ruled Cellmark's test inadmissible based, in part, on Cellmark's failure to comply with all of the CACLD guidelines and failure to follow a laboratory "validation protocol" purportedly used by the FBI and proposed by FBI personnel. Budowle, Deadman, Murch, & Baechtel, "An Introduction to the Methods of DNA Analysis Under Investigation in the FBI Laboratory," *Crime Laboratory Digest* 15(8):18–20 (January 1988).

[144]Some commentators have proposed bringing forensic DNA laboratories under the federal Clinical Laboratory Regulations, 42 C.F.R. 74 (1988), which currently cover many medical diagnostic laboratories.

8. General Admissibility Considerations For DNA Typing Evidence: Let's Learn from the Past and Let the Scientists Decide This Time Around

ROCKNE P. HARMON, Esq.

Many legal treatises dealing with scientific and/or evidentiary matters have been written by law professors[1] with little or no actual trial experience. These studies are generally well written and serve as valuable sources of general legal and technical information for attorneys with very little time for independent research.[2] However, there is danger in relying, as such authors generally do, only on published legal opinions as the bases for the conclusions that they draw on matters of fact and science contained therein.[3] Thus, while such assistance from academia is truly appreciated,

---

[1]See, e.g., Giannelli, "The Admissibility of Novel Scientific Evidence: *Frye v. United States*, a Half-Century Later," 80 Colum. L. R. 1197 (1980). A. Moenssens, F. Inbau, & J. Starrs, "Scientific Evidence in Criminal Cases" 355 (3d Ed., 1986). P. Giannelli & E. Imwinkelreid, "Scientific Evidence" (1986 & 1987 Supp.). Jonakait, "Will Blood Tell? Genetic Markers in Criminal Cases," 31 Emory L. J. 833 (1982)(hereinafter Jonakait).

[2]Giannelli, ibid; Moenssens, ibid.

[3]Jonakait, supra fn. 1. The article is replete with factual and technical errors caused, in the author's opinion, either by faulty research or due to a reliance upon published legal opinions as bases for conclusions of law and fact reached therein. In one discussion on p. 900, the author cited a technical publication (see fn. 217) for a principle it had nothing to do with. In another discussion, the author characterized the bloodstain evidence as "crucial" to the case, while the written opinion cited described it as "weakly probative" and "mildly unfavorable to the defendant " (see fn. 165). These are but a few examples. Perhaps the real danger in relying on legal publications for technical direction on scientific issues is that the authors may not have sufficient scientific expertise to provide that direction. For example, Professor Jonakait also appears to have expertise in another field of science, having authored Jonakait, "Reliable Identification: Could the Supreme Court Tell in *Manson v. Braithwaite*?," 52 U. of Colorado L. R. 511 [1981].

153

more input should be sought from those who have actually waged the legal conflicts.[4]

The following discussion aims to identify the issues that must be addressed during admissibility hearings that, at least for the foreseeable future, are required before evidence derived from DNA identification techniques can be presented in jury trials. Some legal treatises written by nonscientists already provide nontechnical descriptions of the basic identification techniques used in DNA analysis.[5] Therefore, a minimal understanding of the relevant biological principles and a familiarity with forensic DNA identification methods will be assumed, as such an undertaking is beyond the scope of this chapter. Such information is additionally presented in other chapters in this book.

A brief explanation of the legal procedures relating to typical criminal matters will help illustrate what is likely to occur prior to the point where an admissibility hearing might be necessary. Once charges are filed against the defendant, his or her counsel is normally provided access to certain information that the prosecution intends to present in court. This is known as the "discovery" process, wherein scientific or technical evidence is normally disclosed. This disclosure alerts the defense to the nature of the evidence that will be presented and affords it the opportunity to object to the admission of that evidence on various theories, e.g., the suggestiveness of the identification procedures, waiver of Miranda rights, an unreasonable search or seizure, or the need to satisfy Frye or other admissibility standards, but these are but a few examples.

State statutes and local rules of court typically govern when and how far in advance of the trial specific evidentiary objections must be raised. At least one judicial decision requires objections to be made in a "timely" manner because of the nature of the burden imposed on the proponent of the evidence in satisfying the legal admissibility standard.[6] There do not appear to be other published legal opinions that address this specific issue in

---

[4]The author is a trial attorney who successfully presented the prosecution case in *People v. Reilly*, infra, fn. 70. He is currently involved in one of the first hearings involving the admissibility of DNA evidence in California. He has also lectured extensively and written on the subject. See infra, fn. 99.

[5]Long, "The DNA Fingerprint: A Guide to Admissibility," *The Army Lawyer*, October 1988. Note, "DNA Identification Tests and the Courts," 63 Washington L. R. 903 (1988).

[6]*Correll v. State* (1988 Fla.) 523 So. 2d 562, 567. Specifically, under the authority of this holding in Florida, where similar evidence has been presented in a substantial number of other cases in the state, a reliability hearing ". . . for purposes of admissibility is only necessary when the opposing party makes a timely request for such an inquiry supported by authorities indicating that there may not be general scientific acceptance of the technique employed." How would one trial court be aware that the evidence had been presented in a substantial number of other cases unless some form of judicial notice had been used? This subject is discussed in detail, infra fns. 137–147.

this context. If a proper objection is not made before the evidence is introduced, it should not be raised for the first time on appeal.[7]

Legal admissibility standards for novel scientific evidence vary greatly from one jurisdiction to another.[8] Identifying the legal test for admissibility in a particular jurisdiction is but the first step in preparing for an admissibility hearing. The trial attorney must also develop an appreciation for the evolution of the legal standard through its applications to different types of scientific evidence, as well as the different legal considerations necessitated by each new form of scientific evidence.

Unless this history is understood and appreciated, future legal admissibility applications may stray from the limited intent of the early legal decisions. Thus, the evolution of legal standards for the admissibility of new scientific evidence will be traced herein to identify the precise nature and extent of current legal admissibility standards. Finally, the discussion will focus on the applicability of present admissibility standards to various aspects of currently available forensic DNA identification techniques.

THE CURRENT TESTS FOR ADMISSIBILITY

There are presently three "varieties" of legal admissibility tests: the Frye[9] rule, the Federal Rules of Evidence, and the "relevancy" test. Each standard will be briefly discussed in the order presented, with the greatest emphasis being placed on Frye since it is the more frequently debated rule, has the longest history, and has undergone the most startling evolution. One could, in fact, dedicate an entire treatise to a comparison of and a contrast among the various legal tests and still be left with the impression that there is very little difference between or among them.[10] Even to one who recognizes the distinctions between these various standards, it is often difficult to conclude

---

[7]*People v. Poggi* (1988) 45 Cal. 3d 306, 323. The evidence in question was conventional genetic marker evidence and the statistics derived therefrom. The sole trial objection was to the use of statistical probabilities, not the reliability of the test procedures themselves. Since this case was decided after Reilly, infra fn. 70, had decided the admissibility of the test procedures, the court's rationale is understandable. If there were not an already published local legal precedent on the admissibility issue, the Court might well have ruled to the contrary on this point, especially if the record were expanded on appeal by *amicus curiae* briefs, infra fn. 44 or judicial notice, infra fns. 137–147. In any event, a prudent proponent of evidence that might arguably be categorized as "novel" would be wise to either seek an explicit waiver of a hearing or be prepared to conduct an admissibility hearing.

[8]Infra fns. 9–20.

[9]*Frye v. United States*, 293 F. 1013 (D.C. Cir. 1923).

[10]For one state supreme court's impressions on this subject, see *State v. Brown* (Or. 1984) 687 P.2d 751, 758 referring to a symposium of legal and scientific experts on admissibility standards that came to the same conclusion. 99 F.R.D. 188 (1983).

from reading a particular legal opinion which admissibility standard a court has actually applied.[11]

The Frye Rule

This legal screening device, designed to evaluate new forms of "scientific" evidence outside of the presence of the jury, was first developed in 1923. Frye concerned an attempt to present an early form of lie detector test taken by the defendant that would have exonerated him.[12] This technique, known as a "systolic blood pressure deception test," was based on the theory that systolic blood pressure increased when the subject was being deceptive. The trial court's ruling barring the admissibility of the test results was upheld on appeal because the test ". . . had not gained general acceptance in the particular field in which it belongs."[13] The apparent justification for this rule was to prevent juries from being unduly influenced by new scientific evidence that had not yet made the transition from the "experimental" stage to the "demonstrable" stage.[14] The rule is often alternatively described as the "general acceptance" rule,[15] because a showing of general acceptance by qualified experts within the appropriate scientific community is deemed sufficient to allow the proffered evidence to be presented to the jury. This one and a half page legal opinion has generated much spirited debate on issues that the original Court could never have foreseen.

The Federal Rules of Evidence[16]

The Federal Rules of Evidence were enacted in 1975. By one legal commentator's count, they have now been adopted in various forms in 22 juris-

---

[11]See, e.g., *Graham v. State* (Ga. App. 1983) 308 S.E. 2d 413. Just when it appeared that the Court would reverse the conviction, it somehow found a way to uphold it. See also Andrews, infra fn. 111.

[12]Frye, supra fn. 9.

[13]Ibid.

[14]Ibid.

[15]Some legal opinions have characterized the rule as merely a "head count", implying that the quality of scientific-legal decisionmaking may be inferior to other legal tests. *Harper v. State* (1982) 249 Ga. 519,525, 292 S.E. 2d 389. Later discussions of Reilly, infra fn. 70 and Andrews, infra fn. 111, suggest that this pejorative characterization may be inappropriate.

[16]Rule 401—" 'Relevant evidence' means evidence having any tendency to make the existence of any fact that is of consequence to the determination of the action more probable or less probable than it would be without the evidence."

Rule 402—"All relevant evidence is admissible, except as otherwise provided by the Constitution of the United States, by Act of Congress, by these rules, or by other rules prescribed by the Supreme Court pursuant to statutory authority. Evidence which is not relevant is not admissible."

Rule 403—"Although relevant, evidence may be excluded if its probative value is substantially outweighed by the danger of unfair prejudice, confusion of the issues, or

dictions.[17] There are two separate and distinct subjects addressed in the Rules that bear on the issue of novel scientific evidence. The concept of relevant evidence is defined in Rule 401, relevant evidence is presumed admissible in Rule 402, unless the relevant evidence is unduly prejudicial, as defined in Rule 403. Matters governing scientific evidence and opinion testimony are specifically addressed in Rules 702 and 703, respectively. The Federal Rules themselves make no direct reference to Frye, and, until recently, would seemingly have allowed the trial judge to apply Frye in either the relevancy or the scientific evidence/opinion context. In 1985, some of the uncertainty about the continuing viability of *Frye* was resolved by its apparent[18] rejection as the prevailing admissibility standard in favor of Rule 702.[19]

The "Relevancy" Test

The relevancy test is virtually indistinguishable from Federal Rules 402 and 403, which, as previously discussed, are codifications of legal admissi-

---

misleading the jury, or by considerations of undue delay, waste of time, or needless presentation of cumulative evidence."

Rule 702—"If scientific, technical, or other specialized knowledge will assist the trier of fact to understand the evidence or to determine a fact in issue, a witness qualified as an expert by knowledge, skill, experience, training, or education, may testify thereto in the form of an opinion or otherwise."

Rule 703—"The facts or data in the particular case upon which an expert bases an opinion or inference may be those perceived by or made known to him at or before the hearing. If of a type reasonably relied upon by experts in the particular field in forming opinions or inferences upon the subject, the facts or data need not be admissible in evidence."

Rule 704—"Testimony in the form of an opinion or inference otherwise admissible is not objectionable because it embraces an ultimate issue to be decided by the trier of fact."

[17] Giannelli, supra fn. 1, p 1228 fn. 241. The rules have been described as "usually favoring admissibility," whose basic approach is to determine the "helpfulness" of the evidence to the jury. See *United States v. Downing*, 753 F.2d 1225 (3d Cir. 1985) at 1229. Rule 704 specifically allows expert testimony on the ultimate issue. See discussion fns. 122–123 for an unusual contrary view.

[18] Ibid, Downing.

[19] Ibid, Downing, at 1232. General acceptance still constitutes one of many factors for consideration in deciding the admissibility of all scientific evidence, new or old, at 1237. See, e.g., Brown, supra fn. 10 for one state's application of the rule in Downing. Oregon's version, described as a "reasonably reliable" test, is actually a condensed version of a test elaborated in McCormick, "Scientific Evidence: Defining a New Approach to Admissibility," 67 Iowa L. Rev. 879, 911–12 (1982). The Oregon rule considers seven factors for admissibility of all scientific evidence, new or old. The factors are 1) The technique's general acceptance in the field; 2) the expert's qualifications and stature; 3) the use that has been made of the technique; 4) the potential rate of error; 5) the existence of specialized literature; 6) the novelty of the invention, and 7) the extent to which the technique relies on the subjective interpretation of the expert. See also *U.S. v. Gwaltney* (9th Cir. 1986) 790 F.2d 1378 approving admissibilty of a procedure that concededly had not yet gained general acceptance, simply because the proponent had shown the underlying scientific basis of the evidence testing technique.

bility considerations for all types of evidence, scientific or otherwise.[20] Some states follow this apparently simple legal analysis. The following discussion traces the evolution of the Frye test and compares its present form with applications of the Federal Rules and the relevancy test. The analysis demonstrates that the choice of the legal standard to be applied should not necessarily have any impact on the outcome, but should greatly impact on the nature of the issues to be addressed and the form and amount of proof required.

THE EVOLUTION OF THE LEGAL ADMISSIBILITY STANDARDS

The Frye Test

As the oldest of the three admissibility standards, this test has been applied to the greatest variety of novel scientific developments. What may have appeared in 1923 to be a simple, rational attempt to delay admissibility of a new technique until the scientific community had had a chance to pass judgement has not proven to be so simple nor so rational. Some of the obvious difficulties involve the answers to questions such as:

- What is it that must be generally accepted? Is it the underlying principle or the application of the principle to the problem at hand?
- Which is the appropriate community?
- How much agreement constitutes "general acceptance"?
- How is it possible to prove general acceptance in a courtroom setting in view of limitations on time and funding?

In spite of these potential difficulties, Frye continues to be applied with great vitality. It has been criticized as having the potential for withholding valuable evidence from the jury, on the one hand, and as a mere popularity contest among scientists on the other, but it does not appear that Frye will soon be replaced.

Of the three legal admissibility tests, only Frye has undergone substantial transformation from its original form. The other two tests, perhaps because they are dependent upon fixed legal definitions rather than case law, continue to be applied almost universally in their original form.[21] The Frye rule, on the other hand, has been expanded in many jurisdictions to a degree that has resulted in extensive, expensive, repetitive litigation on subjects as diverse as

- Should the scientific community have generally accepted the scientific evidence?
- Are the witnesses the developers of the new science?

---

[20]Graham, supra fn. 11 appears to be an analysis based on the relevancy standard.
[21]It may be that the difference in legal admissibility rules may simply be a matter of form over substance, however. See discussions in fn. 10.

- Should their views alone be sufficient to prove general acceptance?
- Can law enforcement crime lab personnel be classified as "scientists" or are they only "technicians"?
- Should courts be deciding matters of actual scientific reliability or should they defer to the scientists?
- Is scientific peer review publication of every aspect of every analytical procedure a prerequisite to general acceptance?[22]

What could have caused this expansion from the limited caution expressed in Frye? The answer to this question lies in understanding how the rule has been modified in its application to different technical developments over the years.

The earliest cases applying Frye involved varying forms of lie detector tests.[23] Admissibility hearings in this area saw an impressive array of "experts" line up on both sides of the admissibility issue.[24] Subsequent to this initial flurry of legal activity, the next significant scientific development that underwent similar legal scrutiny was the development of voiceprint identification and comparison techniques, which occurred in the 1960s.[25] It was the application of Frye in this area that caused significant changes in the rule, which are still being felt to this date. A brief historical overview will assist the reader in understanding the need for those changes to the early admissibility rules.

Lawrence Kersta was one of the pioneers in the development of the voiceprint comparison and identification techniques.[26] It was while he was an employee of Bell Telephone that the seeds were sown for the development of these techniques. His subsequent career as an expert witness began in the mid-1960s.[27] Efforts to admit these techniques into evidence met with mixed results in the earliest cases.[28] In decisions that ruled the evidence inadmissible, a principal criticism was the lack of a sufficient statistical base for the conclusions that differences in voices could be recognized, identified, and compared by the use of voiceprint analytical techniques.[29] In response to these shortcomings, Dr. Oscar Tosi conducted statistical research under a federal grant at Michigan State University from 1968 to

---

[22]Each of these issues forms the basis of Michigan's legal admissibility standard for electrophoretic analysis of conventional genetic markers, which will be discussed infra in fns. 51–64. The issues addressed seem to far exceed considerations of general acceptance and represent determinations of actual scientific reliability by the trial court.

[23]See Reed and Inbau, "Truth and Deception: The Polygraph ("Lie-Detector") Technique" (2d ed. 1977).

[24]Ibid. See also, *People v. Davis* (1955) 343 Mich. 348, 72 N.W.2d 269.

[25]*People v. Kelly* (1976) 17 Cal. 3d 24.

[26]Ibid, at 35.

[27]*People v. King*, 268 Cal. App.2d. 437 (1968).

[28]Ibid; *State v. Cary*, 56 N.J. 16, 264 A.2d. 209 (1970) declared the evidence inadmissible. Cases supporting admissibility were *U.S. v. Wright*, 17 U.S.C.M.A. 183, 37 C.M.R. 447 (1967), *Trimble v. Hedman*, 291 Minn. 442, 192 N.W.2d 432 (1971).

[29]King, supra fn. 27.

1970[30] in conjunction with Lawrence Kersta, who had by then become the head of the Michigan State Police Voice Identification Unit, and Lieutenant Ernest Nash of the Michigan State Police. Utilizing the newly developed data, these men became involved in a new series of criminal prosecutions dependent on the admissibility of their voiceprint comparison techniques. In spite of the newly developed statistical information, several state supreme courts rejected the admissibility of the voiceprint evidence.[31]

The experiences of California and Michigan in applying the rationale of the Frye test to voiceprint evidence illustrate the reasons behind the expansion of this test, which eventually led to the rejection by the courts of such evidence.[32] For example, Lt. Nash was often the sole prosecution witness testifying on the general acceptance/reliability issue. He had only 50 hours of college credits and no formal degree.[33] The California Supreme Court in Kelly, therefore, expressed serious concern about three issues: a) Nash was the sole witness; b) Since Nash had virtually built his career on the reliability of the technique, he might have been biased in fairly assessing the nature of any opposition to its reliability; and c) in view of his limited college study, his qualifications were those of a technician, not a scientist.[34] In the court's view, only a scientist in regular communication with other colleagues in the field would be competent to express an opinion concerning general acceptance.[35] This standard, i.e., California's version of Frye became known as the Kelly-Frye rule. The part of the decision dealing with Lt. Nash has been characterized as the "disinterested witness rule."[36]

Other than unsuccessful attempts to force various forms of psychiatric/psychological/opinion testimony[37] to undergo a similar pretrial admissibility review, the next significant area for application of Frye/admissibility

---

[30]Kelly, supra fn. 25.

[31]Ibid; *People v. Tobey* (1977) 401 Mich. 141, 257 N.W.2d 537. On the other hand, some courts felt it was admissible; *Commonwealth v. Lykus*, 367 Mass. 191, 327 N.E. 2d 671(1975).

[32]Ibid.

[33]Kelly, supra fn. 25 at 36.

[34]One commentator has described a technician in this way. "The technician merely follows prescribed routines, and is not expected to understand their underlying fundamentals. He knows how, but not why." Giannelli, supra fn. 1 at 1215 citing Kirk, "The Interrelationship of Law and Science," 13 Buffalo L. Rev. 393, 394 (1964).

[35]Kelly, supra fn. 25, at 37–39.

[36]The rule has been extended well beyond its original intent in Michigan. Compare *People v. Barbara* (1977) 400 Mich. 358, 255 N.W.2d. 171 with *People v. Young* (1986) 425 Mich. 470, 391 N.W. 2d 270.

[37]For some reason these areas of expert testimony have avoided the scrutiny of Frye or the other legal admissibility tests. The explanation for this anomalous treatment has been that such testimony merely consists of opinion testimony derived from a body of literature. *People v. Gray*, 187 Cal. App.3d 213 (1986); In re Amber B., 191 Cal. App. 3d 682 (1987). To further confuse this "distinction", these same courts do not hesitate to scrutinize hypnotically induced testimony by the Frye standard. *People v. Shirley* (1982) 31 Cal.3d 18,53, 641 P.2d 775.

standards involved the analysis of conventional genetic markers in physiological fluid evidence.[38]

Analysis of Physiological Fluids for Genetic Markers

Electrophoresis is a method for separating charged molecules, and its use for detecting genetic markers in blood is mechanically uncomplicated. "[A] test sample is placed on a gel medium in an ionized buffer solution. When an electric current is run through the solution, the sample separates and migrates on the medium into characteristic patterns. These patterns are then fixed, dyed, and read visually by the analyst."[39] These electrophoretic typing methods were initially developed for medical research.[40] In order to assign some numerical significance to the results of the analyses of evidence and comparison with known blood samples, population frequency studies based on traditional principles of population genetics were conducted to determine the frequencies of common genetic markers.[41]

Electrophoretic techniques were first introduced into forensic laboratories in the early 1970s; by the late 1970s, nearly 100 analysts from laboratories throughout the United States had been educated in the most commonly utilized methodology.[42]

The first published legal opinion documenting any criticism of the use of electrophoresis to analyze for the presence of genetic markers was *State v. Washington* in 1979, which did not result in preventing the introduction of the evidence.[43] Several years were to pass before further legal criticisms appeared. In the next instance, the same scientist who had been unsuccessful in keeping the evidence from being admitted in *State v. Washington* raised the issue again. Rather than submit to cross examination, which may have contributed to his views being rejected by the Kansas court, however, he arranged to file an *amicus curiae* brief[44] in a case that was then on appeal

---

[38]One definition of genetic markers requires three prerequisites. They must be: a) inherited in a straightforward manner, b) their mode of inheritance must be known, and c) the loci must exhibit genetic polymorphisms. Gaensslen, "Proceedings of the International Symposium on Forensic Application of Electrophoresis," FBI Academy (June 1984) p. 29.

[39]*People v. Reilly*, infra fn. 70 at 1137, citing Jonakait, supra fn. 1.

[40]Sourcebook, infra fn. 128, p. 58. Electrophoresis was developed in the 1930s by Tiselius; He was awarded the Nobel Prize in chemistry in 1948 for developing the technique.

[41]Grunbaum, Selvin, Pace, and Black, "Frequency Distribution and Discrimination Probability of Twelve Protein Genetic Variants in Human Blood as Functions of Race, Sex, and Age," *J. For. Sci.* 23:577 (1978).

[42]229 Kan. 47, 822 P.2d 986 (1981).

[43]Ibid. The conviction was affirmed on appeal.

[44]There are clear limits on the scope of issues that are appropriate to raise in these briefs. The only California legal authority on this point explains " . . . an *amicus curiae* must accept the case as it finds it and 'friend of the court cannot launch out upon a juridical

before the California Supreme Court.[45] The brief questioned the reliability of electrophoretic bloodstain analysis techniques.

As a background to this alleged controversy it is important to note that, at the time of the trial in *Brown* in 1981, there was then no apparent scientific/legal controversy concerning the use of electrophoresis. The only legal precedent was *State v. Washington*,[46] and this decision had clearly resolved the issue in favor of admissibility. The California Supreme Court chose to accept the representations in the *amicus* brief, even though they had not been tested by cross examination. The court determined that the trial record was inadequate to satisfy Frye.[47] In its decision, the court equated the prosecution serologists with Lt. Nash of voiceprint fame, thereby rendering their opinions inadequate to reflect the views of the relevant community of impartial scientists.[48] The two serologists were categorized as "technicians",[49] thereby rendering their opinions invalid. In addition, their affiliations with law enforcement rendered them, in the court's view, too close to the issues to be impartial on the subject.[50] These two serologists were the only witnesses who testified with respect to the electrophoresis issue.

During this period the same scientific-legal issues were also pending before the Michigan Supreme Court in *People v. Young*.[51] However, rather than reverse the defendant's murder conviction, the case was remanded to the trial court for a hearing on the admissibility issue only. A hearing was held, whereupon seven prosecution witnesses[52] and two defense witness-

---

expedition of its own unrelated to the actual appellate record." *Younger v. State of California* (1982) 137 Cal. App. 3d 806. One may attain *amicus* status by filing a timely request and describing the need for additional argument on specific points contained in the existing appellate record. California Rules of Court 14(b). Were there no requirement that issues be limited to those already contained in the record, *amicus* would be able to circumvent the opponent's right to confront and cross examine on the content of the brief by injecting new factual issues. This would appear to be a more serious concern than any confrontation rights involved in judicial notice of other admissibility hearings on the same subject. See discussion, infra fns. 137–147. When the views contained in the *amicus* brief were more thoroughly examined in an adversary setting, they were not deemed significant enough to warrant exclusion of the evidence. See discussion of Reilly, infra fn. 70.

[45]The brief injected many factual issues never presented in the trial record, in obvious violation of Rule 14(b), ibid. *People v. Brown* (1985) 40 Cal.3d 512,736 P.2d 516.

[46]Washington, supra fn. 42.

[47]Brown, supra fn. 45 at 536.

[48]Ibid at 534 fn. 3.

[49]Kirk, supra, fn. 34.

[50]Kelly, supra, fn. 25.

[51](1984) 418 Mich. 1, 340 N.W.2d 805.

[52]Dr. George Sensabaugh, Associate Professor, School of Public Health, University of California-Berkeley; Dr. Rachel Fisher, Michigan State University, Department of Pediatrics and Pathology; Dr. Henry Gershowitz, Professor of Human Genetics, University of Michigan Medical School; Dr. Harvey Mohrenweiser, Michigan State University, Department of Human Genetics; Dale Dykes, B.S./Zoology-Supervisor, Electrophoresis section,

es[53] testified. The "disinterested witness rule"[54] was applied in this case in a curious fashion. During the course of the hearing, each witness was asked whether a decision by the supreme court either approving or disapproving of the admissibility of electrophoretic bloodstain evidence analysis would affect them financially.[55] The trial court made no findings but merely remanded the case to the Michigan Supreme Court for its review.[56] The supreme court disregarded the opinions of both Kearney and Stolorow under the "disinterested witness" test.[57] Because the witnesses were also government employees, the court seems to have automatically classified them as "technicians",[58] thereby placing them on an educational level with Lt. Nash.[59] Only one prosecution witness and one defense witness survived this legal screening process.[60] The legal consequence of this analysis was that there was a "tie". Since the prosecution was required to establish general acceptance by consensus of opinion, the effort to introduce the evidence failed and the murder conviction was reversed. The court also dictated several other scientific requirements that had to be met before any subsequent efforts to introduce this type of evidence could be successful.[61]

The Young rationale continues to be followed, literally, to date. In a recent Michigan trial court decision,[62] evidence of electrophoretic analysis for conventional genetic markers was once again excluded, despite the fact

---

Minneapolis War Memorial Blood Bank; James Kearney, FBI Laboratory Serology Director-B.S. in Bacteriology; M.S. in Microbiology; Mark Stolorow, Serology Coordinator, Illinois State Police, B.S./M.S. in Chemistry /M.B.A. Stolorow had been a principal Prosecution witness in Washington, supra fn. 35.

[53] Dr. Benjamin Grunbaum, retired research biochemist, University of California-Berkeley. B.S., M.S., M. Crim., Ph.D.- Biochemistry; Dr. Diane Juricek, genetic consultant-B.S./ M.S./P.H.D.-Genetics.

[54] Kelly, supra fn. 25; Barbara, supra fn. 36.

[55] It is difficult to comprehend how this rule, which was created to require more than Lt. Nash's testimony alone to satisfy Frye, could be extended to disallow completely the testimony of anyone earning a living pursuing this aspect of forensic science. Since few scientists work for free, this limitation would seem to effectively prevent the reaching of a consensus in Michigan.

[56] Young, supra fn. 36.

[57] Ibid at 276.

[58] Ibid at 276. In view of the two witnesses' impressive academic credentials, this was clearly an unfair judgment, particularly if the Michigan Supreme Court's definition of a "technician" resembles the one previously discussed, supra fn. 34.

[59] Supra, fn. 33.

[60] Drs. Sensabaugh and Grunbaum.

[61] Once the court felt justified in disregarding a witness's opinion because he was either a "technician", not "disinterested", or employed by law enforcement, the entire substance of that witness's testimony was treated as if it had not been presented. The court ignored testimony from several of these witnesses on subjects such as the effects of contamination, the need for further validation studies, and the persistence of certain genetic markers. The court then dictated that specific studies still needed to be conducted, contrary to the overwhelming consensus of opinion contained in the disregarded testimony. Michigan purports to be a Frye jurisdiction. If that were true the court would not be dictating to the scientists how they should be practicing their profession, as the decision clearly does.

[62] Stoughton, infra fn. 64.

that contamination studies had been conducted and published by one of the witnesses.[63] Once again the Michigan courts chose to ignore the testimony of several prosecution witnesses supporting admissibility of the evidence while incredibly, at the same time, pronouncing, "The answer to the question 'Who is right?' is one for the scientists to decide, not the courts."[64]

While Michigan has taken one path, the California decisions have realigned with the rest of the United States in recognizing the need to step back from the rigidity of the expanded voiceprint rule and in returning to a limited pretrial inquiry along the lines originally contemplated in Frye.[65] Based on issues raised for the first time in the *amicus* brief[66] filed in *Brown,*[67] the conviction of a man who had murdered three people was reversed.[68] In the retrial of those charges, an extensive pretrial hearing was held addressing the issues contained in the aforementioned *amicus* brief.[69] The serological evidence was admitted on this occasion and the defendant was convicted once again. The conviction was later affirmed on appeal, the appellate court recognizing that the methodology had been generally accepted in the scientific community.[70] More importantly, the appellate opinion set the tone for how scientific evidence might be analyzed in future admissibility hearings. Some of its ramifications are important to reflect upon:

1. The proponent's burden is not . . . "to create a record that convinces the court that the technique is in fact reliable"[71];
2. Acceptance by a clear "majority" of the community will satisfy the legal test[72];
3. The Michigan interpretation of the "disinterested witness" rule was

---

[63]This was one of the requirements imposed by Young and previously alluded to in fn. 61. An FBI research scientist, Dr. Bruce Budowle, had conducted contamination research since the Young decision. The trial court's scientific opinion was that until someone else duplicated his published contamination study and published it themselves, it could not be relied upon by the court to support admissibility.

[64]*People v. Stoughton*, Wayne County Circuit Court (Michigan) Docket 88–0042–01; October 17,1988.

[65]Supra fn. 6.

[66]Supra fn. 44.

[67]Brown, supra fn. 45.

[68]*People v. Reilly*, A010779, unpublished opinion.

[69]The original trial in Reilly occurred in November 1979, before the trial in Washington, supra fn. 42. At the time of the original trial, Dr. Grunbaum had not yet gone "public" with his criticisms, thereby creating the basis for the legal controversy in the first place. Since there was not yet any legal admissibility controversy, there was no apparent need to satisfy Frye in the first Reilly trial. The principal defense witness in Reilly was the same Dr. Grunbaum who was involved in *State v. Washington*, supra fn. 42, *People v. Young*, supra fn. 36, and *People v. Stoughton*, supra fn. 64. Once the views contained in Dr. Grunbaum's Brown *amicus* brief, supra fns. 44-45, were evaluated under cross examination, they were deemed not sufficient to warrant excluding the evidence from the trial.

[70]*People v. Reilly* (1987) 196 Cal. App. 3d 1127, 242 Cal. Rptr. 496.

[71]Ibid, p. 1152.

[72]Ibid, p. 1148.

rejected. The court chose to consider the testimony of all witnesses for whatever insight they could provide[73];

4. The court refused to impose the defense witness's views concerning quality control guidelines[74] and contamination studies[75] on the scientific community if the community did not feel those factors were a necessary prerequisite to acceptance;

5. The court recognized that if a typing error occurred it would most likely inure to a criminal defendant's benefit by exonerating him when he was really guilty;[76] and

6. The court also recognized that with an issue such as general acceptance it would be appropriate to look at matters beyond the bare record before it.[77]

The Frye rule in many jurisdictions has been thought to consist of three requirements. The first two concern themselves with traditional general acceptance considerations.[78] The third consideration deals with the actual evidence in the case at hand. This latter consideration was first described in *People v. Kelly*[79] in the following manner, "[T]he proponent of the evidence must demonstrate that correct scientific procedures were used in the particular case."[80] It appears that much confusion has arisen concerning the scope of this requirement, much of it being generated by one legal commentator's description of the requirement as, "[T]he proper application of the technique on a particular occasion."[81] This confusion has caused some admissibility hearings to litigate the actual validity[82] of the results obtained, rather than simply determining whether general acceptance has been demonstrated. If there was any doubt about the limited extent of the current Frye admissibility inquiry in California, this doubt was recently dispelled. In a case dealing with footprint comparison evidence, the California Supreme Court finally enunciated what had been hotly debated in earlier admissibility hearings — how the tests were actually performed in the case at hand goes

---

[73]Ibid, p. 1138.

[74]Ibid, p. 1150.

[75]Ibid, p. 1151. See comments by Gaensslen, supra fn. 128.

[76]Ibid, p. 1146.

[77]Ibid, p. 1134. This seems to be a clear reference to the need for methods such as judicial notice, *infra*, fns. 137–147, to ensure that the court is evaluating the real opinions of the scientific community, rather than only those presented in the hearing contained in the record.

[78]The proponent must show that the new scientific evidence has been generally accepted as reliable through testimony elicited from qualified expert witnesses.

[79]Supra fn. 25.

[80]Ibid, at 31.

[81]Giannelli, supra fn. 1 at 1201. The only legal authority cited is Kelly, supra fn. 25.

[82]See fn. 94 for a definition of this term.

to the weight of the evidence, not to its admissibility.[83] This decision appears to put to rest many defense contentions that quality control measures and the actual validity of test results obtained in the case are relevant to California's Frye inquiry.[84]

The Evolution of the Federal Rules

As has been previously discussed,[85] the Federal Rules themselves are codified and have not changed since 1975. Frye considerations seem to have been replaced with a broader test,[86] but they remain as some of the many considerations under both the relevancy test and the expert testimony rules.[87]

The Evolution of the Relevancy Test

All evidence that is sought to be introduced into criminal trials must be relevant to some issue at the trial. If it is not relevant, it will not be admitted. Even if it is relevant it may not be admitted if its probative value is outweighed by its potential prejudicial impact.[88] Perhaps because these principles are not unique to the admissibility of novel scientific evidence, they are frequently overlooked in most legal reviews on the subject.

The most frequently cited case that purports to illustrate the application of the relevancy test is *Coppolino v. State,*[89] in which evidence was derived from a test specifically created for the criminal prosecution to detect the presence of a particular poison. It was not contended by the prosecution that the test had gained general acceptance, but rather that it was probative to a material issue, i.e., the cause of death of the decedent. The imprecision of this test would seem to allow the trial judge to consider as much or more

---

[83]"[T]he Kelly-Frye rule tests the fundamental validity of a new scientific methodology, not the degree of professionalism with which it is applied. Careless testing affects the weight of the evidence and not its admissibility and must be attacked on cross-examination or by other expert testimony." *People v. Farmer* (1989) 47 Cal. 3d 888, 913. The Farmer rationale was recently applied to conventional electrophoretic typing in *People v. Smith*, 215 Cal. App. 3d 19 (1989).

[84]Compare this narrow scope of inquiry with those issues addressed in Young, supra fn. 36, and Castro, infra fn. 98.

[85]Supra fns. 16–19.

[86]Downing, supra fn. 17. See also *U.S. v. Gipson*, 24 M.J. 246 (CMA 1987) for an analysis of the Military Rules of Evidence in a manner similar to the Federal Rules.

[87]For example, the fact that a new scientific development had not yet gained general acceptance could mandate exclusion either because the trial judge felt that this factor caused the prejudicial impact to outweigh the probative value of the evidence (Rule 403) or because the evidence is not " . . . of a type reasonably relied upon by experts in the particular field . . . " (Rule 703).

[88]Federal Rules 401–403, supra fn. 16, are merely codifications of these principles.

[89]223 So. 2d 68 (Fla. Dist. Ct. App. 1968), appeal dismissed, 234 So. 2d 120 (Fla. 1969), cert. denied, 399 U.S. 927 (1970).

material in an admissibility hearing as would be permissible in either a Frye hearing or a Federal Rules review.[90]

While some judges and legal commentators have chosen to characterize the Frye "general acceptance" analysis as a process of "head counting,"[91] clearly the record in Reilly went well beyond that simple process. Had the same testimonial record been presented in a jurisdiction that utilized a Federal Rules[92] analysis or a relevancy[93] analysis, the same legal result would almost certainly have occurred. Each admissibility standard places some emphasis on the issue of reliability — one might seem to require actual proof, another might simply require general acceptance as proof of reliability.[94] Only a semanticist could appreciate the difference![95]

APPLICATION OF CURRENT LEGAL ADMISSIBILITY TESTS TO DNA IDENTIFICATION TECHNIQUES

As the previous discussion has demonstrated, the road from Frye to the present has been a tortuous path with many detours. The electrophoresis cases[96] have signaled a return to the earlier limited screening device clearly contemplated in Frye, rather than the free-wheeling Michigan approach.[97] As such, there are clearly two technical areas where admissibility litigation is necessary: the methodology of the identification process itself and the

---

[90]For example, while the proponent of new scientific evidence has no burden of demonstrating general acceptance, the party seeking to block the evidence might be successful if it could demonstrate a lack of general acceptance to such a degree that the trial judge might feel that the proffered evidence was so unreliable that it should not be admitted.

[91]Supra fn. 15.

[92]Supra fn. 16–19.

[93]Brown, supra fn. 10.

[94]One commentator has given the following explanation, "Although courts use the terms 'validity' and 'reliability' interchangeably, the terms have distinct meanings in scientific jargon. 'Validity' refers to the ability of a test procedure to measure what it is supposed to measure its accuracy. 'Reliability' refers to whether the same results are obtained in each instance in which the test is performed its consistency. Validity includes reliability, but the converse is not necessarily true." Giannelli, supra fn. 1 at 1201 fn. 20.

[95]Even a narrow interpretation of Frye allows for cross examination of experts to probe the reasons why they may have generally accepted the evidence testing techniques.

[96]Thankfully, that legal-scientific controversy has finally been put to rest. The following is a list of some of the many cases that have reviewed the admissibility of conventional electrophoretic stain analysis. They represent analyses under Frye, relevancy, and statutes similar to the Federal Rules. *People v. Morris* (1988) 199 Cal. App. 3d 377; *Commonwealth v. Gomes* (1988) 403 Mass. 258; *Correll v. State* (Fla. 1988) 523 So.2d 562; *State v. Adams* (S.D. 1988) 418 N.W.2d 618; *People v. Partee* (1987) 157 Ill. App.3d 231, cert. denied, (1988) 108 S. Ct. 1043; *People v. Crosby* (N.Y. 1986) 116 A.D.2d 834; *Plunkett v. State* (Okla. Crim. App. 1985) 719 P.2d 834, cert. denied, 107 S. Ct. 675; *Smith v. State* (1985) 62 Md. App. 627; *Graham v. State* (1983) 168 Ga. App. 23; *State v. Chaves* (Ct. App. 1983) 100 N.M. 730; *People v. Borcsok* (N.Y. Sup. Ct. 1982) 114 Misc. 2d 810; *State v. Washington*, supra fn. 35; *Robinson v. State* (1981) 47 Md. App. 558; *State v. Rolls* (Me. 1978) 389 A.2d 824.

[97]Young, supra fn. 39; Stoughton, supra fn. 64.

population frequency statistics assigned to the DNA pattern produced by the identification process. These are separate and distinct issues, as they require expert testimony from separate but related fields and may require different methods to satisfy the burden of proof.

Methodology

A review of several contested DNA admissibility hearings[98] held to date reveals no serious challenges to or questions about the reliability of either the restriction fragment length polymorphism (RFLP) or the polymerase chain reaction (PCR) techniques themselves.[99] Both techniques have their origins in medical genetic research[100] and are performed in substantially the same manner, whether or not the material to be analyzed is described as "tissue" by a cancer researcher or as "evidence" by a police detective. Because the forensic application of DNA techniques is not substantially different from how these techniques are utilized in medical genetics research, a comparison of the transition of conventional electrophoretic

---

[98]Lifecodes was the first private lab to be seriously challenged in an admissibility hearing. *People v. Wesley*, 140 Misc. 2d 306, 533 N.Y.S. 2d 643 (Albany County Ct. 1988). The hearing was held in the latter part of 1988 and resulted in a 49-page written trial court opinion. Cellmark underwent a similar legal challenge in Fort Wayne, IN. Evidence was admitted in both cases and the defendants have been convicted. A contested admissibility hearing on the polymerase chain reaction technology was recently concluded in Paris, TX. The evidence was ruled admissible and the case is still pending. California has undergone a series of extensive, expensive admissibility hearings, all of which have resulted in the evidence being ruled admissible. After several successful admissibility hearings in the state of New York, there has been only one in which the evidence has been ruled inadmissible. That case, *People v. Castro*, in the Bronx, produced a trial court decision wherein the RFLP technology itself was deemed to have gained general acceptance, but the actual results of the RFLP analyses were deemed so unreliable that they should not be presented to the jury. The decision further allows evidence of an exclusion to be presented, but not evidence of matches. Population genetics issues were characterized as issues affecting the weight of the evidence, not its admissibility. In view of the striking similarities between New York and California case law, and in light of the previous discussion in fns. 78–84, it is difficult to comprehend the legal basis for the Castro decision's inquiry into the actual validity of the results obtained in the evidence analysis. See Harmon, "How Has DNA Evidence Fared? Beauty Is In the Eye of the Beholder," 1 Expert Evid. Reptr. 149 (Feb. 1990) for a more complete discussion of Castro. The Castro trial court decision appears to have had little impact on other New York admissibility decisions. See *People v. Shi Fu Huang*, 546 N.Y.S.2d 920 (Co. Ct. 1989). While the trial judge struggled with the reliability of the specific matching results, when the defendant Castro pled guilty, be candidly admitted what Lifecodes' results had claimed, i.e., that the blood on his watch was in fact from the victim.

[99]In a conference held at the Banbury Center, Cold Spring Harbor Laboratory, Cold Spring Harbor, NY in December 1988 involving various members of the nonforensic scientific, forensic scientific, and legal communities, great emphasis was placed on the need for quality control procedures, with little or no concern voiced with regard to the soundness of the technology itself. (The proceedings of this conference will be published in the near future under the title, "DNA Technology and Forensic Science," Banbury Report 32.)

[100]"New Frontiers in Genetic Medicine-UCLA Conference," *Ann. Intern. Med.* 104:527–539 (1986). Ou, Kwok, Mitchell, Mack, Snisky, Krebs, Feorino, Warfield, Schochetman, "DNA Amplification for Direct Detection of HIV-1 in DNA of Peripheral Blood Mononuclear Cells," *Science* 239:295 (1988).

genetic marker analyses with DNA identification techniques from the research to the forensic community reveals that both of these analytical methodologies have had similar transitional histories.

Also, as in the earlier electrophoretic admissibility controversy, the focus of the legal concern to date appears to be on what might occur in the less than perfect environmental conditions present in many forensic situations.[101] As in the earlier studies concerning conventional genetic marker development, studies and experiments have been conducted to determine the limitations of the DNA identification techniques.[102] The clear consensus of opinion seems to be that the techniques themselves produce either a correct result or none at all.[103] Moreover, even if the technology itself were capable of producing an incorrect result, it is highly improbable that the result would be an incorrect identification of an innocent person. It is significantly more likely that an error will erroneously exclude the truly guilty party.[104] While quality control guidelines (to ensure that the correct results are obtained every time) and contamination studies (to provide knowledge of the effect of contaminants) are important factors for scientists utilizing these analytical methods to take into consideration, the legal process should defer to the scientific consensus of opinion, rather than repeat Michigan's misguided scientific dabbling. A recent scientific publication presents an overview of the substantial body of scientific literature that is already in place for some of these techniques.[105]

Population Genetics

As with the analysis of the conventional genetic markers, the DNA methodology allows scientists to identify patterns and to compare results. It is the application of principles of population genetics to the DNA test results that permits scientists to illustrate the uniqueness of one person when com-

---

[101]A detailed discussion of the impact of these factors is beyond the scope of this chapter and will be discussed in other chapters. Suffice it to say, however, that the effects of heat, sun, humidity, and chemical contamination among other factors can impact on the ability to produce typing results and the quality of those results.

[102]Kanter, Baird, Shaler, and Balazs "Analysis of Restriction Fragment Length Polymorphisms in Deoxyribonucleic Acid (DNA) Recorded from Bloodstains," *J. For. Sci.* 31:403–408 (1986).

[103]Andrews, infra fn. 111; Wesley, supra fn. 98; Beeler, supra fn. 5

[104]This is a principle described as the consequence of error—an error would almost in every instance inure to the benefit of the truly guilty person and result in his exoneration. See Reilly, supra fn. 70 and Andrews, infra fn. 111 for legal recognition of the significance of this point. It is always possible in any human endeavor for human error to occur. For example, if a technician were to erroneously mix a known and an evidence sample, an erroneous positive identification could take place. This is a quality control concern and has nothing to do with the reliability of the technology itself.

[105]Fowler, Burgoyne, Scott, and Harding "Repetitive Deoxyribonucleic Acid (DNA) and Human Genome Variation—A Concise Review Relevant to Forensic Biology," *J. For. Sci.* 33:1111 (1988). This reference lists 133 peer-reviewed publications in existence at the time it was written, i.e., December 1987.

pared with another person or with evidence that is of material interest. It is the combining of a restriction enzyme with a probe or series of probes and the subsequent analysis of adequately large numbers of representative blood samples that is the first step in the process of developing a statistical database.[106]

Utilizing a principle known as Hardy–Weinberg equilibrium[107] to ensure that the DNA patterns ("genetic markers") produced in these population frequency studies match what would be expected if the DNA patterns resulted from Mendelian inheritance, it is possible to predict how frequently combinations of patterns might randomly match.[108] Critics of the admissibility of this type of statistical evidence suggest that the size of these studies[109] has been too small to accurately use the results in court. These criticisms are not well founded, however, because once equilibrium is demonstrated, the probabilities derived therefrom will remain unchanged no matter how large the sample becomes.[110]

Four criminal cases have reached the level of published legal precedent.[111] Coincidentally, Andrews, which was the first to be published, was also the first criminal conviction in the United States that was supported by DNA evidence. The court's analysis initially reflected some confusion about which legal admissibility standard should be applied,[112] seemingly analyzing the issues under Frye first[113] and then under a relevancy standard.[114] The decision seems to follow the trend established by the Plunkett/Reilly/

---

[106]Baird, Balazs, Giusti, Miyazaki, Nicholas, et al. "Allele Frequency Distribution of Two Highly Polymorphic DNA Sequences in Three Ethnic Groups and its Application to Determination of Paternity," *Am. J. Hum. Gen.* 39:489–501. (1986).

[107]See Sourcebook, infra fn. 128 pp. 39–42 for a brief but concise discussion of the subject.

[108]Ibid.

[109]Baird, supra fn. 106.

[110]Andrews, infra fn. 111 at 850. Sourcebook, infra fn. 128. See also discussion of the Castro decision, supra fn. 98, as it relates to population genetics issues. These general population statistics concerns are in no way unique to forensic DNA identification techniques. See Thornton, "DNA Profiling: New Tool Links Evidence to Suspects with High Certainty," *C & E News*, November 20, 1989, pp. 18–30.

[111]*Andrews v. State*, 533 So.2d 841 (Fla. App. 5 Dist. 1988). The testing in the case was performed by one of the two labs utilizing RFLP technology, i.e., Lifecodes. In addition, Andrews' second conviction has also been upheld in a one-page opinion, *State v. Andrews*, 533 So.2d 851. The second published appellate decision occurred in Maryland. In *Cobey v. State* (No. 1515), filed June 29, 1989, the Maryland Court of Special Appeals upheld the admissibility of DNA RFLP typing performed by Cellmark. The opinion analyzed the issues under Frye. In addition, the opinion refers to legislation to be effective January 1, 1990, which renders DNA evidence admissible in all criminal trials. Next was *Spencer v. Commonwealth*, 384 S.E.2d 775 (Va. 1989). The evidence was deemed admissible under Virginia's "relevancy" analysis. The court also felt that it would be admissible under a Frye analysis.

[112]Ibid, at 843.

[113]Ibid, at 847, fn. 6.

[114]Ibid, at 849–850. Actually the court combined Florida's codified analysis with the analysis described in Downing, supra, fn. 17.

Gomes[115] line of cases, which reflect a narrow review of admissibility that is similar to what Frye initially prescribed, rather than the Michigan "science court" approach.[116]

As to the "disinterested witness" issue, the court was in full agreement with Reilly[117] when it responded, "Neither Frye nor our evidence code require impartiality" in response to the defense's comparison of one of Lifecodes' scientists to the voiceprint developers.[118] The court also seemed to view several additional factors as important: a) that DNA identification techniques are used extensively in fields other than forensics, b) that there is a body of specialized literature dealing with the technique, and c) that the techniques had already been used to exonerate those suspected of criminal activity.[119] The court recognized that it was virtually impossible to incorrectly identify a person due to an error in the methodology itself.[120] On the issue of the population frequency data produced by these techniques, the court properly recognized that there is nothing new or "novel" about how those calculations are made and, further, that those population genetics principles have been generally accepted by scientists since the 1920s.[121] The only adverse legal admissability decision to date occurred in *State v. Schwartz*, 447 N.W.2d 422 (Minn. 1989). The court analyzed the evidence under Frye because it " . . . facilitates more objective and uniform rulings," but reached a conclusion inconsistent with previous Frye analyses on the same subject.

The use of statistics in criminal cases is not without some legal controversy, however. In Minnesota the prevailing legal view, that the use of statistical evidence is " . . . (U)nfairly prejudicing to a defendant due to its potentially exaggerated impact on the trier of fact," was reiterated as

---

[115]Supra fn. 96.

[116]Supra, fns. 36, 64. These opinions reflect a tendency for Michigan courts to advise scientists what they should be accepting, rather than letting the scientists decide for themselves.

[117]Supra fn. 70.

[118]Andrews, supra fn. 111 at 849, fn. 9. What is most remarkable about this finding is not that it was made, since comparisons between Baird and Lt. Nash should always have produced this judgment upon rational reflection on the issue. The remarkable part is that the legal authority relied upon is in part a Michigan case, *People v. Tobey* (Mich., 1977) 257 N.W. 537, which was reflected upon when the Michigan Supreme Court decided Young, supra fn. 36 and which that court used to totally disregard the opinions of Messrs. Kearney and Stolorow, supra, fn. 59.

[119]Ibid, at 850.

[120]Ibid, at 850. This echoes the Reilly opinion's concern with the same issue, supra fn. 70. This aspect of the Andrews opinion, as well as the others previously discussed, reflects an evaluation of the evidence by the "reasonably reliable" standard, supra fn. 17.

[121]Ibid. This has particular significance in Frye jurisdictions. Since there is nothing "novel" involved, there is no need to prove general acceptance, nor need one be concerned about the disinterested witness rule. Even the "celebrated" Castro decision, supra fn. 98, recognizes this point, having characterized this issue as one going to weight, not admissibility.

recently as 1987[122] in a case involving the use of conventional electrophoretic genetic marker analyses. Interestingly, the rule does not prohibit the use of the typing evidence to illustrate that there is a match in all typable characteristics, nor does it prevent statistics from being used to describe the percent of the population that might share each of the individual marker characteristics. The prohibition is only against multiplying these individual marker characteristics (by use of the "product rule") to depict the small percent of the population that shares all of the markers.[123]

A related topic deserving of legal scrutiny concerns the use of statistical evidence in criminal cases. This analysis involves an inquiry into the actual basis for individual frequency determinations and whether or not there is a basis for using the "product rule" to multiply individual frequencies. Most jurisdictions that have engaged in this exercise have done so citing the California *People v. Collins* decision.[124] In Collins, a robbery case where the

---

[122]*State v. Kim*, 398 N.W.2d 544 at 548 (Minn. 1987). Compare with Rule 704, Federal Rules of Evidence which specifically allow expert testimony, even when it "embraces an ultimate issue."

[123]Ibid at 549. Since research had been conducted to demonstrate that the occurrence of a pattern produced by one conventional genetic marker was independent of the occurrence of another pattern produced by another genetic marker, it was scientifically correct to multiply these individual frequencies to reflect the frequency of concurrence of all the marker types obtained. The genesis of Minnesota's singular view on this subject can be found in *State v. Carlson*, 267 N.W. 2d 170 (Minn. 1978). There were two areas of scientific evidence that produced results with statistical significance—electrophoretic bloodstain analysis and hair comparison. This opinion chose not to proscribe the use of statistical evidence derived from the bloodstains, but limited its decision to preventing the hair comparison statistics from being introduced. For some reason and without apparent explanation for the change, the Kim court chose to apply the rule to bloodstain evidence as well. What would the impact be on applying this rule in a DNA case? After hearing testimony that everyone's DNA is uniquely different, if the population frequency data is banned, a jury could be left with the erroneous impression that the forensic test demonstrated that uniqueness, even if it had not. The statistics provide a truer perspective of the actual "match". Minnesota has recently enacted statutes that require DNA evidence to be scrutinized under a "relevancy" analysis, and that would permit the use of statistics utilizing the product rule. See Harmon, supra fn. 98, for a more complete discussion of the Schwartz/Minnesota experience.

[124]68 Cal. 2d 319, 438 P.2d 33 (1968). These statistics were deficient because there was an inadequate evidentiary foundation for the frequency assigned to individual factors, and there was no proof that these events were statistically independent of one another so that the product rule could be applied.The same issues appear to have been raised by one of the defense witnesses in the Castro case, Dr. Eric Lander. (Dr. Lander was one of the participants in the Banbury Conference, supra fn. 99.) In a non-peer-reviewed commentary in *Nature*, Vol. 339 pp. 501–505, which was rushed to publication while the Castro hearing was still being conducted, Dr. Lander severely criticized the specific work done in the case in both the molecular biology and population genetics aspects. In spite of his criticisms in the latter area, they were not significant enough to play a role in the trial court opinion. Lander has recently come under criticism from one of the other prominent scientists involved in Castro. Dr. Richard Roberts, from the prestigious Cold Spring Harbor Laboratory, subsequently commented, "Lander is a theatrical chap. I think he went overboard in exaggerating the problems in order to stress that there were problems." See "How Barry Scheck and Peter Neufeld Tripped up the DNA Experts," *The American Lawyer*, p. 55 (Dec. 1989).

identity of the robbers was based on partial physical descriptions, a mathematics professor testifying for the prosecution arbitrarily assigned frequencies to factors such as hair styles, racially mixed couples, and automobile characteristics, among other factors. The witness was then permitted to multiply these frequencies together to produce a number larger than the population of Los Angeles. This evidence was touted by the prosecution as tending to prove the identity of the defendants as the robbers.

Many criminal appeals have cited the Collins case while unsuccessfully challenging the use of statistical evidence in blood typing situations.[125] Even Minnesota recognizes that the Collins concerns have been satisfied in calculating conventional blood-typing statistics. The same population genetics principles that were applied in published conventional marker frequency data have also been used in published DNA allele frequency data.[126] Even should these frequencies be legally scrutinized under the Collins rule, there is no reason why the same legal results should not be achieved.

DEFENSE ISSUES

Quite often, defense attorneys involved in hearings relating to the conventional electrophoresis techniques have been successful in broadening the scope of the admissibility hearings by injecting issues well beyond the scope of the legal admissibility standards previously discussed. Some of those issues include:

- Has every step in the technology in use been published in a peer review publication?
- Has there been subsequent critical review of those published methods either concurring or refuting the earlier publication?[127]
- Have there been any changes to any of the peer review published methods? Have these methods undergone this peer review/peer review review process? If not, why not?

---

[125]Carlson, supra fn. 123 at 175; Reilly, supra fn. 70; Brown, supra fn. 45.
[126]Compare Grunbaum, supra fn. 41, and Baird, et al, fn. 106.
[127]The Young, supra fn. 36, and Stoughton, supra fn. 64, rationales do not make sense without their unusual analysis on this subject. These courts took the position that until a scientist repeated another scientist's work contained in a peer-review publication and published his or her concurring opinion, the earlier work had not yet been scientifically validated. The same courts would not apply the converse, however, that if the development of a technique was published and no subsequent published refutation ensued, that would not suffice as validation, no matter how much time had elapsed since the earlier publication. See also fn. 61 on this subject. This latter position was recently taken by a defense witness, Dr. Neville Coleman, in a foundational hearing in Albany, NY, supra fn. 98. He maintained that until Lifecodes' population frequency studies were duplicated by another scientist and these results were also published in a peer-review publication, they could not be relied upon because until then " . . . (I)t's a collection of typed words on a page." Hearing transcript page 406. Dr. Coleman seems clearly to adhere to Michigan's singular legal approach to science, supra fn. 63.

- Have contamination studies been conducted involving all potential sources of contamination known to mankind?[128]
- Does the lab participate in proficiency testing?[129]
- What have the results been?
- Who made the mistake?
- Why?
- What is the nature of the error?[130]
- What quality control/quality assurance methods are in place to ensure that the correct result is produced each time the methodology is utilized?
- If the courts were to exclude the evidence permanently, would this exclusion have an impact on the witness's future earning potential?[131]

Most of these topics are certainly valid topics for discussion at some point. Some bear directly on what is commonly known as the scientific method.[132] Others would seem to bear on the licensing or regulation of laboratories. Yet others reflect on the competence of the person performing the test. The proper forum to discuss these issues, however, is within the scientific community, in publications dedicated to forensic science, such as the *Journal of Forensic Science,* and during the conferences, symposia, and workshops that occur quite frequently. It is only in such settings that free and open debate on the issues can be had and wherein some true measure of the scientific community's opinion can be taken. Forcing these debates to

---

[128]Distinctions must be made about whether these are lawyers' requirements for scientists or whether scientists impose these conditions on themselves. On October 5, 1988, the New York State Assembly Standing Committee on the Judiciary conducted a hearing to investigate the application of DNA fingerprinting. Several prominent scientists spoke to the panel. One of them, Robert Gaensslen (author, *Sourcebook in Forensic Serology, Immunology, and Biochemistry*, National Institute of Justice, 1983) had these comments on the contaminant issue: " . . . (I)t's part of the nature of scientific testing and inquiry that when you do some tests under one set of conditions or with one set of specimens, the results enable you to make some predictions about the behavior of the test under other circumstances and conditions and with other samples. These predictions, if they turn out to be true, uniformly and across the board, can relieve you from the possibility of having to test a procedure under every imaginable condition on earth and with every imaginable contaminant on earth, which clearly is out of the question." Transcript p. 244.

[129]Professor George Sensabaugh, supra fn. 52, in a presentation at a semiannual meeting of the American Chemical Society on September 27, 1988, provided some caution about relying on voluntary proficiency test results as an indication of anything more than the proficiency of the analyst at that time, on that test. Some have tried to equate proficiency test performances in general with part of the "reasonably reliable" test, supra fn. 17, "the potential rate of error." The comparison is misplaced, however. Cases that discuss the error rate factor do so in the context of the error rate inherent in the technology itself and not in the person performing the process. See fn. 104.

[130]Supra, fns. 76, 120.

[131]Young, supra fn. 36.

[132]Imwinkelreid, "The 'Bases' of Expert Testimony: The Syllogistic Structure of Scientific Testimony," 67 N. Car. L. Rev. 1, 2 (1988). "The scientist begins by postulating an hypothesis. She next designs an experiment to verify or disprove the hypothesis and then conducts the experiment and attempts to correlate the experimental results with the hypothesis. The scientist accepts the hypothesis as scientific truth only if the experimental results validate the hypothesis. The essence of the scientific process is, therefore, inductive reasoning."

take place in a courtroom setting, governed by legal rules of evidence, where one side is necessarily for and the other side is necessarily against, can only confuse the issues.[133]

The preceding legal analysis has demonstrated that, despite the misguided Michigan experience,[134] the admissibility inquiry remains today a limited one. The admissibility standards in all their forms were only designed to prevent the premature presentation of novel evidence to juries. No legal test has ever required that actual validity of results be proven before presentation to the jury.[135] Many of these topics appear to be more appropriately addressed to the scientific community at a point before a consensus of opinion has been reached, rather than in courtrooms, after a consensus has been reached and while the taxpayers are footing the bill for the considerable expert witness fees.[136]

SUBSEQUENT HEARINGS—JUDICIAL NOTICE

How long must admissibility hearings continue to be held once there have already been trial court determinations that DNA typing evidence is admissible? In Frye jurisdictions, the obvious answer is until the appellate courts dictate that they need no longer be held. Since there is often a gap of a few years between a conviction and a final appellate decision, this delay imposes a significant burden on the legal system, which may not, in the author's opinion, be absolutely necessary.

The issue is less clear in jurisdictions that adhere to a codified/relevancy/ Federal Rules approach. Since "novelty" may be only one of many permissible considerations in deciding whether or not to admit scientific evidence in these jurisdictions, published legal opinions upholding a trial court's decision to admit such evidence would seem to have less legal impact than in a Frye jurisdiction, wherein published precedent upholding admissibility ends

---

[133]In the Castro case, supra fn. 98, witnesses from both sides met apart from the attorneys in the case and drafted a joint statement, which is mentioned in the *Nature* article, supra fn. 124. They agreed that, based on their courtroom experiences, the adversary system may not be the most appropriate method for reaching scientific consensus.

[134]Young, supra fn. 36; Stoughton, supra fn. 64.

[135]In a forensic odontology presentation given to a California District Attorneys' Association audience in December 1988, one of the bitemark legal admissibility pioneers, Dr. Gerald Vale (*People v. Marx*, 54 Cal. App. 3d 100, 111, *People v. Slone*, 76 Cal. App. 3d 611, 621), commented that, were bitemark evidence to have been scrutinized the way serological evidence has been legally scrutinized, it might have had difficulty passing a Frye inquiry.

[136]To resolve the issues within the scientific community would seem to ensure that the issues are truly scientific ones, investigated as such, rather than trying to resolve them in court, at taxpayer expense, at the current expert witness rates of $150 an hour. In one admissibility hearing in California, an expert witness earned well in excess of $100,000 in consulting fees. Brown "DNA and Kelly-Frye: Who will Survive in California," *Criminal Justice J.* 11:1, 76, fn. 476 (1988).

the need to continue to conduct admissibility hearings.[137] These other admissibility standards appear to allow foundational hearings to continue *ad infinitem*.

Regardless of which admissibility standard applies, there does appear to be an appropriate legal device that permits the proponent of the scientific evidence to alert the trial court that other hearings have been held elsewhere, resulting in decisions to admit the evidence.[138] These admissibility hearings represent one of the few instances when the criminal justice system is concerned with issues of actual reality of an issue beyond the walls of the courtroom in which the admissibility hearing is being conducted.[139] Over the years, appellate courts have routinely taken judicial notice of matters of science and medicine in order to decide issues identical to those currently addressed in legal admissibility hearings.[140] Sometimes these matters are noticed at the request of the parties and sometimes the courts apparently do so on their own initiative.[141] Perhaps it is because these courts recognize that their decision will have a jurisdictionwide impact that they attempt to consider matters well beyond the bare trial court record.

Most jurisdictions have codified the concept of judicial notice. Often these statutes distinguish between mandatory and permissive judicial notice. Using California's statutory scheme as an illustration, the distinction between mandatory and permissive is made according to the nature of the subject matter to be noticed:

1. *Section 451 California Evidence Code* — This is the mandatory section. It includes subjects such as decisional, constitutional, and public statutory laws; rules of professional conduct; rules of pleading, practice, and procedure; and the true signification of all English words, among its topics.
2. *Section 452 California Evidence Code* — This is the permissive notice section. It includes subjects such as any regulations of any public entity, official acts of any federal or state department, facts not reasonably subject to dispute, and the records of any court in California among its many

---

[137]See, e.g., Kelly, supra fn. 25 at 32.

[138]Downing, supra fn. 17 at 1241, actually describes testimony and judicial decisions in other cases involving the same subject matter as areas appropriate for the *in limine* hearing to be held pursuant to the Federal Rules. These same rules would also seem to allow the defense to take judicial notice of any trial court "victories" they achieve in blocking admissibility of this evidence. As of September 1989, Castro, supra fn. 98, is the only case that might be helpful in that regard.

[139]Supra fn. 77. The hearing is an attempt to determine the true status of scientific evidence through the testimony of selected witnesses who purport to represent a cross section of views of the scientific community.

[140]Judicial notice taken of scientific and legal articles. *People v. Kelly*, 17 Cal. 3d 24, 35. *People v. Palmer*, 80 Cal. App. 3d 239. Recently, judicial notice of other trial court Frye transcripts and trial court decisions was approved in *People v. Smith*, supra fn. 83. The trial judge relied on the transcript of the hearing in Reilly, supra fn. 70, and other Alameda County hearings before Reilly had been upheld on appeal.

[141]Kelly, Palmer, ibid; Brown, supra fn. 45.

topics. It is the last provision that applies to legal-scientific disputes such as Frye-admissibility considerations.

A number of California cases permit judicial notice of documents, transcripts of hearings, and findings in other cases.[142] None of these decisions, however, appear to be concerned with the right to confront and cross examine witnesses, perhaps because the California statutes also provide for the appointment of expert witnesses to provide advice on the subject matter sought to be judicially noticed.[143]

The statute further provides each party with an opportunity to present information to persuade the court either to grant or deny the request for judicial notice.[144] Opinions that deem matters in other court's records appropriate for judicial notice do so when there has been some level of scrutiny in that proceeding to ensure reliability of the records.[145] Where the item sought to be noticed is merely an allegation or declaration that has never been ruled upon, judicial notice is deemed inappropriate.[146] Nothing in the statutory scheme prevents either party from presenting any additional evidence in an admissibility hearing to either support or rebut the matters judicially noticed. This would even seem to allow the opponent to the judicial notice request an opportunity to further cross examine witnesses involved in the other proceedings. The only danger involved in this practice would be if appellate decisions were to later pronounce the records judicially noticed to be inadequate to satisfy the legal admissibility standard.[147] If that were to occur, all cases having judicially noticed the record might also suffer the same legal consequences as the underlying case.

There is another practical alternative to judicial notice that should achieve a result that is similar in effect. Since it is impractical and impossible to present testimony from all knowledgeable witnesses in every admis-

---

[142]*People v. Maxwell*, 78 Cal. App.3d 124, 131 (1978) (transcripts), *In re Tanya F.*, 111 Cal. App.3d 436, 440 (1980) (notice taken of juvenile court records in another case to establish material facts).

[143]"Where the advice of persons learned in the subject matter is required in order to enable the court to take judicial notice of a matter, the court may on its own motion or on the motion of any party may appoint one or more of such persons to provide such advice . . . " Section 460 Calif. Evid. Code.

[144]"If the trial court has been requested to take or has taken or proposes to take judicial notice of such matter, the court shall afford each party reasonable opportunity, before the jury is instructed or before the cause is submitted for decision by the court, to present to the court information relevant to (1) the propriety of taking judicial notice of the matter and (2) the tenor of the matter to be noticed." Section 455 Calif. Ev. Code.

[145]*Maxwell, Tanya F.*, supra fn. 142.

[146]*People v. Thacker* (1985) 175 Cal. App. 3d 594. If this rationale were a condition precedent to allowing new information to be presented via an *amicus curiae* brief, supra fn. 44, it is questionable whether California's electrophoresis legal controversy would have occurred.

[147]In California, many cases utilized permissive judicial notice of the Reilly admissibility hearing record and decision to satisfy the initial burden imposed by Kelly-Frye, before Reilly was affirmed on appeal. As luck would have it, Reilly became the precedent case and none of those cases suffered any adverse legal impact as a result thereof.

sibility hearing, transcripts from prior hearings may serve as the basis of other expert witnesses' testimony in subsequent hearings. All that would seem to be required is to provide a copy of the transcript to the witness, court, and opposing counsel. Once the witness has had an opportunity to review the transcript, he or she would then be able to rely on the content as one of the bases for his or her own expert testimony. This would then allow the transcript itself to become an exhibit and to be made a part of the record.

DNA Computer Databases

Much discussion has recently centered on the creation of DNA type databases that would store records of DNA patterns that are similar to those already in existence in many jurisdictions for fingerprint comparisons. While these systems hold a great deal of promise as an asset to law enforcement,[148] they appear to be many years away. At present, each lab providing forensic DNA services has developed its own battery of test components, i.e., restriction enzymes and probes.[149] The DNA pattern produced by one combination of restriction enzymes and probes will not be the same as the pattern produced by a different restriction enzyme-probe combination. Thus, unless all forensic labs performing DNA analyses use the same combinations of enzymes and probes, comparison of different DNA patterns will be meaningless. Since the choice of these test components is currently in a state of flux as forensic labs are constantly seeking to refine their capabilities, attempts to standardize the methodology in order to permit the creation of such a DNA computer database at this point might be premature.

The goal of this type of database would be to compare known, stored DNA patterns of previously identified persons with DNA patterns derived from evidence associated with crimes. In order for such a database to provide a meaningful contribution to law enforcement, all physiological evidence collected from a crime scene or a possible suspect must be immediately typed for DNA patterns, to permit subsequent comparison with patterns stored in the database.

---

[148]Under the authority of Calif. Penal Code Section 290.2, persons convicted of most sex offenses are required to submit blood and saliva samples for typing. Once a computer database is created, it will be possible to compare newly analyzed evidence with types stored therein and also with other newly analyzed evidence arising from other jurisdictions that interface with the database. Depending on the quality of the evidence and the specificity of the results derived therefrom, it will be possible to identify a specific individual if that person's pattern is stored in the database.

[149]The FBI has initially chosen to use three probes used by Lifecodes and one used by Cellmark, as well as a restriction enzyme that is different than those used by either Cellmark or Lifecodes. The patterns generated by these testing components will necessarily be different than those produced by Cellmark or Lifecodes, and cannot be compared with each other.

At present, most government crime labs or private labs would be unable to provide the services necessary to make this assumption a reality. There would have to be a significant increase in staffing of forensic serologists to provide the services necessary to analyze evidence promptly for comparison with the database. Until that occurs, the database should probably be considered a long-term goal, rather than a quick fix.

A third concern related to the development of DNA databases involves the privacy rights of persons whose DNA prints are to be stored therein. The concern is that unauthorized access to this information might reveal genetic information about the person to his or her detriment. These are legitimate concerns that have already been identified, recognized, and discussed.[150] One obvious solution is to restrict access to the information. Another solution lies in the nature of the technology itself. The RFLP technique only utilizes segments of a person's DNA that has no known genetic function. As a result, disclosure of one's known stored DNA pattern could not possibly reveal aspects of one's genetic make-up or predisposition for some genetically caused condition. The PCR technique amplifies and identifies a segment of DNA that has a genetic function.[151] Due to this factor, unauthorized access to a DNA pattern produced by utilizing this technique could conceivably reveal genetic information about a person that could be used to their detriment by prospective employers, insurers, or any other party who would gain an advantage through the disclosure of this information. Other than limiting access, additional safeguards appear to be necessary to prevent abuses of information currently being produced by this technique.[152]

Legal Gamesmanship Versus Science

In virtually all criminal cases in the United States involving DNA evidence, the prosecutor has been the proponent of the evidence. As would be expected, defense attorneys have objected each and every time. The technology has also been used many times as an investigative tool by members of various law enforcement agencies to clear suspects before charging or to dismiss pending cases where science has provided exonerating evidence. In almost all instances, the dismissals have occurred without putting the defense to the task of satisfying the applicable legal foundational test, even though legal precedent imposes the same burden of proof on the defense as is required of the prosecution.

In view of this apparently overwhelming acceptance of DNA identification evidence by prosecutors, one would hope that prosecutors will continue to accept the science at face value without resorting to the legal gamesman-

---

[150]Banbury Conference, supra fn. 99.

[151]Marx, "Multiplying Genes by Leaps and Bounds," *Science* 240:1408 (1988).

[152]Banbury, supra fn. 99. The entire first morning's session was focused on this subject.

ship available to defense attorneys to try to block its admissibility when the tests produce a result inconsistent with their theory of the case. On the other hand, defense attorneys may eventually find themselves in somewhat of a bind if they are successful in blocking the admissibility of DNA evidence that inculpates their client in one case; prosecutors may subsequently be unwilling to concede admissibility of the same type of evidence that could exonerate a different client in a different case.

In summary, it appears that scientific evidence neither suffers nor benefits, depending upon which legal admissibility standard is being applied. Each rule has its strong and weak points, but they all would seem to allow a zealous opponent to the evidence to litigate many of the same subjects under different provisions of the different rules.[153] Differences in admissibility rules simply seem to control the method of litigation and the significance of some of the subjects to be litigated.

The introduction of DNA identification techniques in criminal trials has also demonstrated the willingness of prosecutors and defense attorneys to learn to face a new challenge. The quality of the contested DNA admissibility hearings to date is proof of this willingness; the absence of qualified witnesses voicing concerns relevant to substantial legal admissibility considerations is the strongest indication that DNA identification techniques are here to stay.

---

[153]See, e.g. fns. 19, 86, and 87 for different ways to consider general acceptance.

9. DNA Testing in Criminal Cases: A Defense Perspective

ALLAN D. HYMER, Esq.

PRELIMINARY CONSIDERATIONS

There has recently been an extensive amount of discussion concerning the utilization of DNA evidence by law enforcement agencies and the courts with regard to the identification and conviction of criminals.[1] Moreover, DNA test results have now been admitted into evidence in numerous state trial courts for these purposes.[2] To date, however, there have been only two state appellate decisions affirming the introduction of such evidence.[3] It is thus the intent of this chapter to demystify the use of DNA evidence in criminal cases by focusing on the resolution of some of the legal and scien-

---

[1]This chapter presupposes a general knowledge of the techniques and terminology of DNA testing, e.g., testing procedures such as the restriction fragment length polymorphism (RFLP) and polymerase chain reaction (PCR) techniques, as well as the organizations currently performing these tests, i.e., Cellmark Diagnostics, Lifecodes Corporation, and Cetus Corporation/Forensic Science Associates. Other chapters in this book discuss these matters in greater detail. For additional information regarding the legal ramifications of forensic DNA testing, see, e.g., Note "DNA Identification Tests and the Courts," 63 Washington L. R. 903 (Oct. 1988); Pearsall "DNA Printing: The Unexamined 'Witness' in Criminal Trials," 77 Cal. L. R. 1001; and, especially, Thompson & Ford "DNA Typing: Acceptance and Weight of the New Genetic Identification Tests," 75 Virginia L. R. 45 (Feb. 1989).

[2]It has been estimated that DNA test evidence has led to perhaps 200 convictions and a few acquittals in the United States. See *Scientific American* (August, 1989) "Science and the Citizen", pages 12–12B. See also, "DNA Findings are Disputed by Scientists," *The New York Times*, p. B1, May 25, 1989.

[3]*Andrews v. State*, 533 So.2d 841 (Fla. Ct. App., Oct. 1988); *Cobey v. State*, 559 A.2d 391 (Md. App. 1989); the decision of a New York court of trial jurisdiction has also been published: *People v. Wesley*, 140 Misc.2d 306, 533 N.Y.S.2d 643 (Albany County Court 1988). Moreover, in *People v. Castro*, a murder case in Bronx, NY, the court recently completed a lengthy pretrial admissibility hearing wherein the prosecution's witnesses on the subject of DNA fingerprinting admitted that the testing was improperly performed. See, e.g., "DNA Fingerprinting: Pitfalls Come to Light," *Nature*, 339:89 (1989). In *Minnesota v. Schwartz*, 447 N.W.2d 422 (Minn. Supreme Ct. Nov. 1989) the court found that DNA testing had gained general acceptance in the scientific community but still declared the testing results inadmissible because the testing laboratory (Cellmark) was not shown to

---

tific issues raised by the introduction of this evidence. Along the way, the author additionally hopes to encourage further exploration of a number of as yet uncharted areas of inquiry relating to this new technology.

Introduction of DNA Evidence by the Prosecution

Once a person is suspected or charged with a crime, several scenarios are possible that involve the testing of DNA evidence. For purposes of illustration, the following hypothetical (but perhaps fairly typical) fact pattern is provided. A woman's body is found in a deserted area. During the postmortem investigation, the pathologist gathers semen from her vagina and underclothing. The defendant, who was last seen following the woman out of a bar on the night of her death, is arrested and charged with the crime. The prosecutor then has the evidentiary semen sample and reference blood samples from the defendant and the victim sent either to a private forensic laboratory (see, e.g., fn. 1), the FBI laboratory,[4] or a local municipal laboratory equipped to analyze this type of evidence, with a request for a DNA comparison. The laboratory report concerning this testing might typically read as follows: The patterns derived from the DNA in the defendant's blood and from the semen sample taken from the vaginal swab were indistinguishable. This similarity might be expected to occur in the population 1 time in 45,419,940.[5] Not surprisingly, the prosecutor would like to have these test results admitted as evidence at trial.

Introduction of DNA Evidence by the Defense

There may, however, be many situations in which the prosecution will not have the evidence tested, at least initially. For example, in a typical rape case, the defendant may maintain that he is innocent, but that he has no alibi. The defense attorney in such a situation should seek to obtain the evidentiary semen stain through discovery so that an expert retained by the defense can compare the defendant's control DNA to the DNA contained in the evidentiary stain. If the test indicates that there is no match between the evidentiary stain and the defendant's control sample, the defense will want to introduce the exclusion of the defendant as the semen donor at the trial. However, if there is a match, the defense will seek to keep the evidence out of the trial and will attempt to keep the prosecution from acquiring discovery of the DNA test result. In fact, the defense should seek an order of the

---

have comported with appropriate laboratory standards, nor was proper discovery of testing data and results made to the defense. The court also found that the statistical results were inadmissible because of preexisting Minnesota case law (*State v. Kim* (1987) 398 N.W.2d 544).

[4]The Federal Bureau of Investigation laboratory is the first government laboratory to begin conducting DNA analyses on actual case evidence.

[5]The statistical analysis of DNA test data has recently been questioned in *People v. Castro*, fn. 3 supra. See also "DNA Fingerprinting: Pitfalls Come to Light," *Nature* 339:89 (1989).

court by a motion *in limine*,[6] which prohibits the prosecution from even mentioning at the trial that the defense has done any DNA testing.

Retestinq the DNA Sample

Finally the defense, and in some cases the prosecution, may seek to obtain the remainder of the evidentiary seminal stain through discovery in order to have it retested by an independent expert. If either side thinks it likely that an adverse result will be admitted at trial, or if the initial test is inconclusive, or if there are questions about the bias or reliability of the laboratory conducting the initial test, such retesting should be required.

The sample must not have been depleted by the initial testing procedure, however, if retesting is to remain as an option. Some DNA testing procedures, such as the restriction fragment length polymorphism (RFLP) method of analysis, require far more sample material than do methods such as the polymerase chain reaction (PCR) procedure. Thus the preservation and reanalysis of samples is likely to become a major concern for the defense bar if DNA evidence is routinely accepted by the courts.

Questions have been raised in view of this practice, however, which include: Who is to determine which testing method is to be used to ensure that reliable retesting is possible? What procedures must be followed to preserve a sample for retesting? Should the presence of an expert for the adverse party be permitted during the initial testing? These are but a few of the issues that must be addressed. Moreover, the defense attorney will have to be assured of confidentiality before conducting a retest in case such a test inculpates the defendant.

If defense attorneys are to play an important role in resolving such questions advantageously, they must be prepared to recognize at the earliest stages of the case that DNA testing may be a possibility, either because the prosecution may want to have such tests performed in order to inculpate the defendant or because the defense may want to develop proof that the DNA evidence excludes the defendant from having committed the crime. The defense must then be prepared to file appropriate evidentiary motions, including motions for discovery, to preserve evidence in the hands of the prosecution, to retain portions of the evidence sample for retesting, and to maintain the confidentiality of defense testing, to name but a few.[7]

If the defense does test or retest evidentiary samples for the presence or absence of a DNA match, one question that must be answered is, will the results of the test remain confidential to the defense or is the prosecution to be accorded discovery? There are few criminal defense attorneys who would initiate testing when it might have the result of proving the case against their

---

[6]See, e.g., Rothblatt, et al. "The Motion in Limine in Criminal Trials: A Technique for the Pretrial Exclusion of Prejudicial Evidence," 60 *Kentucky L. J.* 611 (1972).

[7]An excellent text providing useful case authority for such motions is Giannelli & Imwinkelreid, *Scientific Evidence*, The Michie Co. (1986).

own client, even including those who have accepted their clients' protestations of innocence.[8] On the other hand, the prosecution, knowing that the result of defense DNA testing will remain confidential, will be more likely to conduct the testing before turning the evidence over to the defense. Again, this may actually be helpful to a financially strapped defendant.

Admissibility of DNA Evidence Under the Frye Standard

A major issue affecting the reliance by either side upon DNA evidence during trial is whether or not such evidence will pass the Frye test of admissibility discussed infra in the next section. Basically, the Frye test conditions the admissibility of a new scientific technique, such as DNA testing, on proof offered out of the presence of the jury that the test enjoys general acceptance in the particular scientific field in which it belongs. This foundation for admissibility is subscribed to by the majority of state and federal jurisdictions where an opinion based upon new scientific tests or procedures is sought to be admitted.[9] The questions that must therefore be answered include: a) whether DNA testing is still so experimental that its introduction in courts could cause invalid convictions or acquittals and b) how a DNA Frye hearing should be presented. If the hearing is not properly conducted, a case of precedential value could hold that any opinion based on DNA testing would be inadmissible.[10]

Discovery of DNA Test Results

Another issue concerning the introduction of DNA evidence is the extent to which the defense will be granted discovery of any DNA test results obtained by the prosecution. On one end of the scale, a court could allow

---

[8]An expert hired by the defense to perform DNA testing is in an agency relationship. Therefore, all of the work preparatory to the testing, as well as the actual DNA testing, is covered by the work product privilege unless and until the witness is called to the stand. *United States v. Nobles*, 422 U.S. 225, 238–39 (1975). In California, the information is confidential under the attorney-client privilege. *People v. Lines*, 13 Cal.3d 500 (1975). The fact that the defense has conducted a test should not come before a jury, because to do so would require the jury to speculate about the result of the test. As a practical matter, the defense must usually make a tactical decision early on in the proceedings whether it will seek to have DNA testing performed, assuming the prosecution has not already initiated such testing. A defense request for evidence samples will force the prosecution to make a decision whether to conduct a test before the evidence leaves its hands. Thus there is always a calculated risk for the defense in moving for discovery of the evidence for testing in the first instance, but it does have the advantage of forcing the prosecution to stand the costs of such tests.

[9]See generally, Giannelli & Imwinkelreid, supra, note 7, at 9- 35, discussing the Frye test and the competing "Federal test" or "relevancy approach". This reference supplies comprehensive case citations of jurisdictions subscribing to each approach.

[10]See, for example, *People v. Kelly*, 17 Cal.3d 24 (1976), dealing with voiceprints, and *People v. Shirley* , 31 Cal. 3d 181 (1982), dealing with enhancement of a witnesses' memory through hypnosis. In these cases the appellate courts found that an insufficient showing had been made in the trial court. As a practical matter, the cases are cited to prevent any further efforts to introduce these kinds of evidence. On the other hand,

discovery of the laboratory reports alone, regardless of how complicated the analysis might have been. On the other hand, a court could also allow discovery of all laboratory notes made concurrently with the observations, tests, and procedures and, in addition, permit access to physical evidence, such as preserved electrophoretic gels, autoradiographs, and any photographs taken of such evidence.[11] The defense in criminal cases is often limited in its financial resources. Perhaps, therefore, it may even be possible as a matter of discovery to obtain a court order requiring the prosecution to conduct DNA testing in those cases where there is a *prima facie* case that the testing will exonerate the defendant.[12]

At the present time, the organizations primarily engaged in conducting DNA testing, e.g., Lifecodes Corporation, Cellmark Diagnostics, and Cetus Corporation/Forensic Science Associates, are private companies with a proprietary interest in the probes utilized during the testing procedures to bind to genetically variable DNA sequences.[13] It is not clear to what extent information about these probes is available to the public through, for example, the publication of issued patents with claims directed to these probes, in contrast to how much of the information is maintained by these companies as a trade secret. If the defense moves for discovery of information about how these probes are manufactured, the owners of these probes might well object unless a protective order is first obtained to protect the information from being broadcast to its competitors. The defense may,

---

"once a trial court has admitted evidence based upon a new scientific technique and that decision is affirmed on appeal by a published appellate decision, the precedent so established may control subsequent trials, at least until new evidence is presented reflecting a change in the attitude of the scientific community." *People v. Kelly*, supra, 17 Cal.3d at 32.

[11] Here is an example of an expanded discovery order that the defense might use to advantage in a DNA case:

The reports of any scientific tests, examinations or experiments, or physical or mental examinations, or copies thereof, including but not limited to: (1) a statement of all material or other information or sources considered by the examiner in arriving at an opinion, the methodology used, and the findings and conclusions of the examiner, (2) a resume and curriculum vitae of the examiner's qualifications, experience, subject matter of the examiner's testimony, and prior occasions of testimony as an expert, and (3) any worksheets, photographs, notes, or other things used to assist the examiner in reaching an opinion and recording the process and methodology of reaching an opinion. *United States v. Cadet*, 727 F.2d 1453, 1459–60 (9th Cir. 1984).

[12] See, for example, *Evans v. Superior Court*, 11 Cal.3d 617 (1974), which, as matter of discovery, requires the prosecution to conduct a pretrial lineup upon a showing by the defense that there is a likelihood that eyewitnesses may not identify the defendant.

[13] As noted above in fn. 4, in addition to the private laboratories named herein, the Federal Bureau of Investigation laboratory has been performing DNA analyses on case evidence since October 1988, and a number of state laboratory systems, e.g., New Jersey, Florida, and Virginia, are expected to begin such testing within the next year. A California statute provides for the taking of blood and saliva from convicted sex offenders and violent felons for testing in the California Department of Justice DNA laboratory with the results to be maintained in a computerized databank system for criminal identification purposes. Cal. Penal Code sec. 290.2. Currently several laboratories are funded by the Department of Justice. They should be operational during 1990.

however, argue that knowledge of this data is necessary to allow its own experts to judge whether the probe binds in a reliable manner. Without such discovery, the defendant may arguably be denied his or her due process. Similarly, private companies may further assert that their laboratory protocols contain trade secrets as well and may ask courts to limit the dissemination of their contents.[14] In the long run, it is the author's opinion that the economic concerns of private companies conducting DNA tests will have to be made subordinate to the due process concerns of those against whom the tests are offered as evidence.

Preservation of DNA Evidence Samples

How is hair, blood, semen, and other evidence appropriate for DNA testing to be preserved to ensure the viability of the test, and, if any retesting is to be done, to ensure the viability of that procedure? A recent United States Supreme Court case holds that sanctions for failure to preserve evidence that thereafter leads to its destruction will be imposed only where there has been "bad faith" on the part of law enforcement personnel.[15] Does this decision mean, therefore, that DNA evidence is unlikely to be utilized as evidence in court because the prosecution will rely on more traditional means to prove the guilt of the defendants?

In Youngblood, a semen stain that had been deposited on the victim's clothing was not properly preserved. Serological testing was not attempted until over a year after the crime. Since the stain had not been frozen to preserve the evidence, the classic forensic serological methods of analysis, including ABO and enzyme tests, were not possible. In rejecting the defendant's contention that the case must be dismissed because the tests *might* have exonerated the defendant, the Court held that sanctions could be imposed only when there was "bad faith" in the failure to preserve the evidence. "Bad faith" was, however, left undefined. In his dissent, Chief Justice Rehnquist commented:

> What constitutes bad faith for these purposes? Does a defendant have to show actual malice, or would recklessness, or the deliberate failure to establish standards for maintaining and preserving evidence, be sufficient? Does "good faith police work" require a certain minimum of diligence, or will a lazy officer, who does not walk the few extra steps to the evidence refrigerator be considered to be acting in good faith?[16]

---

[14]See Thompson & Ford, supra, note 1, pp. 59–60, describing the position taken by Cellmark in a recent Frye hearing. There has been criticism of the practice of restricting access to probes when the information is necessary to evaluate population databases that are used to calculate identification frequencies. See King "Invited Editorial: Genetic Testing of Identity and Relationship," *Am. J. Human Genet.* 179–180 (1989).
[15]See *Arizona v. Youngblood*, 488 U.S _____, 102 L.ED. 281, 109 S.Ct 333 (1988).
[16]Ibid, 102 L. Ed. at 295, 109 S. Ct. at 342.

The *Youngblood* majority stated:

> We think that requiring a defendant to show bad faith on the part of the police both limits the extent of the police's obligation to preserve evidence to reasonable bounds and confines it to that class of cases where the interests of justice most clearly require it, *i.e.*, those cases in which the police themselves by their conduct indicate that the evidence could form a basis for exonerating the defendant.[17]

The message to the defense in DNA cases is thus clear: In every case where discovery indicates that evidence susceptible to DNA analysis exists and that there is a substantial issue about the identity of the perpetrator, the defense should obtain a court order to require the preservation of the evidence (by drying and freezing, in the case of blood, semen, or other fluids) on the grounds it may need to be subsequently tested with the hope that it will then exonerate the defendant. A subsequent failure to preserve such evidence would therefore be far more likely to be found to be in "bad faith". In cases where it is anticipated that the prosecution will conduct DNA tests, the defense should also move to require that a sufficient amount of the sample be retained to permit retesting by a defense expert. Finally, in cases where RFLP testing has already occurred, the defense should move that the test membrane be preserved for possible later reprobing, since it is technically possible to strip the membrane of old probes after an autoradiograph has been produced, to apply new probes, and to produce new autoradiographs that may either prove or disprove the original test.

THE FRYE ADMISSIBILITY REQUIREMENT

General Acceptance and Correct Scientific Procedures

In the hypothetical example cited at the beginning of this chapter, two propositions were asserted to be true. The first was that the DNA patterns from the control sample, derived from the defendant's blood, and the DNA patterns from the evidentiary semen stain were indistinguishable. Therefore, the defendant was part of the population group that could have deposited the semen. The second proposition was that the donor population group is a very small proportion of the total population: here 1 in 45,419,940.[18] If these propositions are true, they are quite relevant to show that the defendant committed the crime. If they are not true, they are quite likely to mislead a jury into convicting an innocent defendant. This raises the question of whether there should be a prejury procedure, such as a

---

[17]Ibid, 102 L. Ed. at 289, 109 S. Ct. at 337.
[18]It is extremely difficult to demonstrate that such a number is even reasonably accurate. Necessarily, an inference must be made about a large population based on the characteristics of a small sample. Because of resolution problems inherent in gel electrophoresis,

foundational hearing, to narrow the possibility that invalid opinions based on nonreliable experimental procedures will be presented to the jury.

The Frye court attempted to accomplish this result through an admissibility test based upon the general acceptance of "the thing from which the deduction is made" in the relevant scientific community.[19] The proponent of the evidence bears the burden of proving such general acceptance; otherwise the evidence cannot be admitted. In Frye, the defendant wanted to place before the jury evidence that he had passed the 1923 version of a polygraph examination, which measured his systolic blood pressure in response to certain questions. Based upon the test results, the expert would testify that the defendant was telling the truth when he denied committing the crime. The court held that before such evidence, based upon an unrecognized scientific discovery, can be admitted:

> . . . the thing from which the deduction is made must be sufficiently established to have gained general acceptance in the particular field in which it belongs. We think the systolic blood pressure deception test has not yet gained such standing and scientific recognition among physiological and psychological authorities as would justify the courts in admitting expert testimony deduced from the discovery, development, and experiments thus far made.[20]

It would seem that the "thing", i.e., the test, experiment, or procedure, must reliably give rise to a valid "deduction". For the "thing" to reliably do this, it must be "generally accepted" in the "field". The question arises, however, by whom and in what field? In Frye, it was "physiological and psychological authorities." For DNA, one would suppose that the "field" would involve general acceptance of authorities in relevant disciplines, such

---

frequencies must be projected utilizing a grouping of nondiscrete alleles—called *binning*—rather than discrete single alleles, as is utilized in conventional blood or serum typing. As one increases the size of the *bin* the frequency becomes more conservative. This frequency bin must not be smaller than the standard used to declare a match, otherwise a spuriously small statistic will be generated. Also it can be argued that confidence levels should be applied to correct for small sample sizes; thus, a frequency of a given bin might have to be increased from 3% to 10%, for example, to attain a 99% confidence level. Finally, the most difficult problem may be in demonstrating that the sample population is homogeneous and is representative of the larger population. If the sample population is heterogeneous, or substructured, then the allele frequencies it demonstrates will not be representative of the population of interest. Thus, it must be shown that the alleles of each genetic locus are in "Hardy–Weinberg equilibrium" and that all probed loci are in statistical "linkage equilibrium" with one another. These issues are currently very alive, much debated, and unresolved. See Lander "DNA Fingerprinting on Trial," *Nature* 339:501, 503–504. For a text generally discussing population genetics issues see Hartl, D.L. and A.G. Clark Sunderland, MA: Sinauer Associates *Principles of Population Genetics*. See also Cohen "DNA Fingerprinting for Forensic Identification: Potential Effects on Data Interpretation of Subpopulation Heterogeneity and Band Number Variability," *Am. J. Human Genet.* 46:358–368 (1990); Lander, "Population Genetic Considerations in the Forensic Use of DNA Typing," in 32 Banbury Report *DNA Technology and Forensic Science* (1989) 143–156.

[19]*Frye v. United States*, 293 Fed. 1013 (D.C. Cir. 1923).
[20]Ibid at 1014.

as biology, molecular biology, chemistry, biochemistry, genetics, statistics, and related subdisciplines.

The proponent of DNA evidence in a Frye jurisdiction may thus be met with an objection of "no foundation" upon attempting to introduce his or her expert's opinion. The proponent must then introduce evidence to establish this foundation. The Frye court itself gave no clues about who is a qualified witness to establish the foundation of general acceptance of the scientific test and how many such expert witnesses would be required. The Frye court also did not discuss whether the experiments or tests must be conducted in a particular manner in order to be reliable. These determinations, however, have been the subject of later case law.[21]

The Frye rule was recently clarified in a California decision, which held that to show general acceptance of a new scientific technique in the particular field in which it belongs:

> The proponent of the evidence bears the burden of proving a consensus of opinion and must establish (1) the reliability of the method, usually by expert testimony; (2) the qualifications of the witness providing the testimony; and (3) that correct scientific procedures were used in the particular case. The expert witness must possess academic and professional credentials that permit him to understand the scientific principles involved and any differing viewpoints regarding reliability. The witness must also be impartial—not so personally invested in establishing the technique's acceptance that he might not be objective about disagreements within the relevant scientific community. Additionally, the trial court must exercise restraint and cautious scrutiny of the general acceptance of the new process or technique when it is offered to identify the perpetrator of a crime. The trial and the reviewing courts may examine the trial record, decisions from other jurisdictions and relevant scientific literature in deciding whether a technique is generally accepted.[22]

Frye itself did not require that a witness who testifies concerning general acceptance have any particular qualifications. As might be expected, proponents seeking to establish such general acceptance normally call the witnesses who cost the least money and who are most readily available. These witnesses are usually the technicians who have done the testing or persons

---

[21]See Giannelli, et al., note 9, infra, for case citations to various jurisdictions that have further modified or developed the original Frye rule.

[22]*People v. Morris*, 199 Cal. App.3d 377, 387 (1988) (citations to authorities within quote omitted). For a discussion of the evolution of the Frye rule in California, see *People v. Kelly*, 17 Cal.3d 24 (1976) (voiceprints); *People v. Shirley*, 31 Cal.3d 181 (1962) (hypnosis); *People v. McDonald*, 37 Cal.3d 351, 372 (1984) (rule does not apply to eyewitness identification expert testimony); *People v. Brown*, 40 Cal.3d 512 (1985) (electrophoresis); *People v. Reilly*, 196 Cal. App.3d 1127 (1987) (electrophoresis).

who had some personal or financial interest in establishing the new technique.[23]

> Criticism laid upon experts in some California cases has stressed the need to ensure that the court hears the views of the whole scientific community. Thus, in cases where the *sole* (or a *crucial*) witness has a significant financial or professional interest in promoting the new technique or lacks theoretical training, that witness's ability to speak for all concerned has been questioned.[24]

Thus the proponent of DNA evidence must be prepared to call qualified scientists who are knowledgeable about the scientific techniques utilized in DNA testing of forensic evidentiary samples. Obviously, careful thought must be given to this issue before the hearing. Too great a reliance upon "forensic" scientists may raise the spectre that the witnesses are overinterested. It is probably safest to combine the testimony of "interested"[25] scientists with "disinterested" scientists from the broader sciences of molecular biology, genetics, chemistry, and statistics. "Nevertheless, to the extent that those scientists in broader disciplines are knowledgeable about bloodstain typing, their opinions should be considered as part of the relevant scientific community."[26]

These qualified experts may then offer their opinions about whether there is general agreement that the DNA testing procedure utilized can, with any degree of reliability, reach a valid result.[27]

It is not the court's role to decide whether a particular DNA testing technique may provide valid results or whether it can be utilized reliably. Rather, the court's function is to decide, based upon the opinions offered by the "experts", whether there is or is not substantial agreement concerning

---

[23]See, e.g., *People v. Brown*, supra. (Technicians of the laboratory who had done blood enzyme testing were not qualified to establish general acceptance of gel electrophoresis for this purpose).

[24]*People v. Reilly*, supra, at 1139. For a more extensive discussion of this issue, see Giannelli "The Admissibility of Novel Scientific Evidence," 80 Colum. L. Rev. 1197 (1980); see also, *People v. Young*, 425 Mich. 470, 391 N.W.2d 270 (1986).

[25]"Interested" scientists may include those whose "livelihood [is] intimately connected with the new technique" (*People v. Young*, 391 N.W.2d at 275–276), although their opinions may be accorded less weight than "disinterested" scientists. See Pearsall, infra, note 1 at 1020–21; Burk "DNA Fingerprinting: Possibilities and Pitfalls of a New Technique", *Jurimetrics J.* 28:455, 471 (1988).

[26]*People v. Reilly*, supra, at 1138.

[27]"Although courts use the terms "validity" and "reliability" interchangeably, the terms have distinct meanings in scientific jargon. "Validity" refers to the ability of a test to measure what it is supposed to measure—its accuracy. "Reliability" refers to whether the same results are obtained in each instance in which the test is performed—its consistency. Validity includes reliability, but the converse is not necessarily true. Giannelli & Imwinkelreid, *Scientific Evidence*, The Michie Co., 1986, pg. 1, fn. 1. There is some dispute as to whether questions of scientific reliability are really Frye issues going to the admissibility of the evidence. It would seem, however, that even if it is theoretically possible to obtain valid DNA test results, if it remains out of reach of most laboratories to reliably perform the analysis, then reliability should be part of the Frye equation.

validity and reliability. "Thus, as a matter of satisfying their initial burden, the People are not required to create a record that convinces the court that the technique is reliable."[28] It would seem, however, that if the court is to make a judgment concerning substantial agreement or disagreement, it will have to make some sort of normative judgment about which problems are significant and which are not.

In the initial DNA Frye hearings, it is likely that the party seeking to introduce the evidence will introduce a series of expert witnesses who will testify that there is no substantial disagreement about the general theory underlying DNA testing. In addition, it can be anticipated that the opponent of the proffered evidence will produce experts who will testify that the tests are so difficult to apply that unreliable results will occur too often for DNA testing to be safely admitted into evidence in trials at this time, or, similarly, that the test results require such subjective interpretation that unreliable and biased results will ensue. It is doubtful that a court will rule that a substantial disagreement exists simply because opposing experts disagree. Instead, the court will likely accept the opinion of the experts on one side or the other as to whether a dispute about a particular issue constitutes a substantial disagreement about the validity or reliability of the method.

As we have seen, the California version of the Frye test additionally requires that the proponent of the evidence must demonstrate that correct scientific procedures were used in the particular case. This requirement was imported in *People v. Kelly*,[29] a voiceprint case, which cited a California polygraph case, *People v. Adams*[30] stating:

> Furthermore, *general acceptance* is not necessarily a proper test since it does not invariably equate with reliability. A better test for admissibility of novel scientific test results should require proof of reliability.

Adams held that reliability was not shown in the administration of a lie detector test because an incorrect scientific procedure was used in the case. That is, the "Defendant, 18 days after the accident, took a unilateral test from a polygrapher of his own choosing."[31] The court found support in the literature that such a procedure could produce an unreliable result and, on that ground, refused to admit an opinion based upon the polygraph.

Thus, California does not simply rely upon the Frye rule of admissibility. It has instead developed the Kelly/Frye rule of admissibility, combining the holding of these two cases. In addition, therefore, to the scientists who must establish substantial agreement that a particular DNA testing technique is valid and can be applied reliably, there must also be proof submitted concerning the reliability of the procedures used, as well as proof that these

---

[28]*People v. Reilly*, supra at 1152.
[29]*People v. Kelly*, supra.
[30]*People v. Adams*, 53 Cal. App.3d 109, 115–116 (1975).
[31]Ibid. at 115.

procedures were actually followed in the particular test in question. For example, the three private laboratories who currently test forensic DNA samples have the facilities and licensing necessary to utilize radioactively labeled probes. At such time in the future that local crime laboratories attempt DNA testing, however, they may find it unfeasible to use radioactive probes. These laboratories may thus seek an alternate method of labeling, such as with biological stains or enzymes, rather than radioactive probes. These alternate methods may perhaps result in a comparison of DNA patterns that might be less than optimum. Such comparisons, involving a greater degree of subjectivity, might therefore be less than reliable.[32] A court faced with this issue might find that such testing does not pass the Kelly/Frye test.

> Essentially, this part of the *Kelly/Frye* standard insures that the technique was performed reliably *in each particular case* before the evidence can be put to the "trier of fact". The fact that our courts impose this case-specific burden bolsters our conclusion that potentially unresolved questions of deterioration or contamination do not invalidate the technique as a whole. Rather, if those questions are serious enough on the facts of a particular case, they can be addressed in the second phase of *Kelly/Frye* and, of course, before the trier of fact at trial should the evidence be ruled admissible.[33]

Although it is not stated explicitly, it is implied that the second phase of the admissibility hearing does not involve the question as to whether there is general agreement about what the procedures have to be; rather, the court may find whether the proponent of the evidence has carried its burden of proof as to which procedures should be followed to ensure reliability and whether, in fact, they have been followed.

It is certain, nevertheless, that the initial Kelly/Frye hearings will be complicated and lengthy. For the court to rule knowledgeably on whether proper procedures have been followed, the intricacies of the science will have to be presented in a palatable manner. Under this standard, it can be argued that no laboratory results should be admitted unless the laboratory

---

[32] All DNA comparisons of two bands require a degree of subjectivity to determine whether two bands "match" or, more appropriately, are indistinguishable. Disputes currently center around whether a visual matching rule is sufficient, perhaps by reference to the patterns shown by all the bands in the system, or whether a more objective method involving measurement of migration of the band on the gel with reference to size standards within and without the sample lane must be utilized, in order to accurately estimate the length of the band in base pairs. See Lander, note 18, supra.

[33] *People v. Reilly*, supra, at 1153. This does not mean that the defense is entitled to a Kelly/Frye hearing outside the presence of the jury every time there is a question of whether the test was done correctly. Evidently, if the neglected procedure goes to the "fundamental validity" of the test, the defense can obtain an admissibility hearing outside the presence of the jury in this second phase of Kelly/Frye. If, however, the procedure is not done with the required "degree of professionalism", it is a matter of weight, not of admissibility, and there would not be a right to a hearing outside of the jury's presence. See *People v. Farmer* (1989) 47 Cal.3d 888, 913.

performing the tests is properly accredited by professional agencies that enjoy the uniform respect of scientists working in the field. Moreover, the examiners of such evidence should have a track record of having passed blind DNA proficiency tests administered by independent regulatory agencies.[34] Finally, these results should not be admissible unless a sufficient sample is retained to allow for retesting.

Some Specific Frye Issues

Scientists are better qualified than judges or lawyers to discuss the validity and reliability of particular DNA typing systems. Some issues occur to the technically minded attorney, however, which may have the value of providing a focus concerning the issues of admissibility.

For example, are false-positive results possible?[35] The answer would likely be affirmative if no precautions are taken to prevent the suspect's reference sample from contaminating the evidence sample, in which case the DNA patterns would match because the reference sample would be compared to itself.

In the case of RFLP analysis, the problem may be effectively minimized by keeping evidence and reference samples widely separated on the electrophoretic gel. There may be more chances for things to go wrong when the amplification or polymerase chain reaction (PCR) method is used. With the use of this method, a tiny segment of DNA is isolated and then amplified several million times. If even a minute amount of the DNA isolated from the suspect contaminates the reference DNA during any of the procedures prior to amplification, there is, of course, the possibility of a false-positive result. On the other hand, PCR has the virtue of requiring far less DNA at the outset. In many cases much of the evidence sample can be preserved so the experiment can be repeated, which should provide a control against contamination by the suspect's DNA.

An invalid exclusion would more likely show a pattern mismatch than a pattern match. This would mean that persons who should be included among those who could have left the DNA evidence will be excluded. Interpretation involving band shifting and band intensity variations are examples of situations where false exclusions could occur. If DNA testing regularly exonerates guilty defendants, it is as good an argument for inadmissibility under Frye as a false identification. Thus, all of the ways a particular DNA typing system might be misinterpreted must be evaluated and procedures should be established to prevent such problems from occurring before the evidence is admitted.

---

[34] See Thompson & Ford, supra, note 1, page 92, fn. 207; Lander, supra, note 18, 339 Nature at 501.

[35] A "false positive" results when a suspect is falsely included as the source of a DNA sample; similarly, a "false negative" results when the suspect is falsely excluded as the source.

The particular probe used in the testing system must be independently evaluated. Cellmark Diagnostics and Lifecodes corporation utilize a system that measures variations in DNA fragment lengths. Are the band patterns that are visualized so distinct from one another that every expert would read them in the same way? If not, the validity of the test becomes compromised by subjective interpretation, which can be an argument for Frye inadmissibility.[36]

Validating one probe system along with a particular restriction enzyme will not serve to validate the same probes using a different restriction enzyme, nor will the validation of one type of probe validate another type of probe. In the same manner, multilocus and single-locus systems, allele-specific amplification systems, and sequencing systems would have to be validated separately before any decision involving one would have precedential force as to the admissibility of the other.[37]

A successful Frye hearing, i.e., resulting in the validation of a particular DNA technique when used on one type of evidentiary sample, e.g., semen, would not necessarily validate the technique as to another type of sample, such as blood. A similar argument regarding the stability of stains due to aged or relatively unpreserved samples, as distinguished from fresh samples, is applicable.[38] Finally, one may make an argument that the testing cannot be as reliably done when there are contamination problems, such as those caused due to the presence of bacteria, or when mixture conditions

---

[36]See *People v. Harbold*, 124 Ill App.3d 363, 464 N.E.2d 734, 746–748 (1984). See also note 32 *supra*. At this stage the "Proposed Standards for Tests Involving DNA Polymorphisms November 1987" of the American Association of Blood Banks Parentage Committee" might be profitably perused. They provide, in part:

    I. The use of a particular DNA probe system should be validated by extensive family and population studies that show that the particular system exhibits Mendelian inheritance and a nondetectable or acceptably low frequency of mutation and/or recombination.

    VI. Autoradiographs or membranes must be read independently by two or more individuals.

    X. Confirmatory testing by an independent laboratory shall be possible for all DNA tests.

Other standards include the use of size markers, control systems, methods to ensure complete endonuclease digestion, chromosomal location of size fragments, and a kilobase listing of all size fragments. Other concerned organizations also have or will develop similar validation protocol standards. They should be garnered as a checklist to test the reliability of the testing in the initial Frye hearings. For example, a group called the Technical Working Group on DNA Analysis Methods (TWGDAM) comprised of FBI and state crime laboratory personnel has prepared a draft document entitled "Guidelines for a Quality Assurance (QA) Program for a DNA Restriction Fragment Length Polymorphism (RFLP) Analysis." (Note: these guidelines are provided as an appendix to Chapter 10 by Jan Bashinski.) It should prove useful to measure the quality control of a particular laboratory.

[37]See *People v. Young*, note 24 supra (holding that a "multi-system" where multiple enzymes are developed on the same gel does not meet Frye reliability standards).

[38]For further information concerning this topic, see the chapter entitled "Validation With Regard To Environmental Insults of the RFLP Procedure For Forensic Purpose" appearing in this book.

prevail, such as when there is both a male and female contribution.[39] In such situations, difficulties in the interpretation of test results can occur.

THE OBJECTIVITY OF THE LABORATORY

Concerns have been voiced that when government laboratories perform DNA testing they will usually be aligned with law enforcement.[40] Thus, if there is any room for subjective interpretation, it is believed that the opinion in court will reflect a bias to identify the charged defendant. If there is an opportunity for the defense to retest the sample, it alleviates this concern about the reliability of the initial test result. The question is whether the retention of a sample for retesting should be made a condition of admissibility. Thus, enough of the evidentiary sample sufficient to permit testing by the PCR technique should be retained if at all possible. This raises a different issue, however, in that difficulties have been encountered with the use of the PCR technique on very small samples, since, along with the DNA present, any contaminants are also vastly amplified. Even remaining mindful of such potential difficulties, the retention of sufficient sample to permit retesting could provide a control to ensure the reliability of the initial test. In essence, therefore, retaining a sample for this purpose would become a necessary "procedure" that would have to be followed before the result of the test would be admissible. Also, in those cases where there is insufficient sample for more than one test, the defense could be given notice and the opportunity to have their own expert present during the test.

Another argument that may be raised at an admissibility hearing is that an analyst whose DNA testing is being offered should have a track record of having passed blind proficiency tests involving the same DNA test system on the same kind of unknown evidentiary materials. Again, the institution of such a requirement would be expected to raise the reliability of DNA test results to an acceptable level for Frye purposes.

No doubt there are many more questions that could be raised about the validity of any DNA test result. For instance, on a basic level, is there certainty that probes will bind where they are supposed to bind, that is, could there be adventitious binding that would show or create a band that is not really endemic to the individual? Is there a possibility that the band

---

[39]The probe itself may be contaminated either by human DNA from another probe or by bacterial DNA contaminating the probe in the laboratory or in the process of cloning the probe. This foreign DNA can potentially be radioactively labeled and can cause spurious bands if it finds like bacterial or human sequences in the sample DNA lanes. It can be argued that a control probe should test for this type of contamination to ensure the validity of the result. See Lander, note 18, supra, 339 Nature at 503.

[40]See "Increased Testing Leads to Concerns About Lab Scientists," by Peter Applebome, The New York Times News Service, December 1987, stating in part: "Also in question is the objectivity of forensic testimony, since the vast majority of crime laboratories are part of police agencies."

from the evidence sample interpreted by the analyst as identical to the band from the reference sample from the suspect really is a band resulting from the DNA of another organism such as bacteria? How much subjective interpretation is to be allowed an analyst in stating whether banding patterns are or are not identical? We will have to wait for the testimony of qualified scientists at Frye hearings on these and other issues.

Statistical Issues

Prosecution experts will testify not only that the defendant or the victim is included in the segment of the population that left the evidentiary sample, but will also testify as to what proportion of the population could have been the source of the sample. Much of the excitement about DNA testing comes from these statistical opinions. Consider the impact on a jury that hears that only 1 in 50 million people, including the defendant, could have left the sample.

Taken by itself, most courts find such statistical evidence relevant.[41] The statistical principles involved, that is, extrapolation of population statistics from sample populations and utilization of the product rule on independent segments, are not new and are probably not subject to a Frye objection. However, the application of these statistical principles to the hypervariable alleles revealed by RFLP probes is very new and should therefore be subject to a Frye objection.[42]

Typically, DNA analysis may involve the use of several probes. Each RFLP probe will bind to a finite number of nucleotide length variations. Each nucleotide length variation is hypothesized to correspond to a certain percentage of the population, based on extrapolation from smaller sample populations to which the probe system (together with a certain cutting enzyme) has been applied. To obtain a final population statistic, the product of the percentages is taken, for example, if the percentage of the population possessing the length variation obtained using probe 1 is 1 in 1587, using probe 2 is 1 in 180, and using probe 3 is 1 in 159, the product is 1 in 45,419,940.

For this calculation to be meaningful, however, certain assumptions must be proven. First, the length variations brought out by a probe must be shown to be in Hardy–Weinberg equilibrium; that is, in the population there must be a statistically independant allelic contribution from the mother and the father. It is usually assumed that the sample population is in Hardy–Weinberg equilibrium, and therefore it holds that the frequency of two different band sizes (heterozygous alleles) occurring is twice the product of their individual frequencies, or, if the band sizes are the same, the

---

[41] See *People v. Brown*, supra, 40 Cal.3d 512, 536, fn. 6; *People v. Lindsey*, 84 Cal. App.3d 851, 863–866 (1978); *People v. Vallez*, 80 Cal. App.3d 46, 56 (1978); see also *United States v. Gwaltney*, 790 F.2d 1378, 1382–1383 (9th Cir. 1986).

[42] See note 18, supra.

frequency is the square of the band's individual frequency (homozygous alleles). Otherwise, there would be no basis to assume that the percentage of the population sample would correspond to the percentage of the general population.

Second, the population sample must be of sufficient size and share the characteristics of the general population. Otherwise, the percentages derived from the nucleotide length variations may bear no relationship to the general population and the percentages derived using the product rule will bear no relationship to reality.[43]

Third, all nucleotide length variations must be shown to be inherited independently, that is, the length variations within one probe system cannot be inherited together. In addition, any length variation of one probe may not be dependent in its inheritance with any length variation of another probe, nor should the use of one probe cause adventitious binding of a length variation by another probe. Otherwise the population statistics derived from the length variations will not be independent and the product of the statistics will bear no relationship to reality.[44]

Since statistical opinions are here being offered about a new and, by definition, unproven technique, it seems those opinions should be subject to and part of the Frye hearing. There may be no general agreement about the independent assortment of length variations in a particular DNA typing system, for instance. On the other hand, if the validity of the statistical opinion cannot be proven in a pretrial hearing, it would be inadmissible in a California Kelly/Frye hearing because proper procedures were not used.[45]

Aside from the Frye question, defense counsel would be well advised to object to the admissibility of the statistical probability of the concurrence of DNA patterns on the ground that the relevancy of the evidence will be outweighed by its tendency to be confusing, time consuming, and prejudicial. See Federal Rules of Evidence, section 403; California Evidence Code. section 352. For example, in current RFLP analysis, even if two length sequences are of exactly the same length, only actual sequencing would

---

[43]See *People v. Collins*, 68 Cal.2d 319 (1968). To date, population studies deriving from use of DNA probes have been based largely on unpublished information, which has therefore not been subject to criticism by authorities in the field.

[44]See *People v. Collins*, supra. In this case the court held that statistical evidence, even if "conservatively estimated", should not be admitted.

[45]During any ensuing trial, defense counsel should be alert to obtain an instruction that the statistical evidence alone cannot establish guilt and that the small proportion of the population who could have left the sample should not be equated with the chance that the defendant is guilty. Also defense counsel can argue that the error rate of the person who conducted the test should be applied to each component, and the product taken, to establish the probability that the test was completely wrong. Counsel should argue that the jury is likely to overemphasize the probative value of the statistics and that therefore the evidence should be limited to the fact that the defendant is included in the group of people who could have left the evidence sample, not that a particular minute percentage of people could have left it. See *State v. Carlson*, 267 N.W.2d 170, 176 (Minn. 1978); *State v. Kim*, 374 N.W.2d 814, 816 (Minn. Ct. App. 1985). It may also be argued that the

demonstrate that their base pair sequences are the same, so that the source of one band could be demonstrated not to be excluded as the source of the other band. Further, because of resolution problems, one cannot be certain that bands that look like they are the same length are really the same length: They might actually vary from one to perhaps hundreds of base pairs. [See Sarkar "Letter," *Science* 247:1018 (1990)].

Thus, the most that can be said is that the pattern of "bins" may have a certain probability in the population, not that actual biological "alleles" have that probability. Therefore a criminal defendant may be part of an unknown small group of the population who has inherited the biological genotype that is identical to the evidence sample, or he or she may be part of an unknown group of the population that has not inherited the biological genotype but has inherited one that looks similar upon visual comparison. A jury is likely to be highly confused by the ramifications of all this; and, in fact, if told that the chances of a random concurrence are a particular number, whether one in a thousand or one in a trillion, will probably equate that number with the probability that the defendant is guilty. Thus, a court may be convinced that the statistical evidence should not be admitted. Once that ruling is obtained, the defense can argue that the fact of matching DNA patterns should not be admitted either, since the jury may prejudicially speculate about what the match means.

CONCLUSION

It is likely that the debate concerning the evidentiary admissibility of DNA testing will center on whether a particular analyst in a particular laboratory conducting the test can produce reliable results, not whether a valid result is possible when the test is performed by a Nobel prize winning scientist using state-of-the-art instrumentation under ideal conditions. Probably some error rate will be allowed. In such cases, the fact of error would go to the weight of the evidence and could be argued before the jury, but would not keep the DNA testing from being admitted.

On the other hand, at some point the question of unreliability becomes an

---

percentage of the population sharing the defendant's DNA pattern is irrelevant, since it is speculative whether it was the defendant who left the sample or some other member of the population group who shares the DNA characteristic. See, on the latter point, Jefferson, "California Evidence Benchbook," §21.6, pp. 569–570.

This paper has concentrated on pretrial admissibility issues of DNA testing in criminal cases. If, as is to be expected, the evidence is found to be admissible, the question for the defense attorney is how to deal with the evidence before a jury at trial. Counsel should call on their own and their colleagues' experience in defending traditional fingerprint cases: Can the analyst be impeached for bias, lack of knowledge, etc.? Jurors have a healthy skepticism of statistics and of experts. If there are aspects of the case that can be emphasized to create a reasonable doubt, counsel for the defense should not assume the case is lost simply because DNA evidence is coming in against their client.

admissibility question and Frye experts will have to examine whether there is general agreement in the field as to whether DNA testing can currently be reliably done in a typical law enforcement crime laboratory.

Also, the validation in court of one method of DNA testing will not necessarily validate another method of testing: Already there are competing methods, such as RFLP typing, which relies upon different probes and restriction enzymes; PCR methods, which look for sequence variations, and direct sequencing. Population studies should be completed and published before any statistical opinions are offered in court.

Thus, it will be a slow, arduous process to qualify DNA testing in criminal cases, but both sides will seek to introduce DNA evidence. The importance for the prosecution of this kind of evidence in sexual assault and homicide cases cannot be underestimated. For the defense, literally every case presenting an eyewitness identification issue is ripe for DNA testing if any testable evidence has been left at the crime scene, since it may prove the eyewitness was wrong. We can expect, therefore, that both the defense and prosecution will be offering and opposing DNA evidence. In that ordeal by fire we may hope and expect that the correct decisions about the admissibility of this evidence in criminal cases will be made.

10. Managing The Implementation and Use of DNA Typing in the Crime Laboratory

JAN S. BASHINSKI, M.S.

INTRODUCTION

The potential for forensic DNA testing using the Jeffreys multilocus probes was first reported in England by Gill in 1985.[1] Much discussion has ensued since that date of how this powerful technology should be implemented in the crime laboratory.[2-4] As recently as January 1988, public officials in the United States questioned whether DNA typing was sufficiently well documented for forensic purposes.[5] Since then, the progress made by researchers in the private sector, academia, and government forensic laboratories has been such that there is now widespread acceptance within the legal and scientific communities of the concept of using DNA for forensic purposes. The potential of DNA typing to identify criminal offenders and to exonerate those falsely accused has become obvious.[6] In fact, the quantum leap between the discriminating power of DNA typing and that of conventional genetic marker testing has created a mandate that crime laboratories develop DNA testing capability.

The forensic DNA procedures described elsewhere in this text are now rapidly being introduced into the working crime laboratory. Some laboratories (notably the Federal Bureau of Investigation, the British Home Office, the Royal Canadian Mounted Police in Ottawa, Canada, and the Virginia State Crime Laboratory) are already providing casework service. Several others (for example, Metro-Dade, Florida; Washoe County, Nevada; Nassau County, New York; New Jersey State Laboratory System; Raleigh, North Carolina; Orange County, California; Phoenix, Arizona; the Michigan state laboratory system; and Toronto) are developing DNA testing programs for implementation in the near future. DNA testing by private consulting laboratories (Lifecodes, Cellmark, Forensic Science Associates/ Cetus) and by the FBI laboratory has been accepted in the courts of more than two dozen states.[7,8]

There is no question that DNA typing can be successfully accomplished in the crime laboratory setting or that the use of DNA will enhance the value of physiological evidence. The question has now become, "What is the most effective way to implement and oversee this powerful new technology in our laboratories to insure that it best serves the cause of justice?" This chapter reviews some of the issues to be considered by a crime laboratory, its parent agency, and its clients in answering this question.

CASELOAD ISSUES

A major issue is the estimation of the potential demand for DNA typing services in serology cases. A related concern is whether or not a laboratory's caseload will provide sufficient "critical mass" to maintain the experience level of the staff once they are trained in DNA analysis. A crime laboratory whose conventional serology caseload occupies at least one full time serologist, for example, may have enough casework to justify an in-house DNA program but may not be able to divert staff from other critical work to complete the background validation and training necessary to implement DNA testing. In order to support an appropriate level of quality assurance and case review, a laboratory should be in a position to train at least two DNA analysts or to participate in a collaborative peer review arrangement with another DNA testing facility.

In projecting the laboratory's caseload for planning purposes, it can be anticipated that adding DNA testing to the laboratory's battery of routine serology tests will initially increase the number of analyses performed per case. DNA testing will tend to complement conventional work rather than supplanting all traditional testing, particularly in the early phases of implementation. Many preliminary examination procedures, such as the detection, identification, and microscopic characterization of body fluid stains and mixtures, will remain an integral part of the analysis. In addition, many laboratories plan to validate their DNA testing methods in part by running them in tandem with conventional protein marker testing. Indeed, this sort of cross check of new DNA probes has been recommended in paternity testing by the American Association of Blood Banks (AABB) Parentage Testing Committee.[9]

With the availability of DNA testing, the laboratory should also anticipate that the total number of cases in which serology examination is requested will increase. Investigators will be quick to understand the value of DNA typing for screening potential suspects or for establishing a link between a series of unsolved crimes. As DNA identification databases become established, public demand for analysis in "suspectless" rape cases and other unsolved serial crimes will escalate. Prosecutors will request analysis of biological evidence in cases they would previously have prosecuted on the strength of other evidence alone, anticipating that jurors educated by the popular press may expect to hear DNA results. A recent Nevada case where an acquittal resulted from the prosecution's failure to conduct a DNA analysis underscores this point.[10]

The increased discrimination power of DNA testing will create demands for additional testing in which conventional serology previously proved of little value. A case in point is that of Gary Dotson, an Illinois man accused and convicted of rape on the testimony of a woman who later recanted her story. Dotson was eliminated as the source of a semen stain on the woman's underclothing by a DNA test performed 9 years later.[11] The exclusionary potential of DNA is demonstrated by the experience of both the Home Office and the FBI laboratories, who have found an exclusion rate of approximately 25% in their casework thus far.[12]

Most crime laboratories are operated by public law enforcement agencies, many of whom currently do not conduct testing at the request of the defense. In view of the potential of DNA to eliminate a falsely accused person, public agencies should consider the effect of their case acceptance policies on the quality of justice. In New York, for example, the Advisory Panel to the State Director of Criminal Justice recently recommended[13] that DNA testing be equally available to defense and prosecution, stating, "Justice demands that any technique with the power to include or exclude a suspect with a high degree of certainty be made available to all parties."

RESOURCES AND FACILITIES

Existing staff, equipment, and facilities in most crime laboratories are unlikely to be adequate to meet the demands presented by a new DNA program. The costs/benefits of acquiring these resources must be weighed against the alternatives of contracting to a private vendor or referring the work to another agency, such as the FBI laboratory or a centralized state facility. Experienced laboratories estimate that DNA typing is generally required on two to four samples per case. Estimates of productivity of the individual DNA analyst vary more widely—from 25 casework samples per month[15] to 75 per month.[14,15]

Using the current restriction fragment length polymorphism (RFLP) technology, the laboratory should anticipate spending up to 1 year or more in the development, training, and proficiency testing stages of implementation. Training and implementation time may decrease in the future as more validation work is published on existing procedures and as standardized training and simpler typing technologies are developed. Improved and simplified technology may also lead to increased productivity and a faster turnaround time for casework.

The availability of trained staff is a major factor in implementation. Most forensic serologists have academic backgrounds and practical experience in immunology and/or protein electrophoresis techniques. They may have little background in molecular biology, or their academic training in this rapidly developing field may be dated. In-service training in forensic DNA typing procedures is available at the FBI Academy at Quantico, via short courses provided by forensic science associations and other professional groups, and through private consulting laboratories, such as Lifecodes, Cellmark, Cetus, and Analytical Genetic Testing Center.[16]

Although in-service practical training courses are extremely valuable, they are not intended to substitute for a sound theoretical background. The crime laboratory should encourage its forensic serologists to pursue continuing education in molecular biology, biochemistry, and genetics, and should recruit experienced molecular biologists to complement existing staff. The laboratory would be well advised to establish collaborative relationships with a local university molecular biology/biochemistry department or hospital medical genetics facility. Professionals from the biotechnology industry can also provide valuable support.

In most respects, the laboratory space requirements of a DNA program are similar to those of other functional units of the crime laboratory. An allotment of 1000 square feet per scientist has been recommended.[17] To maintain the integrity of the evidence, access to the laboratory space must be limited and controlled by an adequate security system. Ample refrigerator and freezer storage must be available for biochemicals and reagents, as well as for proper preservation of biological evidence samples and long-term storage of reference samples. Adequate ventilation and fume hoods must exist for organic extraction procedures and for safe handling of liquid blood samples.[18]

The Southern blotting procedures traditionally employed in an RFLP analysis require the use of ^{32}P-labeled probes. For this work, the laboratory must obtain a license from the Nuclear Regulatory Commission (NRC). Staff must be trained in the safe use and disposition of radioisotopes. Space needs include a "hot room" or dedicated hood and sink for handling isotopes, an area for holding waste prior to its disposal, and a photographic darkroom. If the laboratory is already performing radioimmunoassay work, its existing NRC license can be amended for ^{32}P.[19]

The polymerase chain reaction (PCR) technology requires careful isolation of the evidence extraction/preparation process from the amplification process. Contamination of evidence extracts with even small amounts of amplified PCR product can swamp the amplification of the evidence DNA and produce spurious results. Physical separation of the equipment, reagents, and work area in which amplification is conducted from the other aspects of the analysis is strongly recommended.[20]

Estimates of the total cost of the equipment required for Southern blot RFLP analysis range up to $100,000, although much of the equipment may already be available in the laboratory.[21] The cost of probes and other reagents has been estimated at approximately $50 per sample.[15] The basic equipment for PCR costs an additional $10,000, with reagent costs of approximately $25 per sample.[22]

CENTRALIZED VERSUS LOCAL/REGIONAL DNA TESTING LABORATORY

In establishing the basic organization of the DNA program at the state level, the question of how much centralization is necessary and/or desirable must be addressed. Within an individual laboratory, the organizational question revolves around whether or not the DNA program should be a separate unit or should be integrated into the existing serology unit. The decision as to the best administrative structure for a forensic DNA program must balance a number of related, and often competing, factors. Among those are cost effectiveness, quality control, standardization, and responsiveness to the needs of the local criminal justice system. The implementation strategy is likely to vary considerably among jurisdictions as a function of the differing histories of their existing systems for the delivery of forensic services.

In order to provide the most effective analysis and interpretation of the evidence in the context of a particular case situation, the DNA analyst should have full knowledge of the investigative information and analytical data developed by the forensic serologist who conducted the preliminary examination of the evidence. Regardless of its organizational placement, the DNA program is a part of the crime laboratory's forensic serology service. For example, in an inspection conducted by the American Society of Crime Laboratory Directors Laboratory Accreditation Board (ASCLD/LAB), the DNA program will be evaluated in combination with the other serology services, even if they are administered as separate units of the laboratory.[23] If the DNA and conventional typing functions are bifurcated, the laboratory administration should encourage close coordination and interaction between the two units.

Some states, such as Connecticut and North Carolina, have only a single state-run crime laboratory, which provides a natural base for a centralized DNA program. Others, for example Florida, New York, California, and New Jersey, have numerous well-established city and county-run laboratories serving urban population centers, in addition to state-run laboratory systems, which tend to service the more rural areas. The forensic laboratory communities in both New York and California are considering programs with a network of regionalized DNA laboratories serving both state and local jurisdictions.[13,24,25]

It has been suggested[26] that it might be most appropriate to use the clinical experience as a model and to utilize a few large centralized medical genetic testing facilities for the analysis of specimens referred from the crime laboratories. This mass screening approach is unlikely to prove viable in the forensic arena for a number of reasons. The clinical model implies a series of rigidly controlled routine procedures applied to samples by technicians who are generally not involved in selection of testing methods or in the interpretation of the results. This approach may be ideal for a setting in which the samples to be tested can also be well controlled. However, in the forensic context, the condition and purity of the sample are unknown. There are also uncontrollable factors that may require modification of sample preparation procedures, which will require careful initial evaluation of the sample and of the analysis as it progresses. It is critical that forensic testing be approached on a case-by-case basis, with attention given to the characterization of each individual sample by persons trained and experienced in both forensic serology and molecular biology.[27,28]

State systems with multiple laboratory sites or states contemplating the creation of regional forensic DNA testing centers must balance the potential efficiency and cost effectiveness to be gained from a centralized operation against the need to remain responsive to the needs of local administration of justice. Studies have shown that use of crime laboratory services falls exponentially with the distance between the police agency and the crime lab that serves it and becomes vanishingly small when that distance exceeds 50 miles.[29] This same phenomenom may be observed between the referring crime laboratories and a centralized forensic DNA facility. Distance creates logistical problems with evidence transport and can compound problems of maintaining the chain of custody of the evidence. Establishing casework priorities can also prove to be a problem for a centralized facility trying to meet the demands of many police and court jurisdictions.

In addition to efficiency and cost effectiveness, there are two compelling reasons to consider centralizing and specializing the forensic DNA function. One issue is concern for quality control of the testing; the second is interest in establishing DNA identification data banks. The former requires the development of standards of training, practice, and proficiency; the latter requires agreement regarding standardization of methodology and acceptable levels of reproducibility in the results. Both are of significant interest to the courts, legislators, and public interest groups, as well as to the crime laboratory community. Both demand the attention and active involvement of forensic practitioners and their professional societies, as outlined in more detail later in this chapter.

METHOD SELECTION AND VALIDATION

In many respects, the process of selecting and implementing DNA testing in the crime laboratory is analogous to the introduction of any new technology into the forensic arena. Significant parallels exist between current work with forensic DNA typing and the experience with the introduction of protein genetic markers over the past 20 years, and there are lessons to be drawn from that history. On the other hand, DNA typing differs from conventional genetic marker testing in the extent to which practitioners in the private sector have borne the burden of method development and validation, and have met the initial court challenges. Further, the unprecedented individualizing power of DNA testing has produced great pressure on the publicly funded laboratories to accelerate the pace with which they have traditionally assimilated new technology.

Historically, a variety of factors have been considered in developing or selecting genetic marker typing procedures for use in the forensic context. Among these are the stability and robustness of the marker under typical crime scene conditions, the sensitivity of detection in case type samples, cost, and the ease of application of the technology.[30,31] Before application to casework, the procedure must have been properly validated.[32] This process generally involves a progression of experiments, beginning with application to pristine samples, then to simulated case samples that have been subjected to a variety of environmental insults, and finally to nonprobative casework specimens. The method must be subjected to blind trial testing. If the method has been developed in house, this phase should include the exchange of blind samples with other independent laboratories. There is universal agreement in the forensic community[9,28,33,34] that DNA probes and procedures should be readily available so that confirmatory testing by an independent laboratory is possible.

If a procedure is transferred into the crime laboratory from the research or clinical setting, modifications may be needed to address the specific problems encountered in crime–scene type samples. In forensic DNA testing, for example, problems with mixed body fluids in sexual assault cases have been addressed by Gill et al.[1] by developing a procedure for the differential analysis of epithelial and sperm cells. The FBI and the RCMP have approached the problem of maximizing discrimination between small fragments in partially degraded evidence samples by selecting the four–base cutter *Hae*III as a restriction enzyme.[35] The effect on DNA of crime scene contaminants and other environmental factors has been explored by a number of workers[36–40] and is still an area of active research.

The extent to which a crime laboratory should conduct its own validation studies before implementing a previously published method in casework is a matter of professional judgement. However, it is generally recognized that use of a method based strictly on a literature report is not appropriate.[32] The process of replicating portions of previous validation work can be a useful training exercise for the staff and can buttress their confidence when they testify about the method. At the very least, the analysts must demonstrate analytical competence by completion of a series of proficiency tests before applying the method to casework. Significant modifications to published procedures must also be appropriately validated by comparison with the original method.[18,34]

STANDARDIZATION

The extent to which forensic DNA methods should be standardized is presently a topic of considerable discussion.[6,13,27,41,42] Standardization in this context means the use of identical procedures and/or procedures that give comparable results. *Standardization* (which is a means of restricting *what* methods can be used) differs from the term *standards* (which define the minimum quality assurance measures needed to achieve control over *how* the methods are used). The importance of quality assurance standards in general has been widely recognized by the forensic science profession. A number of specific DNA quality assurance proposals are discussed later in this chapter.

Clearly some standardization (in the sense of procedures that give comparable results) must exist if DNA profiling data are to be shared for criminal identification purposes. The FBI has taken a leadership role in this area by convening a working group of North American forensic DNA laboratories, the Technical Working Group on DNA Analysis Methods (TWGDAM), to identify a basic methodology (e.g., *Hae*III, core set of probes) to produce the core of an RFLP database. Strong support for the DNA identification database concept has been expressed by the American Society of Crime Laboratory Directors (ASCLD)[43] and by the legislatures of several states (including Virginia, California, Washington, North Carolina, Florida, Louisiana, Colorado, and Illinois) that have enacted statutes requiring convicted offenders to submit biological samples for DNA profiling.[44]

Standardization is also helpful to the collaborative method validation process and to the delivery of a massive training and technology transfer effort, such as is currently being undertaken by the FBI Forensic Science Research and Training Center. By the same token, rigid standardization can become a bottleneck to progress. Care must be taken that the database system is flexible enough to evolve with changing technology and that method selection is responsive to input from the entire forensic community. Crime laboratories should be free to investigate and implement additional testing methods, as long as they are subjected to the appropriate validation procedures. Limiting acceptable procedures only to those that are most

widely known or used would in the long run lead to stagnation and techno-
logical obsolescence.

QUALITY ASSURANCE STANDARDS

Quality assurance includes all those activities that the laboratory under-
takes in order to assure itself and its users that it meets defined standards of
quality. Every crime laboratory should have a quality assurance program
that addresses a) preservation and chain of custody of samples; b) competence of analysts; c) methods, materials, equipment, and procedures used in
the testing; and d) casework documentation, reporting, and testimony. General guidelines for crime laboratory quality assurance have been adopted by
the American Society of Crime Laboratory Directors (ASCLD)[32]; additional standards are articulated in the ASCLD/LAB (Laboratory Accreditation Board) *Accreditation Manual.*

The TWGDAM has developed specific RFLP quality assurance recommendations, endorsed by the ASCLD (reproduced in Appendix A), that
provide a framework upon which individual crime laboratories may con-
struct written quality assurance procedures for their DNA programs.[34] The
TWGDAM guidelines stress the need for analysts and supervisors to be
experienced in both conventional serology and forensic DNA typing, as well
to have completed coursework in genetics, biochemistry, and molecular
biology. The guidelines require a formal training program that includes
both written and practical proficiency tests. Periodic follow-up proficiency
tests and audits are recommended.

The TWGDAM recommendations regarding validation of probes parallel
those of the AABB Parentage Testing Committee and the International
Society for Forensic Haemogenetics.[9,33] Loci selected for forensic RFLP
analysis must have known Mendelian inheritance and chromosomal designation, and must be somatically stable; the restriction endonuclease and
probes used must be documented in the literature; and statistical evaluation
should be supported by an appropriate database. Probes used should be
readily available to the forensic science community and must have been
properly validated.

The TWGDAM guidelines also delineate the requirements for internal
controls and standards. The quantity and quality of DNA recovered from
specimens are to be estimated. Restriction should be monitored by testing
each lot of enzyme and by the use of a test gel. Controls for the analytical
gel must include visual markers, molecular weight size markers, and a
human DNA control. A procedure should be in place to identify and com-
pensate for possible migrational differences (i.e. band shifts) in the DNA
fragments. There must be independent review of the results by a second
examiner/analyst. Notes, autoradiograms, and other documentation that

support the conclusions in the report must be available for review. Reports should identify the DNA locus, as defined by the probe, and the restriction enzyme used.

LIAISON OUTSIDE OF THE LABORATORY

It is axiomatic that the quality of the analysis in the crime laboratory cannot exceed the quality of the submitted evidence. Further, the effectiveness of an analysis ultimately resides in its impact on significant decision-making in the case.[45] The laboratory has a vested interest in improving the ability of its client agencies to recognize, collect, and properly preserve physical evidence and an equally strong interest in seeing that its work product is presented appropriately in court.

The crime laboratory would do well to establish a strong outreach program through which the scientific staff can provide information regarding the value and limitations of physical evidence to all quarters of the criminal justice system. Periodic training seminars for medical examiners, crime scene investigators, detectives, and attorneys on the value and limitations of biological evidence and genetic marker typing will go a long way toward increasing support for the laboratory's DNA program, in addition to improving the quality of the evidence the laboratory has to work with. Feedback from investigators, prosecutors, and defense attorneys regarding the laboratory's services and the quality of its reports and testimony can also be a valuable quality assurance tool for the laboratory manager.

A concerted effort to train victim advocates and health practitioners involved in the examination of sexual assault victims will prove especially fruitful in view of the potential impact of DNA testing in cases of rape. The crime laboratory should be actively involved in developing and delivering training on evidence collection for hospital emergency rooms and/or trauma centers. Many states have already established excellent protocols for the examination of sexual assault victims.[46] These should be reviewed in the light of DNA testing and should be updated where necessary.

Training on evidence collection and preservation should stress the fact that DNA evidence, like conventional protein markers, is highly susceptible to degradation in the presence of moisture.[47] Therefore, collection protocols should emphasize the need to thoroughly dry evidence stains and samples collected on swabs before packaging. Once dried, samples should be stored frozen. The degradation of DNA by restriction nucleases is diminished in the presence of the chelating agent EDTA. It is advisable to collect reference blood standards from victims and suspects in EDTA (purple-topped) vacutainers.

Close liaison between the crime laboratory and the attorneys who will be presenting DNA results is vital to the effective presentation of this sophisticated evidence in the courtroom. Especially during the initial implementation phase, there may be extensive admissibility hearings. An inadequate record caused by lack of preparation on the part of the attorney can result in adverse rulings that have an impact far beyond the instant case. Crime laboratory staff should be prepared to help the attorney to understand the basic science of the analysis and to become aware of the significance and the limitations of the data generated in the case. The laboratory can also assist the attorney by identifying supportive literature and independent expert witnesses to participate in the hearings. The laboratory must be prepared to make full disclosure of the data generated in the validation experiments, the documentation of its quality assurance program and population database, and the documentation (notes, autorads, calculations, etc.) generated in the case that supports the conclusions of the analyst.

In addition to contacts within the criminal justice system, liaison with the relevant scientific community (e.g., molecular biology, population genetics) outside of forensic science is also important for the crime laboratory. To strengthen the rigor of its procedures, the crime laboratory would be wise to subject proposed analytical procedures and validation experiments to outside review. Such a peer review process will serve the additional purpose of establishing a pool of knowledgeable scientists who can provide supporting testimony in hearings on the admissibility of DNA testing. The state of New York, for example, has proposed the creation of a scientific review panel to approve new DNA typing methods before implementation in the state's laboratory system.

Finally, proposals to establish DNA databases have raised concern[13,42,48] over public policy issues, such as privacy rights and the reliability of laboratory work. It is wise for the agency preparing to implement a DNA program to acknowledge these concerns and to address them openly at public hearings and meetings. If the laboratory's quality assurance and information security measures are subjected to public review and comment, potential areas of conflict can be identified and resolved before they develop into significant problems.

MECHANISMS FOR PROFESSIONAL REVIEW

Like other professions, forensic science has both the right and the obligation to set standards for its own practice and to establish mechanisms for peer review of its practitioners. Crime laboratory managers have formally acknowledged their responsibility to provide leadership regarding standards for DNA implementation through their professional societies, e.g., the ASCLD and the California Association of Crime Laboratory Directors (CACLD). A laboratory implementing forensic DNA testing should comply with the general standards for crime laboratory operation articulated in the

ASCLD *Management Guidelines*[22] and ASCLD/LAB *Accreditation Manual,*[18] as well as with specific DNA guidelines and standards such as those outlined by the TWGDAM,[34] CALCD, and the International Society for Forensic Haemogenetics.[33]

The ASCLD/LAB accredits crime laboratories in the functional areas of serology, controlled substances, toxicology, trace evidence, documents, firearms/toolmarks, and latent prints. After the initial inspection, the applicant laboratory has up to a year to remedy deficiencies before the final decision to accredit is made by the ASCLD/LAB. The accreditation period is 5 years, and reaccreditation requires another on-site inspection.

The heart of the accreditation process is the on-site inspection, during which a team of trained inspectors examines the laboratory's facilities, equipment, and written and technical procedures, as well as interviewing the technical staff and reviewing case records. A crime laboratory must meet the accreditation standards in all of the functional areas in which it provides services in order to become accredited. The ASCLD/LAB regards DNA typing as a part of the serology function of the crime laboratory. A laboratory applying for accreditation by the ASCLD/LAB can expect the accreditation inspectors to apply the ASCLD-endorsed TWGDAM guidelines to the inspection of its DNA program.

The ASCLD/LAB accreditation program has been in existence since 1981. Since then, 64 laboratories from 18 federal, state, and local agencies have been accredited. This total represents approximately 20% of the nation's crime laboratories and is growing at a steady rate each year. Because the program is voluntary, it is unlikely that it will achieve the active participation of all eligible laboratories. However, its published standards are widely available and provide a yardstick against which the performance of any crime laboratory can be measured.

Proficiency testing by an external body is another important component of professional peer review. The ASCLD and the American Academy of Forensic Sciences sponsor a voluntary crime laboratory proficiency testing program administered by Collaborative Testing Services (CTS) in which approximately half of the crime laboratories in the country participate.[49] Many crime laboratories also subscribe to the AABB Parentage Proficiency Testing Program in Serology, which has recently added a DNA component. The establishment of a proficiency testing system in conjunction with the national DNA database is also on the agenda for the TWGDAM.

Another basic mechanism for professional review is the certification of individual analysts. Presently there is no formal program for certification of forensic serologists or DNA analysts, although it can be anticipated that the recently formed American Board of Criminalistics will eventually establish one. A certification program must be based on the development of a professional consensus regarding minimum standards of education, training, and practice. The TWGDAM guidelines regarding personnel qualifications could form the nucleus around which such a consensus could be built. Indeed, the need for standards in DNA analysis may prove to be the catalyst needed for forensic serologists to agree on standards of training and education leading to certification.

CONCLUSION—TOWARD THE FUTURE

It is clear that DNA testing should be a part of the crime laboratory's serology services, and it appears that DNA typing will eventually supplant much of the protein-based genetic testing that currently forms the backbone of forensic serology. It is anticipated that many local forensic laboratories will implement DNA testing within the next 2–5 years, although some may elect to continue referral of cases to the FBI laboratory or to private vendors.

Some standardization of methodology is necessary to allow training and technology transfer on such a large scale and to support the development of a national DNA identification database. Within these boundaries, however, it is important to remain flexible and to encourage advances in technology. The "acid test" of the acceptability of a method should not be its widespread use but rather acceptability should be based upon the demonstration that it gives reliable results and that it is being applied by competent people.

The intense legal interest in forensic DNA typing has attracted considerable attention recently from the scientific community at large[13,42,50,51] and has prompted a proposal for a review by the National Academy of Sciences as well.[52] Through professional mechanisms such as the ASCLD/LAB and the TWGDAM, the forensic science community has demonstrated the willingness and ability to assume its proper role in establishing and enforcing professional standards. In order to meet the rigorous challenges ahead, the community must continue and intensify these and other efforts to meet its professional responsibilities.

REFERENCES

1. Gill, P. "Forensic Applications of DNA Fingerprints," *Nature* 318:577–579 (1985).
2. Dodd, B. "DNA Fingerprinting in Matters of Family and Crime," *Nature* 318:506–507 (1985).
3. Sensabaugh, G. F. "Forensic Biology—Is Recombinant DNA Technology in its Future?" *J. Forensic Sci.* 31:393–396 (1986).
4. Thompson, W. and S. Ford "DNA Typing: Acceptance and Weight of New Genetic Identification Tests," *Virg. Law Rev.* 75(1), 45–103 (1989).
5. Van deKamp, J. Speech to California Attorney General's Conference on Forensic DNA Testing, Los Angeles, January 7, 1988.

6. Hicks, J. "DNA Profiling: A Tool for Law Enforcement," *FBI Law Enf. Bull.* 1–3 (August 1988).
7. Ferrara, P. "Report of the DNA Implementation Committee to the American Society of Crime Laboratory Directors' Board of Directors," May 1989.
8. Bashinski, J. "Report of the California Association of Criminalists DNA Committee," July 1989.
9. "Standards for Tests Involving DNA Polymorphisms," American Association of Blood Banks Parentage Testing Committee, November 1987.
10. "Rape Murder Jury Did Not Fail Its Job; The Authorities Did," editorial in *Reno Gazette-Journal* February 16, 1989.
11. "Rape Case Clemency Appeal," article in the *San Jose Mercury News*, August 16, 1988.
12. Werrett, D. and W. Eubanks, personal communication (1989).
13. Poklemha, J. *"DNA: Report of New York State Forensic DNA Analysis Panel,"* Office of Director of Criminal Justice and Commissioner, September 6, 1989.
14. Eubanks, W. "Cost, Implementation and Training for DNA Analysis," paper presented at the International Symposium On the Forensic Aspects of DNA Analysis, Quantico, VA, June 22, 1989.
15. Stuver, W. "DNA Analysis in the Metro-Dade Laboratory," paper presented at the International Symposium On the Forensic Aspects of DNA Analysis, Quantico, VA, June 22, 1989.
16. Cellmark Diagnostics, 20271 Goldenrod Lane, Germantown, MD 20874; LifeCodes, Old Saw Mill River Road, Valhalla, NY 10595; Cetus Corporation, 1450 53rd Street, Emeryville, CA 94608; Analytical Genetic Testing Center, 7808 Cherry Creek South Drive #201, Denver, CO 80231.
17. McLaren, J. and M. Mount "Forensic Laboratory Planning and Design," paper presented at the Symposium on Crime Laboratory Development, Quantico, VA, September 29, 1989.
18. *Accreditation Manual,* American Society of Crime Laboratory Directors/Laboratory Accreditation Board (1985).
19. Riley, J. "Radiation Aspects of DNA Analysis," *Crime Lab. Dig.* 15(Suppl. 1):15–16 (1988).
20. von Beroldingen, C., E. Blake, R. Higuchi, G. Sensabaugh, and H. Erlich, "Applications of PCR to the Analysis of Biological Evidence" in *PCR Technology*, H. Erlich, Ed. (New York: Stockton Press, 1989), 209–223.
21. Eubanks, W. "Expenses Associated with DNA Typing Methods," *Crime Lab. Dig.* 15(Suppl. 1):12–14 (1988).
22. Reid, S., Cetus Corporation, personal communication (1989).
23. Resolution of the American Society of Crime Laboratory Directors/Laboratory Accreditation Board, September 24, 1989.
24. "Final Report to the Legislature," California Attorney General's Advisory Board, July 27, 1989.

25. *CA Penal Code* Section 290.2, as amended by Senate Bill 1408, October 1, 1989.
26. Caskey, C. T. "A Critical Evaluation of the Laboratory Techniques," paper presented at the Banbury Conference on DNA Technology and Forensic Science, Cold Spring Harbor, NY, November 29, 1988.
27. Bashinski, J. "Laboratory Standards, Accreditation, Training and Certification of Staff in the Forensic Context," in *DNA Technology and Forensic Science,* Banbury Conference #32, (Cold Spring Harbor, NY: Cold Spring Harbor Laboratory, 1989).
28. "Position on DNA Typing of Forensic Samples," California Association of Crime Laboratory Directors, November 20, 1987.
29. Benson W., J. Stacy, and M. Worley "Systems Analysis of Criminalistics Operations Kansas City, MO," (Midwest Research Institute, 1970).
30. Sensabaugh, G. F. "Biochemical Markers of Individuality" in *Forensic Science Handbook*, R. Saferstein, Ed., (New Jersey: Prentice-Hall, 1982), 338–415.
31. Budowle, B., H. Deadman, R. Murch, and F. S. Baechtel "An Introduction to Methods of DNA Analysis Under Investigation in the FBI Laboratory," *Crime Lab. Dig.*, 15(1):8–21(1988).
32. "ASCLD Guidelines for Forensic Laboratory Management Practices," *Crime Lab. Dig.* 14(2):39–46 (1987).
33. "DNA Recommendations," Executive Committee of the International Society for Forensic Haemogenetics (1989).
34. Technical Working Group on DNA Analysis Methods "Guidelines for a Quality Assurance Program for DNA Restriction Fragment Length Polymorphism Analysis" *Crime Lab. Dig.* 16(2):40–59 (1989).
35. Budowle, B., J. Waye, G. Shutler, and F. S. Baechtel "Hae III: A Suitable Restriction Endonuclease for Restriction Fragment Length Polymorphism," *J. Forensic Sci.*, (in press, 1989).
36. McNally, L., R. Shaler, A. Guisiti, M. Baird, and I. Balazs "The Effects of Environment and Drying Surfaces on DNA: The Use of Casework Samples from New York City," *J. Forensic Sci.*, 34:1070–1077 (1989).
37. Adams, D. "Validation of the FBI Procedure for DNA Analysis: A Summary," *Crime Lab. Dig.* 15(4):106–108 (1988).
38. Buoncristiani, M., C. von Beroldingen, and G. F. Sensabaugh "Effects of UV Damage on DNA Amplification by the Polymerase Chain Reaction," poster presented at the International Symposium On the Forensic Aspects of DNA Analysis, Quantico, VA, June 22, 1989.
39. Konzak, K., R. Reynolds, C. von Beroldingen, M. Buoncristaini, and G. F. Sensabaugh "Effects of DNA Damage and Degradation on RFLP Analysis," poster presented at the International Symposium On the Forensic Aspects of DNA Analysis, Quantico, VA, June 22, 1989.
40. Reynolds, R., C. von Beroldingan, and G. F. Sensabaugh, "Effects of DNA Degradation on Amplification by the Polymerase Chain Reaction," poster presented at the International Symposium On the Forensic Aspects of DNA Analysis, Quantico, VA, June 22, 1989.
41. "The Combined DNA Index System (CODIS): A Theoretical Model,"

Data Base Subcommittee of the Technical Working Group on DNA Analysis Methods, October 15, 1989.

42. "Forensic Uses of DNA Tests," Project Director Robyn Nishimi (U. S. Congress Office of Technology Assessment, in press 1989).

43. Resolution adopted by the ASCLD Board of Directors, May 1989.

44. Gordimer, D. "Report of the ASCLD Legislative Committee," American Society of Crime Laboratory Directors Annual Meeting, Quantico, VA, September 27, 1989.

45. Peterson, J., S. Mihajlovic, and M. Gilliland, *Forensic Evidence and the Police: The Effects of Scientific Evidence on Criminal Cases* (Washington D.C.: U.S. Govt. Printing Office, 1984).

46. *California Medical Protocol for Examination of Sexual Assault and Child Sexual Abuse Victims* (Sacramento, CA: Office of Criminal Justice Planning, 1987).

47. McNally, L., R. Shaler, A. Guisiti, M. Baird, and I. Balazs "Evaluation of DNA Isolated From Human Bloodstains Exposed to Ultraviolet Light, Heat, Humidity, and Soil Contamination," *J. Forensic Sci.* 34:1059–1069 (1989).

48. Reilly, P. "Regulation of Access to Genetic Data," paper presented at the Banbury Conference on DNA Technology and Forensic Science, Cold Spring Harbor, NY, November 29, 1988.

49. Lucas, D., C. Leete, and K. Field "An American Proficiency Testing Program," *Forensic Sci. Int.* 27:71–79 (1985).

50. *DNA Technology and Forensic Science*, Banbury Conference #32 (Cold Spring Harbor, NY: Cold Spring Harbor Laboratory, 1989).

51. Lander, E. "DNA Fingerprinting on Trial," *Nature* 339:501–505 (1989).

52. Kearney, J. FBI Forensic Science Research and Training Center, personal communication (1989).

APPENDIX A

GUIDELINES FOR A QUALITY ASSURANCE PROGRAM FOR DNA RESTRICTION FRAGMENT LENGTH POLYMORPHISM ANALYSIS*

Technical Working Group on DNA Analysis Methods (TWGDAM)

James J. Kearney, TWGDAM Chairman
FBI Laboratory
Quantico, Virginia

Quality Assurance Subcommittee
James L. Mudd, Subcommittee Chairman
FBI Laboratory
Quantico, Virginia

John M. Hartmann
Orange County Sheriff-Coroner Department
Santa Ana, California

Margaret C. Kuo
Orange County Sheriff-Coroner Department
Santa Ana, California

Mark S. Nelson
North Carolina State Bureau of Investigation
Raleigh, North Carolina

Lawrence A. Presley
FBI Laboratory
Washington, D.C.

Willard C. Stuver
Metro-Dade Police Department
Miami, Florida

*Reprinted with permission from *Crime Laboratory Digest* Vol. 16. No. 2 April-July 1989.

INTRODUCTION

With the advent of DNA typing technology in the forensic laboratory, the forensic examiner now has the potential to individualize various body fluids and tissues. In addition, since the tests performed by crime laboratories can have a significant impact on the outcome of a trial, it is important that any test procedure used by the laboratory possess a high degree of accuracy and reproducibility. Consequently, the use of appropriate standards and controls is essential in order to ensure reliable results.

As any technology becomes more discriminating and precise, it is essential that the quality of the analytical data be more closely monitored. A detailed and flexible quality assurance program can assist in establishing a basis for scientifically sound and reliable forensic analysis.

Although often used interchangeably, quality assurance (QA) and quality control (QC) refer to different, specific quality functions.[1-4] The function of the QA program is to provide to all concerned the evidence needed to establish with confidence that the QC function is being performed adequately. This is accomplished in part through the use of proficiency tests and audits. The QC measures are employed by the DNA analysis laboratory to ensure that the quality of the product (DNA typing) will meet and satisfy specified criteria.

Although the application of formal QA programs in forensic laboratories is currently not widespread and little information has appeared in the forensic science literature,[4-6] a great deal has been written on the application of QA programs to clinical and federally operated laboratories.[7-18]

In November 1988, the first meeting of the Technical Working Group on DNA Analysis Methods (TWGDAM) was hosted by the FBI Laboratory at the FBI Academy. This group consisted of 31 scientists representing 16 forensic laboratories in the United States and Canada and 2 research institutions. The purpose of this group is: a) to pull together a select number of individuals from the forensic science community who are actively pursuing the various DNA analysis methods, b) to discuss the methods now being used, c) to compare the work that has been done, d) to share protocols, and e) to establish guidelines where appropriate. During the first meeting, a subcommittee was established to formulate suggested guidelines for a QA program in crime laboratories conducting restriction fragment length polymorphism (RFLP) DNA analysis.

These guidelines represent the minimum QA requirements for DNA RFLP analysis and are intended to serve only as a guide to laboratory managers in establishing their own QA program for DNA RFLP analysis.

These QA guidelines were designed, using established quality functions[19-24] to follow systematically the DNA RFLP typing procedure and to cover all significant aspects of the laboratory process. In addition, they provide the necessary documentation to ensure that the DNA analysis process is operating within the established performance criteria, and they provide a measure of the quality of the results.

The guidelines form the basis of a quality assurance program for RFLP analysis and are subject to future revisions as the state of the art and experience dictate.

1. Planning and Organization

1.1   Goals: It is the goal of the (organization's name) to:
- 1.1.1   Provide the users of laboratory services access to DNA typing of selected biological materials associated with official investigations using RFLP DNA testing.
- 1.1.2   Ensure the quality, integrity, and accuracy of the DNA typing data through the implementation of a detailed QA program.

1.2   Objectives: It is the objective of the QA program to:
- 1.2.1   Monitor on a routine basis the analytical testing procedures for DNA typing by means of QC standards, proficiency tests, and audits.
- 1.2.2   Verify that the entire DNA typing procedure is operating within the established performance criteria and that the quality and validity of the analytical data is maintained.
- 1.2.3   Ensure that problems are noted and that corrective action is taken and documented.

1.3   Authority and Accountability
- 1.3.1   Organization Structure: Defines the relationships within the laboratory between individuals, job responsibilities, and operational units. It defines the relationship of the QA program to DNA analysis and related laboratory operations, as well as to the laboratory management.
- 1.3.2   Functional Responsibilities: The job function and responsibility for each position within the laboratory should be clearly established. It should specify and describe the lines of responsibility to developing, implementing, recording, and updating the QA system.
- 1.3.3   Levels of Authority: Clear lines of authority and accountability should be established between personnel responsible for the QA program and those assigned to manage and perform the DNA analysis. It should be established as to who may take what action, whether approval is required, and from whom approvals are needed.

2. Personnel

   2.1 Job descriptions
   The job descriptions for all DNA personnel should include responsibilities, duties, and skills
   2.2 Qualifications
   The criteria for qualifications and training of technical personnel within the DNA testing laboratory will be established by each laboratory. Each individual engaged in the typing of DNA should have, at a minimum, the education, training, and experience as specified in Sections 2.2.1 through 2.2.3.
   2.2.1 Supervisor
   2.2.1.1 Education — Must have a minimum of a BA/BS degree in a biological, chemical, or forensic science.
   2.2.1.2 Training — It is highly desirable that this individual have the following:
   (a) Training in DNA analysis technique with individuals, agencies, or other laboratories having an established training program that meets American Society of Crime Laboratory Directors (ASCLD) accreditation standards (ASCLD 1985),
   and
   b) Undergraduate or graduate courses in genetics, biochemistry, and molecular biology (molecular genetics or recombinant DNA technology).
   2.2.1.3 Experience — Technical supervisors should have a minimum of 2 years of experience as a forensic science analyst/examiner and 6 months of DNA laboratory experience.
   2.2.1.4 Qualification — It is highly desirable that a supervisor meets the same requirements as those specified for an examiner/analyst in 2.2.2.4.
   2.2.1.5 Continuing Education — Supervisors should stay abreast of developments within the field of DNA typing by reading current scientific literature and attending seminars, courses, or professional meetings. Management should provide supervisors with an opportunity to comply with the above.
   2.2.2 Examiner/Analyst
   2.2.2.1 Education — Must have a minimum of a BA/BS

degree in a biological, chemical, or forensic science.

2.2.2.2 Training — Must include as minimum the following:

(a) Training in DNA analysis technique with individuals, agencies, or other laboratories having an established training program that meets ASCLD accreditation standards (ASCLD 1985).

and

(b) Undergraduate or graduate courses in genetics, biochemistry, and molecular biology (Molecular genetics or recombinant DNA technology).

2.2.2.3 Experience — Prior to any DNA typing and reporting on case work samples, the examiner/analyst must have a minimum of 6 months of forensic DNA laboratory experience. It is highly desirable that the examiner/analyst have minimum of 1 year forensic laboratory experience.

2.2.2.4 Qualification — The minimum requirements for qualification of examiner/analysts within a laboratory must be based on the experience, training, and job knowledge of the individual and on the successful completion of a formal system of training, which requires the passing of specified tests and a demonstration of a thorough knowledge of the theory and practice of DNA typing. These minimum requirements also must include the successful completion of a series of proficiency samples.

2.2.2.5 In-House Qualification Standards for Examiner/Analyst — It is highly recommended that the examiner/analyst complete the requirements for any in-house certification, which should include the following:

(a) Knowledge of the scientific literature and procedures with reference to DNA typing. This will be evaluated by written testing after training or from grades received in courses taken.

(b) Skills and mechanical abilities to perform the test can be evaluated by the observation of qualified personnel and by seeing if the proper test results are obtained.

(c) The ability to correctly interpret the test results is of paramount importance. All examiners should go through a well-documented and rigorous set of proficiency test samples while in training. After completion of the training program, examiners should undergo periodic in-house and blind proficiency testing administered by an outside agency.

2.2.2.6 Continuing   Education — Examiners/analysts must stay abreast of developments within the field of DNA typing by reading current scientific literature and through attendance at seminars, courses, or professional meetings. Management must provide examiners/analysts with an opportunity to comply with the above activities.

2.2.3   Technicians

2.2.3.1 Technicians not performing analytical techniques should have the experience and education commensurate with the job description.

2.2.3.2 Technicians involved in performing analytical techniques related to DNA analysis should have a minimum of a BS/BA degree and receive on-the-job training by a qualified analyst. It is understood that technicians will not have the responsibility for the interpretation of results, preparation of reports, or providing testimony concerning such.

3.   Documentation

The DNA laboratory must maintain documentation on all significant aspects of the DNA analysis procedure, as well as any related documents or laboratory records that are pertinent to the analysis or interpretation of results, so as to create a traceable audit trail. This documentation will serve as an archive for retrospective scientific inspection, reevaluation of the data, and reconstruction of the DNA procedure. Documentation will exist for the following topic areas:

3.1   Test Methods and Procedures for DNA Typing

3.1.1   This document must describe in explicit detail the protocol currently used for the analytical testing of DNA. It must include the date the procedure was adopted and the authorization for its use. Revisions must be clearly documented and appropriately authorized.

3.2　Population database

3.3　Quality control of critical reagents and materials to include lot and batch numbers, manufacturer's specifications, and in-house evaluations.

3.4　Case files/case notes — Must provide foundation for results and conclusions contained in formal report.

3.5　Data analysis and reporting

3.6　Evidence handling protocols

3.7　Equipment calibration and maintenance logs

3.8　Proficiency testing

3.9　Personnel training and qualification records

3.10　Method validation records

3.11　Quality assurance and audit records

3.12　Quality assurance manual

3.13　Equipment inventory

3.14　Safety manuals

3.15　Material safety data sheets

3.16　Historical or archival records

3.17　Licenses and certificates

4.　Materials and Equipment

Only suitable and properly operating equipment should be employed. Chemicals and reagents should be of suitable quality, correctly prepared, and demonstrated to be compatible with the methods employed.

4.1　Instruments and Equipment

　　4.1.1　Inventory — A list of equipment essential for DNA analysis which includes the manufacturer, model, serial number, agency inventory number, and purchase and replacement dates.

　　4.1.2　Operation Manual — The manufacturer's operation manual should be readily available.

　　4.1.3　Calibration and Maintenance Procedure — There should be written calibration and maintenance procedures and schedules.

　　4.1.4　Calibration and Maintenance Logs — There should be a permanent log of calibration and maintenance of equipment essential for DNA typing.

4.2　Chemicals and Reagents

　　4.2.1　Logs must be maintained of all commercial supplies and kits (such as probes and restriction enzymes), as indicated in Section 3.3.

      4.2.2   Formulation—There must be a written procedure for the formulation of reagents, standards, and controls.

      4.2.3   Labelling Requirements—To include identity, concentration, date of preparation, identity of analyst preparing reagents (storage requirements, and expiration date where appropriate).

      4.2.4   Storage and Disposal—All chemicals and radioactive materials must be stored, used, and disposed of in a manner conforming to established safety requirements.

      4.2.5   Material Safety Data Sheets (MSDS)—There should be a file of MSDS received from the manufacturer for all chemicals used in the laboratory. These data sheets should be readily available to all laboratory personnel.

      4.2.6   A current inventory should be maintained to include information on supplier, catalog number, lot number, date received, and storage location.

  4.3   Glassware and Plasticware

      4.3.1   Preparation—There should be specific procedures for cleaning, preparation, and sterilization.

      4.3.2   Disposal—There should be specific procedures for the safe disposal of contaminated or broken glassware or plasticware.

5.   Validation of Analytical Procedures

  5.1   DNA Probes

      5.1.1   The DNA probe(s) selected for use in forensic analysis should be readily available to the forensic science community.

  5.2   DNA Loci for RFLP Analysis[25,26]

      5.2.1   Inheritance—DNA loci used in forensic testing shall have been validated by family studies to demonstrate that the loci exhibit Mendelian inheritance as reported in scientific communications. For those DNA loci used in parentage testing, the frequency of mutation and/or recombination should not be greater than 0.2%.

      5.2.2   Gene Mapping—The chromosomal location of the polymorphic loci (single-locus polymorphisms) used for forensic testing shall be submitted to or recorded in the Yale Gene Library or by the International Human Gene Mapping Workshop.

      5.2.3   Documentation—The polymorphic loci shall be documented in the literature stating the restriction endonuclease and the probes used to detect the polymorphism.

5.2.4 Polymorphism—The type of polymorphism detected shall be known (that is, single locus or multiloci).

5.2.5 Population Studies—Population distributions for at least the commonly recognized racial groups should be determined for the restriction enzyme and locus combination.

5.3 Developmental Validation of the DNA Analysis Procedure

During the development of a RFLP procedure and prior to the adoption of the procedure by a DNA laboratory, validation studies must have been conducted by the scientific community. These validation studies form the basis for evaluating the validity, accuracy, and reproducibility of a particular DNA analysis procedure. This validation should include the following.[27]

5.3.1 Standard Specimens—The typing procedure should be evaluated using fresh body tissues, and fluids that have been obtained and stored in a controlled manner. Determine if DNA isolated from different tissues from the same individual yields the same typing profiles.

5.3.2 Consistency—Using specimens obtained from donors of known phenotypes/genotype, evaluate the reproducibility of the technique both within the laboratory and among different laboratories.

5.3.3 Population Studies—Establish population distribution data in different racial groups for restriction fragment bands detected by a given restriction enzyme-DNA probe pair.

5.3.4 Reproducibility—Prepare dried stains using body fluids from donors of known phenotypes and analyze to ensure that the stain specimens exhibit accurate, interpretable, and reproducible DNA typing profiles that match the profiles obtained on liquid specimens.

5.3.5 Time/Temperature Studies—Determine if the polymorphic patterns in dried stains change as a function of time and temperature.

5.3.6 Degradation Studies—Expose laboratory-prepared body fluid stains to a variety of commonly encountered substances to assess the impact of these substances on DNA profiles.

5.3.7 Nonprobative Evidence—Examine DNA profiles in nonprobative evidentiary stain materials. Compare the DNA profiles obtained for the known liquid blood versus questioned blood deposited on typical crime scene evidence.

5.3.8 Nonhuman Studies—Determine if DNA typing methods designed for use with human specimens detect DNA profiles in nonhuman source stains.

5.3.9   On-Site Evaluation — Set up newly developed typing methods in the case working laboratory for on-site evaluation of the procedure.

5.3.10   It is essential that the results of experimental studies be shared as soon as possible with the scientific community through presentations at scientific/professional meetings. It is imperative that the complete details of the experimental study be afforded the opportunity for peer review through timely publications in scientific journals.

5.4   In-House Validation of Established Procedures[28]

Prior to implementing a new RFLP procedure, or an existing RFLP procedure developed by another laboratory that meets the developmental criteria described under Section 5.3, the forensic laboratory must first validate this procedure in its own laboratory. This same prerequisite would apply to any existing procedure to which significant modifications have been made. This validation study forms the basis for assessing the specificity, reproducibility, and limitations of the particular RFLP procedure. This validation must include the following:

5.4.1   The method must be tested using known samples.

5.4.2   The method must be tested using proficiency test samples. The proficiency test may be administered internally, externally, or collaboratively.

5.4.3   If a significant modification has been made to an analytical procedure, the modified procedure must be compared to the original using identical samples.

5.4.4   Measurement imprecision must be determined by repetitive analyses for establishing matching criteria.

6.   Evidence Handling Procedures

Evidence and samples from evidence must be collected, received, handled, sampled, and stored so as to preserve the identity, integrity, condition, and security of the item. Destructive testing of evidence and evidence samples should be performed so as to provide the maximum utility from the most economical consumption.

6.1   Sample Labeling — Each sample must be labeled with a unique identifier in accordance with agency policy.

6.2   Sample Handling — Each agency will prepare a written policy to ensure that evidence samples will be handled so as to prevent loss, alteration, or contamination.

6.3 Chain of Custody—A clear, well-documented chain of custody must be maintained from the time the evidence is first received until it is released from the laboratory.[29]

7. Internal Controls and Standards

7.1 Procedures for Estimating DNA Recovery
A procedure must be used for estimating the quality (extent of DNA degradation) and quantity of DNA recovered from the specimens. One or more of the following procedures may be employed to evaluate the effectiveness of the DNA recovery:

7.1.1 Yield Gel—Yield gels must include a set of high molecular weight DNA calibration standards for quantitative estimate of yield. This procedure provides an estimate of the quantity of DNA recovered and the degree of DNA degradation, or

7.1.2 UV Absorbance—260/280 nm absorbance to provide measures of the quantity of DNA extracted from liquid blood. This procedure provides an estimate for the quantity of DNA recovered and assesses organic solvent and protein contamination in the recovered DNA, or

7.1.3 Fluorescence—Approximate quantitation of extracted DNA by comparison with known concentration of high molecular weight DNA. This procedure provides only an estimate of the quantity of DNA recovered, or

7.1.4 Hybridization—Hybridization with probes to repetitive DNA specific to human/primate DNA. This procedure provides an estimate of the quantity of human DNA recovered.

7.2 Restriction Enzymes
7.2.1 Prior to its initial use, each lot of restriction enzyme should be tested against an appropriate viral, human, or other DNA standard that produces an expected DNA fragment pattern under standard digestion conditions. The restriction enzyme should also be tested under conditions that will reveal contaminating nuclease activity.

7.3 Demonstration of Restriction Enzyme Digestion—Digestion of extracted DNA by the restriction enzyme should be demonstrated using a test gel that includes:
7.3.1 Size Marker—Determines approximate size range of digested DNA.
7.3.2 Human DNA Control—Measures the effectiveness of restriction enzyme genomic human DNA.

7.4   Analytical Gel — The analytical gel used to measure restriction fragments must include the following:

    7.4.1   Visual Marker — Visual or fluorescent markers that are used to determine the end point of electrophoresis.

    7.4.2   Molecular Weight Size Markers — Markers that span the RFLP size range and are used to determine the size of unknown restriction fragments. Case samples must be bracketed (as defined by the sample lanes) by molecular weight size markers.

    7.4.3   Human DNA Control — Documented human DNA control of known phenotype/genotype that produces a known fragment pattern with each probe and serves as a system check for the following functions:

        a. electrophoresis quality and resolution

        b. sizing process

        c. probe identity

        d. hybridization efficiency

        e. stripping losses

    7.4.4   A procedure should be available to identify and compensate for possible migrational differences in the DNA fragments.

7.5   Southern Blots/Hybridization — The efficiency of blotting, hybridizations, and stringency washes is monitored by the human DNA control and size markers.

7.6   Autoradiography — The exposure intensity is monitored by the use of multiple x-ray films or by successive exposures in order to obtain films of the proper intensity for image analysis.

7.7   Image and Data Processing — The functioning of image and data processing is monitored by the human DNA control allelic values.

8.   Data Analysis and Reporting

8.1   Autoradiographs and data must be reviewed independently by a second examiner/analyst. If a detection method other than autoradiography is used, the analytical results must be reviewed independently by a second examiner/analyst. Both examiners/analysts must agree on the interpretation of the data to be reported.

8.2   For proper data interpretation, the measured sizes of the restriction fragment bands of the human DNA control must fall within the established tolerance limits. Visual matching of the restriction fragment bands must be confirmed with statistical analysis based on tolerance limits.

8.3   The matching restriction fragment bands are assigned a frequency of occurrence calculated using a scientifically valid and accepted method from an established population database.

8.4 The human DNA controls should be monitored by means of established statistical quality control methods.[30-38]

8.5 Report Writing and Review — Laboratories should have policies, checks, and balances in place that ensure the accuracy and completeness of reports. It is highly desirable that the laboratory reports be signed by the reporting analyst.

    8.5.1 Contents — In addition to the presentation of the findings and conclusions of the examiner/analyst, the DNA locus (defined by the Nomenclature Committee of the International Gene Workshop), as identified by a particular probe, as well as the restriction enzyme used to digest the DNA, should be included.

    8.5.2 All reports should be reviewed by appropriately designated personnel.

9. Proficiency Testing

9.1 Open Proficiency Test — Open proficiency tests must be submitted to the DNA testing laboratory on a semiannual basis (minimum) such that each analyst is tested at least annually. These are labeled as proficiency test specimens and may be prepared internally and/or may be part of an external proficiency-testing program.

9.2 Blind Proficiency Test — Blind proficiency test specimens must be submitted to the DNA testing laboratory on a regular basis and are prepared in such a way as to appear as routine case specimens. These specimens may be prepared internally and/or may be part of an external or proficiency-testing program. Each analyst should be tested at least annually.

9.3 A file will be maintained of all proficiency test results. Each laboratory will have a written policy for dealing with deficiencies. When deficiencies are noted, the file will identify the cause of the deficiency and the corrective action taken.

10. Audits

Audits are an important aspect of the quality assurance program. They are an independent review conducted to compare the various aspects of the DNA laboratory's performance with a standard for that performance. The audits are not punitive in nature, but are intended to provide management with an evaluation of the laboratory's performance in meeting its quality policies and objectives.

10.1 Audits or inspections should be conducted annually by individuals separate from and independent of the DNA testing laboratory. It is highly desirable that at least one auditor be from an outside agency.

10.2 Records of each inspection should be maintained and should include the date of the inspection, area inspected, name of the person conducting the inspection, findings and problems, remedial actions taken to resolve existing problems, and the schedule of next inspection.

11. Safety

11.1 Policy—The DNA testing laboratory shall operate in strict accordance with the regulations of the pertinent federal, state, and local health and safety authorities.

11.2 Written Manuals—Written general laboratory safety and radiation safety manuals shall be prepared by the laboratory and be made available to each member of the DNA analysis laboratory and/or other persons affected.[40-49]

PARTICIPANTS
TECHNICAL WORKING GROUP ON DNA ANALYSIS METHODS

Lucy A. Davis
Kentucky State Police
   Forensic Laboratory
1250 Louisville Road
Frankfort, KY 40601

Terry L. Laber
Minnesota Forensic Science
   Laboratory
1246 University Avenue
St. Paul, MN 55104

Michael A. DeGuglielmo
North Carolina State Bureau
   Investigation
3320 Old Garner Road
Raleigh, NC 27626

Henry C. Lee
Connecticut State Police
294 Colony Street
Meriden, CT 06450

Jacqueline A. Emrich
Commonwealth of Virginia
   Crime Laboratory
401-A Colley Avenue
Norfolk, VA 23507

Don McLaren
Washington State Patrol
   Crime Laboratory
Public Safety Building
Seattle, WA 98104

Ronald M. Fourney
Royal Canadian Mounted
  Police Central
  Forensic Laboratory
1200 Alta Vista Drive
Ottawa, Ontario, Canada
K1G 3M8

Richard A. Guerrieri
Commonwealth of Virginia
  Crime Laboratory
401-A Colley Avenue
Norfolk, VA 23507-1966

M. Roger Kahn
Metro-Dade Police Department
1320 N.W. 14th Street
Miami, FL 33125

Kenneth C. Konzak
California Department of
  Justice
140 Warren Hall
Berkeley, CA 94720

Margaret C. Kuo
Orange County Sheriff's-
  Coroner Office
601 Ross Street
Santa Ana, CA 92701

Willard C. Stuver
Metro-Dade Police Department
1320 N.W. 14th Street
Miami, FL 33125

Scott A. Wanlass
Nassau County Police
  Department
1490 Franklin Avenue
Mineola, NY 11501

Susan D. Narveson
Arizona Department of Public
  Crime Laboratory
Post Office Box 6638
Phoenix, AZ 85005

Mark S. Nelson
North Carolina State Bureau of
  Investigation Crime
  Laboratory
3320 Old Garner Road
Raleigh, NC 27626

Pamela J. Newall
Centre for Forensic Sciences
25 Grosvenor Street
Toronto, Canada M7A 2G8

James M. Pollock
Florida Department of Law
  Enforcement
Post Office Box 4999
Jacksonville, FL 32211

George F. Sensabaugh
University of California
  School of Public Health
Berkeley, CA 94720

Bruce Budowle
Forensic Science Research Unit
FBI Laboratory

Catherine T. Comey
Forensic Science Research Unit
FBI Laboratory

John S. Waye
Royal Canadian Mounted
  Central Forensic
  Laboratory
Post Office Box 8885
1200 Alta Vista Drive
Ottawa, Ontario, Canada
  K1G 3M8

Raymond White
Howard Hughes Medical
  Institute
University of Utah School
  of Medicine
Salt Lake City, UT 84132

Dwight E. Adams
DNA Analysis Unit
FBI Laboratory

Stephen P. Allen, Jr.
Forensic Science Research
  Unit
FBI Laboratory

F. Samuel Baechtel
Forensic Science Research
FBI Laboratory

William Eubanks
DNA Analysis Unit
FBI Laboratory

George F. Foresen
Technical Services Division
FBI

Keith L. Monson
Forensic Science Research Unit
FBI Laboratory

James L. Mudd
Forensic Science Research Unit
FBI Laboratory

Lawrence A. Presley
DNA Analysis Unit
FBI Laboratory

REFERENCES

1. American National Standard ANSI/ASQC A3–1978 "Quality Systems Terminology," American Society for Quality Control, Milwaukee, Wisconsin (1978).
2. Kilshaw, D. "Quality Assurance. 2. Internal Quality Control," *Med. Lab. Sci.* 44:73–83 (1987).
3. Kilshaw, D. "Quality Assurance. 3. External Quality Assessment," *Med. Lab. Sci.* 44:178–186 (1987).
4. Kilshaw, D. "Quality Assurance. 1. Philosophy and Basic Principles," *Med. Lab. Sci.* 43:377–381 (1986).
5. Bradford, L. W. "Barriers to Quality Achievement in Crime Laboratory Operations," *J. Forensic Sci.* 25:902–907 (1980).
6. Brunelle, R. L., D. D. Garner, and P. L. Wineman "A Quality Assurance Program for the Laboratory Examination of Arson and Explosive Cases," *J. Forensic Sci.* 27:774–782 (1982).
7. Pereira, M. "Quality Assurance in Forensic Science," *Forensic Sci. Int.* 28:1–6 (1979).
8. Alwan L. C. and M. G. Bissell "Time Series Modeling for Quality in Clinical Chemistry," *Clin. Chem.* 34:1396–1406 (1988).

9. Box, G. E. P. and S. Bisaard "The Scientific Context of Quality Improvement," *Quality Progress* 20(6):54–61 (1987).
10. Bussolini, P. L., A. H. Davis, and R. R. Geoffrion "A New Approach to Quality for National Research Labs," *Quality Progress* 21(1):24–27 (1988).
11. Ford, D. J. "Good Laboratory Practice," *Lab. Practice* 37(9):29–33 (1988).
12. Gautier, M. A. and E. S. Gladney "A Quality Assurance Program for Health and Environmental Chemistry," *Am. Lab.* July, pp. 17–22 (1987).
13. Hay, R. J. "The Seed Stock Concept and Quality Control for Cell Lines," *Anal. Biochem.* 171:225–237 (1988).
14. Kenney, M. L. "Quality Assurance in Changing Times: Proposals for Reform and Research in the Clinical Laboratory Field," *Clin. Chem.* 33:328–336 (1987).
15. Kidd, G. J. "What Quality Means to an R & D Organization," in *41st Annual Quality Congress Transactions*, May 4–6, American Society for Quality Control, Milwaukee, Wisconsin (1987).
16. Simpson, J. "National Bureau of Standards Approach to Quality," *Test and Measurement World*, December, p. 38 (1983).
17. Taylor, J. K. *Quality Assurance of Chemical Measurement* (Chelsea, MI: Lewis Publishers, 1987).
18. Taylor, J. K. "The Quest for Quality Assurance," *Am. Lab.*, October, pp. 67–75 (1985).
19. Whitehead, T. P. and F. P. Woodford "External Quality Assessment of Clinical Laboratories in the United Kingdom," *J. Clin. Pathol.* 34:947–957 (1981).
20. American National Standard ASQC Standard C1–1968 "Specification of General Requirements of a Quality Program," American Society for Quality Control, Milwaukee, Wisconsin (1968).
21. American National Standard ANSI/ASQC Z1.15 1979 "Generic Guidelines for Quality Systems," American Society for Quality Control, Milwaukee, Wisconsin (1979).
22. American National Standard ANSI/ASQC Q90–1987 "Quality Management and Quality Assurance Standards–Guidelines for Selection and Use," American Society for Quality Control, Milwaukee, Wisconsin (1987).
23. American National Standard ANSI/ASQC Q90–1987 "Quality Management and Quality System Elements–Guidelines, American Society for Quality Control," Milwaukee, Wisconsin (1987).
24. Juran, J. M. "Quality Policies and Objectives," in *Quality Control Handbook*, 3d ed., J. M. Juran, Ed. (New York: McGraw Hill, 1979).
25. Ruzicka, R. K. "Documentation: Configuration Management," in: *Quality Control Handbook*, 3d ed., J. M. Juran, Ed. (New York: McGraw Hill 1979).
26. Baird, M. "Quality Control and American Association of Blood Bank Standards," presented at the American Association of Blood Banks National Conference, April 17–19, Leesburg, Virginia (1989).

27. AABB Standards Committee "P7.000 DNA Polymorphism Testing," in *Standards for Parentage Testing Laboratories.* (Arlington, Virginia: American Association of Blood Banks, 1989).
28. Budowle, B., H. A. Deadman, R. S. Murch, and F. S. Baechtel "An Introduction to the Methods of DNA Analysis Under Investigation in the FBI Laboratory," *Crime Lab. Dig.* 15:8–21 (1988).
29. ASCLD. "Guidelines for Forensic Laboratory Management Practices." American Society of Crime Laboratory Directors, Laboratory Directors, September (1985).
30. ASCLD *ASCLD Accreditation Manual*, American Society of Crime Laboratory Directors, Laboratory Accreditation Board, (February, 1985).
31. American National Standard ANSI/ASQC Z1.1-1985 "Guide for Quality Control Charts," American Society for Quality Control, Milwaukee, Wisconsin (1985).
32. American National Standard ANSI/ASQC Z1.2-1985 "Control Chart Method of Analyzing Data," American Society for Quality Control, Milwaukee, Wisconsin (1985).
33. American National Standard ANSI/ASQC Z1.3-1985 "Control Chart Method of Controlling Quality During Production," American Society for Quality Control, Milwaukee, Wisconsin (1985).
34. American National Standard ANSI/ASQC A1-1987 "Definitions, Symbols, Formulas, and Tables for Control Charts," American Society for Quality Control, Milwaukee, Wisconsin. (1987).
35. AT&T Technologies "Statistical Quality Control Handbook," AT&T Technologies, Indianapolis, Indiana (May, 1985).
36. Bicking, C. A. "Process Control by Statistical Methods," in *Quality Control Handbook*, 3d ed., J. M. Juran, Ed. (New York: McGraw Hill, 1979).
37. Gryna, F. M. "Basic Statistical Methods," in *Quality Control Handbook*, 3d ed., J. M. Juran, Ed. (New York: McGraw Hill, 1979).
38. National Bureau of Standards "The Place of Control Charts in Experimental Work," in *Experimental Statistics*. National Bureau of Standards Handbook 91. (Washington, D.C.: U. S. Government Printing Office, 1966).
39. Westgard, J. O., P. L. Barry, M. R. Hunt, and T. Groth "A Multi-Rule Shewart Chart for Quality Control in Clinical Chemistry," *Clin. Chem.* 27:493–501 (1981).
40. Bond, W. W. "Safety in the Forensic Immunology Laboratory," in *Proceedings of the International Symposium on Forensic Immunology* (Washington, D.C.: U. S. Govt. Printing Office, 1987).
41. Code of Federal Regulations (1988a) Title 10, Part 19 - "Notices, Instructions, and Reports to Workers; Inspections," (Washington, D.C.: U. S. Government Printing Office, 1988).
42. Code of Federal Regulations (1988b) Title 10, Part 20 - "Standards for Protection Against Radiation," Washington, D.C.: U. S. Government Printing Office, 1988.
43. Gibbs, F. L. and C. A. Kasprisin "Environmental Safety in the Blood

Bank," American Association of Blood Banks, Arlington, Virginia (1987).

44. National Fire Protection Association "Standard on Fire Protection for Laboratories Using Chemicals," (Batterymarch Park, Quincy, MA: National Fire Protection Association, 1986).

45. National Research Council "Prudent Practices for Disposal of Chemicals from Laboratories," (Washington, D.C.: National Research Council's Committee on Hazardous Substances in the Laboratory, National Academy Press, 1983).

46. National Research Council "Prudent Practices for Handling Hazardous Chemicals in Laboratories," (Washington, D.C.: National Research Council's Committee on Hazardous Substances in the Laboratory, National Academy Press, 1981).

47. Sax, N. I. and R. J. Lewis *Hazardous Chemicals Desk Reference.* (New York: Van Nostrand Reinhold, 1987).

48. Steere, N. V., Ed. *CRC Handbook of Laboratory Safety*, 2d ed. (Cleveland, OH: The Chemical Rubber Co., 1971).

49. Wang, C. H., D. L. Willis, and W. D. Loveland *Radiotracer Methodology in the Biological, Environmental, and Physical Sciences.* (Englewood Cliffs, NJ: Prentice-Hall, 1975).

Glossary

AGAROSE – Support medium for electrophoresis.

ALLELE – One of two or more alternative forms of a gene occupying the same locus on homologous chromosomes.

AMPLIFICATION – Increasing the number of copies of a desired DNA molecule.

ANNEAL – Pairing of complementary single strands of DNA to form a double-stranded helical structure.

AUTORADIOGRAPHY – The detection of an image on photographic film caused by radioactive molecules.

BASE – Four chemical units (adenine, thymine, guanine, and cytosine) whose order in DNA molecules controls the genetic code.

BASE PAIR – Partnership of adenine with thymine or cytosine with guanine in the DNA double helix.

CHROMOSOME – One of the rodlike bodies that carries the genes that convey heredity characteristics and are constant in number.

CLONING – Technique of producing identical DNA sequences.

CODON – Sequence of three adjacent nucleotides that will code for an amino acid.

DENATURATION – Conversion of DNA from double-stranded to single-stranded state by use of heat or high pH.

DNA (deoxyribonucleic acid) – Double-stranded molecule that carries the genetic information in living organisms.

DNA LIGASE – Enzyme that covalently joins two pieces of double-stranded DNA.

ELECTROPHORESIS – Technique for the separation of molecules through their movement on a support medium such as agarose under the influence of an electrical charge.

END-LABELING—Incorporation of nucleotides at the 5′ end of a strand of DNA by the use of specific enzymes.

ENZYME—Protein that speeds up the rate of chemical reactions in the body but is unaltered itself in the reaction.

ENDONUCLEASE—Enzyme capable of cutting the DNA strand at a specific site.

GENE—Chromosomal segment, organized in a linear arrangement, that codes for a polypeptide chain or RNA molecule.

GENOME—Entire set of heredity factors of an organism, contained in the chromosomes.

GENOTYPE—Particular combination of genes present in the cells of an individual.

HYBRIDIZATION—Process of complementary base pairing between two single strands of DNA, or DNA and RNA.

HOMOLOGOUS CHROMOSOME—Two chromosomes that have identical sets of loci.

INTERCALATION—Binding of dyes to DNA molecule that will affect mobility during electrophoresis, resulting in a potential band shift.

KILOBASE (kb)—Unit of 1000 base pairs of DNA.

LINKAGE—Two genes on the same chromosome that are not inherited independently but are transmitted together.

LOCUS—Position a gene occupies on a chromosome.

MUTATION—Any change in the sequence of DNA.

NUCLEOTIDE—Combination of a base with a sugar and phosphoric acid.

PHENOTYPE—Visible characteristics of an individual as determined by the genes.

PLASMID—Small circular self-replicating piece of DNA found in some bacteria.

POINT MUTATIONS — Changes involving single base pairs.

POLYMERASE CHAIN REACTION (PCR) — Process by which a small amount of DNA can be amplified to yield a larger quantity of DNA.

POLYMORPHISM — Occurrence in a population of two or more genetically determined alternative phenotypes with frequencies greater than could be accounted for by mutation.

RECOMBINANT DNA — DNA molecule produced from inserting DNA from one organism into another piece of DNA by using genetic engineering techniques.

RESTRICTION ENZYME — Derived from bacteria, catalyzes the cleavage of DNA at specific points, also called restriction endonuclease.

RESTRICTION FRAGMENT LENGTH POLYMORPHISM (RFLP) — Variation in the size of DNA fragments produced by restriction enzyme digestion of a genomic DNA. Pattern is recognized using a probe after electrophoresis, Southern blotting, and hybridization.

RIBONUCLEIC ACID (RNA) — Single-stranded nucleic acid. Three types are messenger RNA, which codes for proteins; transfer RNA, an adapter molecule used for protein synthesis; and ribosomal RNA, which contributes to the composition of the ribosome.

SIZE MARKER — DNA fragment of known size used to calibrate an electrophoretic gel.

SOUTHERN BLOT — Procedure for transferring denatured DNA from an agarose gel to a membrane where it can be hybridized with a complementary DNA probe.

STAR ACTIVITY — Relaxation of the strict canonical recognition sequence of a restriction enzyme specifically resulting in the production of additional cleavages within DNA.

STRINGENCY — Conditions of hybridization that increase the specificity of binding between two single-strand portions of nucleic acids, usually the probe and an immobilized fragment. Increasing the temperature or decreasing the ionic strength results in increased stringency.

TRANSCRIPTION — Process of producing an RNA copy from a DNA template.

TRANSLATION—Production of protein from messenger RNA.

VARIABLE NUMBER OF TANDEM REPEATS (VNTR)—Copies of identical-sequence DNA fragments (30–50 bp) arranged in direct succession within a chromosome. The number of copies varies in random fashion at any locus from one individual to another.

For a complete molecular biology glossary, see *Clinical Chemistry* 35(9):1816 (1989).

General Index

adenine 4, 26, 33
admissibility hearing for DNA evidence 16-17, 97, 125, 211
admissibility standards for DNA evidence 153-155
  disinterested witness rule 163, 171
  Federal Rules of Evidence 155-157, 166, 197
  Frye standard 16-17, 155, 156, 158-161, 184, 187-195
  lab objectivity and 195-198
  relevancy test 155, 158, 166-167
agarose gels 4, 83
AIDS 1, 10
allele 52, 56
allele frequency 39, 47-48, 53, 59
allele specific amplification in detecting genetic variation 67-68
allelic dropout 98, 132
altered enzyme specificity 120-129
Alu family 37
*Alu*I 37
ambiguity, other sources of 136-137
American Academy of Forensic Sciences 212
American Association of Blood Banks (AABB) Parentage Testing Committee 194*n*, 202
American Board of Criminalistics 212
American Society for Human Genetics 14
American Society of Crime Laboratory Directors Laboratory Accreditation Board (ASCLD/LAB) 211
  accreditation program for 205, 209, 212
  proficiency testing program 212
amino acid spacing 2
Analytical Genetic Testing Center 204
annealing 31
Asilomar meeting 9-10, 17

Astbury, Bill 2, 3
automated thermocycling 66
autoradiography 43-44
autosomes 12, 54
Avery, O. T. 2-3

bacterial bands 128-130
bacterial contamination 88, 128, 195
bad faith in preservation of DNA evidence samples 186-187
Baltimore, David 4, 9
band(s)
  extra 110-111, 127, 130
    sample cross-contamination and 111-116
  faint 136-137
  intensity variations 193-194
  missing 132
    degradation 132-135
    lower 135
    middle 135
bandshift 95, 98-100, 193-194
  causes of 100-105
  problems of interpretation raised by 105-109
  sources of ambiguity in 95
base pairing 4, 32
Bell, Florence 2, 3
Berg, Paul 7, 9
bins 56-60, 198
biological evidence, use of polymerase chain reaction in analyzing 63-78
biotechnology, public attitude on 17
blood group analysis 63
bloodstain analysis 85
body fluid stains, genetic marker typing in characterizing 83-90
Boyer, Herb 8, 9
Bragg, W. H. 2
Bragg, W. L. 2
Brenner, Sydney 10, 12

Index of Cited Cases

.